Robert Helpmann
A Rare Sense of the Theatre

The Wanderer   *(Gordon Anthony)*

Robert Helpmann
A Rare Sense of the Theatre

Kathrine Sorley Walker

DANCE BOOKS • ALTON

By the same author

Ninette de Valois: Idealist without Illusions
De Basil's Basil Russes
Eyes on the Ballet
Eyes on Mime
Dance and its Creators
Brief for Ballet
Robert Helpmann
Ballet for Boys and Girls (with Joan Buller)
The Royal Ballet: a Picture History (with Sarah C. Woodcock)
Writings on Dance 1938-68 by A. V. Coton (edited with Lilian Haddakin)
Cyril W. Beaumont: Dance Writer and Publisher

verse
Emotion and Atmosphere
Late Century Poems
New Century Reflections
Thoughts and Impressions

First published 2009
Dance Books Ltd, The Old Bakery,
4 Lenten Street, Alton, Hampshire GU34 1HG

ISBN 978-1-85273-133-5

A CIP catalogue record for this title
is available from the British Library

Printed in Great Britain by Latimer Trend and Company Ltd,
Plymouth, Devon

Contents

Acknowledgements

Some of the material in this book appeared earlier in the scholarly journal *Dance Chronicle* (New York), with a different set of illustrations, and the author and publisher would like to acknowledge this, and thank the then editors, George Dorris and Jack Anderson. The numbers in question are Volume 21, Nos 1, 2 and 3, 1998.

Additionally, the author would like to acknowledge, with great gratitude, my publisher, David Leonard, and the splendid editorial help of Dr Rod Cuff and Liz Morrell.

1

The passage of time can lead to clear perspectives. It can also confuse issues, falsify context, and create myths that replace the truth of an artist's contribution and capability. To a large extent, this is what has happened with Robert Helpmann, and it is time for a more accurate picture to go on record. At present, for those who have little or no memory of him, the image is more like a police artist's sketch than the complex and protean personality who played a dominant part in the theatre of his time. To a certain extent the emphasis must rest on his place in ballet history. Nevertheless, this has to be related to his overall importance as a memorable man of the theatre. His work as an actor, and as a director of plays, operas and musicals, is of equal weight with his contribution to ballet in the consideration of his life. It was not a sideline, not a dancer's resettlement programme; it was an integral part of a multimedia career of exciting range and accomplishment, a closely woven fabric of performance achievement.

Probably the most difficult task a writer can tackle is to try to capture in words the lost quality of a stage artist, a vibrant personality, an entertaining talker and raconteur. The second hard labour is to conjure up the instantaneous effect, the swift firework excitement, of a brilliant stage comedian. Both problems face me in writing about Helpmann. Additionally, I have to remember how varied my readers are likely to be. There are those who knew him and his work and cherished both; those who, with similar experience, held opposing views, as must always be the case with an eminently controversial man. There are many who know only late performances, such as the bossy Stepsister in *Cinderella*, Dr Coppelius, Don Quixote, or the Red King in *Checkmate*. These people have probably also seen some of the very mixed bag of films in which he appeared – especially, of course, *The Red Shoes*, *The Tales of Hoffmann* or *Chitty Chitty Bang Bang* – and they may have picked up a certain amount of confusing hearsay and amusing anecdotes. Finally, there are many others for whom he is barely a name in theatre records. How, then, to flesh out a very much more substantial range of gifts and accomplishment?

An irrepressible clown and mimic, Helpmann could also play tragedy with point and poignancy. He could be outrageously uninhibited and impressively reticent. By no means a great dance technician (but it has to be remembered that in those days this was not the prime qualification for supremacy that it is now), he had remarkable qualities of line, grace and musicality. He was an inspired partner in *grand adage* – the Aurora *pas de deux* has never been more superbly and dramatically handled than when he danced it with Margot Fonteyn. His complete identification with theatre meant that he approached all types of performance with the same relish and respect: from traditional ballet to pantomime, from Shakespeare to musicals. It also inculcated in him an acute awareness of audiences, their differences, their reactions. Like all great theatre artists, he had a magnificent sense of timing; like them, too, he inevitably altered the atmosphere of any theatre in which he appeared.

2

The qualities Helpmann brought to major roles and ballets will be analysed later in this book. However, as always in the consideration of an individual, a life's chronology must also be filled in. Robert Murray Helpman was born on 9 April 1909, in the small country town of Mount Gambier, South Australia, to a non-theatrical family; but he was conditioned from infancy to think of the theatre as a goal. The eldest by some years of three children of a young mother, Mary Gardiner Helpman, whose parents had frustrated her passionate ambition to go on the stage, he was nourished by her on dramatic poetry (principally Shakespeare), music from the popular shows of the time, and the idea of acting and dancing.

His maternal grandmother had talent. Her daughter Mary (known all her long life as Maytie) described her as being 'a good pianist, a good singer, and a devastating mimic' who produced 'not always kind impersonations of visitors who came to the house.'[1] Her daughters also studied singing and music, and, at a boarding school in Melbourne run by 'an English lady named Mrs Spooner', Maytie was discovered to have a considerable gift for elocution and recitation – a favoured activity in late Victorian society.

With a remarkable teacher, Nellie Veitch, she studied drama seriously, reading plays and poetry and learning elocution. She spent weekends with her maternal aunt's family, when she and her cousins went regularly to the theatre, seeing straight plays and melodramas, variety shows and operettas. 'I lived in the drama and tragedy of Shakespeare's heroines,' she wrote ironically, 'coming down occasionally to comedy.' At sixteen she was encouraged by Nellie Veitch to audition for a small part in a professional production of J.M. Barrie's *The Little Minister.* She was offered the job, but the news was greeted with fury and a strict veto from her parents. It was the professional aspect, of course, that was considered absolutely out of the question.

Back in Mount Gambier, Maytie went on, with her sisters, to sing in concerts, to give local poetry recitals and to collaborate in amateur directing and acting. Undaunted by practical difficulties, at eighteen she put on a successful local production of *The Merchant of Venice* with 'a cast of local boys and girls, some of whom had never heard of Shakespeare'. Little wonder, therefore, that after her marriage (in 1907) and when she had a baby son to rear, she should share with him all her enthusiasm for the lost heaven of her dreams. From the beginning, she found that reciting to him stopped his crying: the rhythms seemed to please him. In a year or two he was proving to be a quick study of poetry and before long was able to act out scenes from Shakespeare with her. He loved dressing up, as she did, and learned sword dancing from his delighted Scottish grandmother. In addition, he never forgot a childhood experience of watching an aboriginal corroboree.

When Robert was four, the family moved to Adelaide, the South Australian capital city, where he graduated from the Mount Gambier playschool to an under-ten school run by a Miss Dunn. Maytie immediately arranged for him to have dancing lessons with a first-rate teacher, Nora Stewart. She records that Miss Stewart 'soon discovered his sense of drama and gave him "story dances" and declared that "a child is either a born dancer or he isn't. Bobby is; he will go a lot farther than I can take him". In May 1914, his brother, Maxwell (Max) Gardiner, was born, and in August World War I broke out. Maytie threw herself energetically into war work, which soon included fund-raising by concert parties touring the streets in decorated carts. Six-year-old Robert went with her, standing up to sing patriotic songs, and also helping to pack parcels for soldiers overseas and writing little notes to send with them. In March 1916 the family was completed by the birth of a daughter, Sheila Mary. Both Max and Sheila made careers in the theatre, Max in Canada and Sheila in Australia. They also followed Robert in adding a second 'n' to the original name of Helpman.

There are various accounts of why and when he did this. One says it was suggested by Anna Pavlova, another that a numerologist told him fourteen letters would be luckier for him than thirteen. In a BBC broadcast in 1960, the actress Margaret Rawlings claimed the idea as hers: 'I suggested he should change the spelling – at least stick on another "n". In the war, I thought he'd be interned, that I'd sent him to his death.'[2] The change seems to have been made after his first season with the Vic-Wells Ballet. Stage names were frequently adopted at that time, and in a publicity leaflet he was listed as 'Robert Helgar' (presumably made up from the Hel of Helpmann and the Gar from his mother's maiden name of Gardiner). This was firmly opposed by his mother – and quite possibly this was the moment when Rawlings suggested the extra 'n' as making the name more glamorous.

It did mislead some people into thinking that the family had German or Austrian origins. His ancestry was, in fact, purely British. His father, James Murray Helpman (known as Sam), who eventually owned a flourishing wholesale meat-marketing company in South Australia, was descended from a Devonshire family of Helpmans with strong Royal Navy and British Army connections. In the early nineteenth century three Helpman brothers entered the Forces. One, Philip Augustus, became a Rear Admiral in the Navy; another, Robert John Crichton, also served in the Navy and is known for his paintings.

Tthe third, Benjamin Francis (Frank), served in the Navy as a 23-year-old surveying officer and later lieutenant on *HMS Beagle* from 1837 when, on its third voyage, it completed the survey of the northern coastline of Australia. His diary of this long voyage is lodged in the LaTrobe Library in Melbourne and is an invaluable record of the expedition until he left the ship in 1840. Quotations from it are included in Keith S. Thomson's fascinating book, *HMS Beagle: The Ship that Changed the Course of History*,[3] and show that for Frank the expedition was not a happy one, quite apart from the fact that he had reluctantly left a sweetheart back home in England. He got on badly with the captain, John Wickham, and with the lieutenant and assistant surveyor, John Stokes, but took well to his wide experiences of Australia, which included landfalls in Perth, Hobart and Sydney. Thomson describes Sydney in 1838 as being 'a round of parties, walks, picnics in the country, theatrical and musical performances, and a stream of new faces appearing and reappearing with tales of the outback, of farming life, or news from home'. Frank must have already been considering the possibility of making a life for himself in the Antipodes.

In 1839 the voyage continued north past the Barrier Reef and Cape York to the small settlement of Port Essington, which Frank wrote about at length and enthusiastically. It was 'vastly pretty' with 'a most perfect appearance': 'the Botanic Gardens have melons, pineapples, bananas, and cocoa nut trees apparently flourishing. They have found no trouble with the Natives, on the contrary they are the most civil, friendly creatures imaginable.' They saw aboriginal dances, and there was a good deal of fun when Owen Stanley, the captain of another ship in port, the *Britomart*, got up a play called *Cheap Living* (the first theatre performance in the north of Australia), which delighted the audience. The voyage, with land explorations, continued beyond Port Essington down the coast of Western Australia; but at Swan River, on 4 March 1840, Frank applied for the vacant post of captain of the colonial schooner *Champion*. He got the command and left the Royal Navy for good.

Frank married Ann Pace, whose father was a captain in the East India Service, in 1842, but continued to have links with Australian exploration. In the 1840s he took part in expeditions to Shark Bay and other Western Australian sites, producing the first hydrographic report on Port Gregory in 1844. In 1846 there was an expedition to report on coal that had been discovered on the Irwin River. In 1861, when John McDouall Stuart was planning an expedition to Northern Australia, Frank Helpman gave his advice as 'the only person in Victoria who has been to the top of both' (the Adelaide River and the Victoria Estuary, when he was serving on the *Beagle*). Stuart took his advice and paid him the tribute of naming a hill near the Waterhouse River 'Mount Helpman'. From 1859 Frank was harbour master in the coastal town of Warrnambool in Victoria and held the position until 1868. His son Walter was to become Robert's grandfather.

Walter, a bank manager in Warrnambool, married Isabella Murray, whose father owned grazing properties and racing stables. Her brother John became a prominent politician and premier of the state of Victoria. Apart from Robert's father Sam, they had three other children. Francis Murray (Frank) married May Harman but had no children. Gordon, an Anzac, survived World War I but later died of blackwater fever in New Guinea; he never married. The only daughter, Jean, married twice – a Hungarian medical doctor, Theophilus Duka, who gained a DSO with the RAMC in World War I, and by whom she had a son, Theo; and, after a divorce, her second cousin, Colonel Robert Rudyerd-Helpman, an English-resident descendant of Benjamin Francis Helpman's elder brother, Rear Admiral Philip Helpman; they had no children.

On his mother's side, Robert's forebears were all Scottish. Maytie's parents (a Gardiner and a Graham) were both born in Scotland. Robert Gardiner was the son of a shipbuilder, born in Dunbar in 1812. In Australia, he became a commander of whaling ships, made money at the time of the Gold Rush, and married Susan Foley in Hobart in 1834. Their son (Maytie Helpman's father), Robert Melville Gardiner (known as Mel), born in 1850, eventually owned a sheep station at Mount Schank near Mount Gambier, and this led to a mistaken idea in England that Helpmann was the son of 'a rich sheep station owner'. Maytie's mother was Catherine Glendinning Graham, born in 1846 in Holywood near Dumfries, whose family moved to Australia in the 1850s. Because Susan Foley's grandfather John sailed as a marine with the First Fleet, Maytie's own Australian roots went impeccably far back.

3

In Adelaide the Helpman family, including Sam who shared his wife's love of plays, went regularly to the theatre, and Robert went to everything with them. He was particularly keen on shows that included dancing. He absorbed dances by watching and later trying them out at home. Soon he was allowed to go backstage afterwards and talk to the cast about another fascination – make-up. He took to piano lessons with great ease and pleasure. When Allan Wilkie's Shakespeare company came to Adelaide, Nora Stewart's pupils were recruited as fairies and gnomes, and Robert was at last on stage. 'From that moment,' Maytie writes, 'there was no other life for him'.[4]

Robert and Sheila were both child performers, she the more celebrated as an actress. Anecdotes have been perpetuated. One in particular is well known: when he was eleven, Robert danced in a charity concert at which the Australian prima donna Dame Nellie Melba was guest of honour. He persuaded Miss Stewart to let him do the pizzicato solo from *Sylvia* (which he had picked up as the girls learned it in class), on *pointe*, wearing a blond curly wig and a silver and white tutu. It was a great success, and he enjoyed the joke of pulling off the wig at his curtain calls to show he was a boy. Melba was apparently much amused and she, and the English writer Beverley Nichols who was with her, congratulated him afterwards. At another charity concert, he and his six-year-old sister gave an Apache dance. Sheila had to hold a rose between her lips, but did not let it go easily when her brother snatched it, so that her front tooth came out along with it. Neither young Helpman allowed that to interfere with the performance.

Sheila was making more ripples as a young prodigy than Robert – at the age of six she acted in Sydney in a production of the play *Eyes of Youth* staged by a company starring the American actress Emilie Polini, and than had a lead in a mystery play called *The Flaw*. Max also made a stage debut in *Eyes of Youth*. Sheila went on to a part in *A Message from Mars*, and got Robert his first acting role in the production as a messenger boy. She continued acting, and, in a play called *The Squaw Man* where, according to Maytie, an Indian dog saved a child's life, 'Another Helpman took the stage – our working sheep dog Wandi. He acted it perfectly, dragging Sheila out of the make-believe river; and they took a curtain call together with Wandi standing on his hind legs with his paws on her shoulders.' (There would be an interesting parallel in 1957, when Robert acted Launce in *The Two*

Gentlemen of Verona with Keith Michell's golden Labrador, Duff. He was photographed in a curtain line-up before Queen Elizabeth II, kneeling down and pointing the Queen out to the splendid dog.) Another popular story about Sheila concerned a school performance of *A Midsummer Night's Dream* in which she was acting Oberon. At the dress rehearsal, after she said the line, 'I do but beg a little changeling boy to be my henchman', and her Titania replied, 'Set your heart at rest – the fairy land buys not the boy of me', Sheila turned to the audience – fortunately only schoolmates and relatives – and said with a shrug, 'We may be poor but, by gosh, we're proud!'.

Regular education was of little interest to Robert. He was a pupil at Adelaide's Prince Alfred College (one of Australia's equivalents of British 'public schools'), starting at its prep school at the age of ten; but, as his mother wrote, he 'was pretty selective about the subjects he liked and disliked, and I think he only liked history, geography and music'. In sport, he rode horses, played a great deal of tennis on the family court in the garden, and excelled at swimming, diving and surfing. He concentrated not at all on formal schooling, and gained an unenviable reputation for insubordination, refusing to wear the school cap and illicitly smoking, so that the masters were not saddened by his leaving early to work in the theatre. The college was not slow, however, to welcome him back when he was starring with Katharine Hepburn in an Old Vic company tour of Australia in 1955.

As a dance student, he went on from Nora Stewart to Louise Larsson. Before she opened a school in Adelaide, Larsson's career was in all forms of stage dancing rather than in classical ballet. She had worked from the age of five in shows put on by the prestigious theatre company J.C. Williamson Ltd. Robert then graduated to Minnie Everett's theatre school (Everett and her associate Minnie Hooper were leading figures in musical theatre, and choreographers to J.C. Williamson), where he learned more about dancing and partnering in musicals and revues than in a context of ballet.

This was balanced after a couple of years when, in March 1926, Anna Pavlova began an Australian tour at His Majesty's Theatre in Melbourne. A family story goes that Sam Helpman decided to go backstage to meet her and somehow persuaded her to take on his theatre-mad sixteen-year-old son as a pupil and apprentice dancer while she was in the Antipodes. As a result, Robert was introduced to the ballet world, taking classes with Pavlova's partner, Laurent Novikov, as well as having an invaluable opportunity to appear as an extra and learn ballets by watching them night after night. Her large and basically Russian repertoire included *The Fairy Doll, Chopiniana* (choreography attributed to Ivan Clustine), *The Awakening of Flora, The Magic Flute, Autumn Leaves* and *Walpurgis Night*, as well as the celebrated divertissements. Harcourt Algeranoff recorded Helpmann's advent:

> The next time we did *Don Quixote* we were treated to a prophetic vision of a future great dance comedian – in the centre of the stage was Bobbie, dressed in a Korovine-designed yellow toreador suit with a huge white hat, looking for all the world like Little Lord Fauntleroy shorn of his curls. [5]

Helpmann's own version (he loved adding ironical footnotes to anecdotes) was that he sat at the side of the stage at a café table with a large red cloak to throw over the droppings if the (live) horse misbehaved. This production of *Don Quixote* by Novikov was a two-act condensed version of the Alexander Gorsky staging of 1902.

The Pavlova Ballet tour continued to Sydney (17 April) and on to New Zealand until July. Returning to Australia, the company appeared at His Majesty's Theatre, Brisbane (12 July), briefly in Sydney and Melbourne, then went on to the Theatre Royal, Adelaide, until 4 August. Here Maytie Helpman saw the company and had a meeting with Pavlova, who told her that she had regularly watched Helpmann in class and was sure of his potential. She suggested he should go overseas to further his career, but his parents considered him too young, so instead he accepted a five-year contract with J.C. Williamson. Helpmann's admiration for Pavlova and her art was always unshaken. She constituted a standard that he recognised as an artistic goal. Although he could not join her company on its return to Australia in 1929, he managed to see some performances, including her Giselle. This appreciation of Pavlova later became an important bond with Frederick Ashton, for whom she was also a goddess of the dance.

Sam Helpman died in September 1927, and Maytie was glad to have her elder son within reach at that time. During the Williamson years, Helpmann appeared in a succession of popular musicals, operettas and revues: *Frasquita, Katinka, The Merry Widow, The New Moon, Queen High, This Year of Grace, Tip Toes.* He made a considerable name for himself, appearing with such stars as Marie Burke, Gladys Moncrieff and Maisie Gay. His vitality and bravura presentation of dances stopped various shows. Marie Burke, in a BBC broadcast in 1960, recalled him in Franz Lehar's operetta *Frasquita* as 'doing a very interesting and nice dance'.[6] This was a

tango *pas de deux* with Sylvia Miller in Act II, 'The Night Cabaret'.
Helpmann danced the first performances in New Zealand (December 1926
to March 1927) in a version by Minnie Everett, and was dismayed when
Alexis Dolinoff was brought in for the Sydney opening. However, Dolinoff's
different arrangement of the duet was unpopular, and when he left the
company Helpmann got the role back. Together Burke and Helpmann
travelled with the show to Perth in Western Australia in August 1927.
She said,

> I remember him as very slim, with wonderful dark flashing eyes. He was
> always laughing, and always asking questions from everyone about
> Europe. He had masses of books about theatre and music. He said, 'I
> shall end up in England, you'll see me there.' When I met him in London,
> he said, 'You see I've made it, I made up my mind.'

Noël Coward's *This Year of Grace* was given its Australian premiere in
Melbourne in March 1929, starring Maisie Gay. Helpmann had cameo
roles as The Patient in Ronald Jeans's sketch 'The Ministering Angel', a
waiter in 'Love, Life and Laughter' and the drag role of Baroness Kurdle in
'The Lido Beach'. He was also one of the small group of dancers in numbers
such as 'Dance Little Lady' and 'Teach Me to Dance Like Grandma'. In
Katinka in 1930 the star was Gladys Moncrieff, but Helpmann and Frances
Ogilvy were Russian dancers and cabaret dancers. With a regular pay
cheque plus a supplementary allowance from his family, he could amuse
himself in his spare time, spending money on clothes (the more fantastic
the better), partying and gambling. He later told Elizabeth Salter 'I would
go anywhere I was invited, and I was invited everywhere'.[7] He had inherited
from his mother a zest for life and a delight in company; fortunately, he
had also inherited, from both sides of his family, a healthy leavening of
realism, common sense and a basic seriousness of purpose that would never
desert him.

At last, in 1932, his life changed dramatically. He was appearing in
Melbourne during the Christmas season of 1931/32 in a pantomime,
Sinbad the Sailor, in which he partnered Frances Ogilvy in 'The Rose Ballet'
and later in a spectacular scene called 'The Spider's Web' – when, perhaps
for the first time, he was given a small photograph in the programme. This
item was based on a number performed in 1916 by Ivy Schilling and Fred
Leslie in a revue, *Come Over Here*. As a child, Helpmann had seen it and
been enthralled. It involved a good deal of gymnastic work on a vast steel
web, which was taken out of storage for the revival. He was seen by visiting

actors from England, the 24-year-old Margaret Rawlings and her husband, Gabriel Toyne. They were impressed and, as Helpmann's contract with Williamson was coming to an end, they recruited him for their stage company, giving him the tiny acting role of Octavius Barrett in *The Barretts of Wimpole Street* and asking him to stage a curtain-raiser ballet as well. This, with a scenario by Toyne, was called *Business à la Russe,* the steps echoing typewriter rhythms. They went on tour to New Zealand, after which, with Maytie's willing permission and financial help from his maternal grandfather, he left Australia for Europe in December 1932. He would not return until 1955.

4

Helpmann was now setting his sights on ballet rather than musical shows. All too aware that years in commercial theatre had eroded his classical ballet technique, he had been working for some months in Adelaide with a teacher, Vera van Rij, whom he had met as a dancer with the Pavlova Ballet. Interviewed after a recital she organised in September 1932, Helpmann emphasised what a splendid coach she was. Apart from her technical knowledge of ballet, 'she has had that valuable stage experience which is so necessary, combining as it does the theory and the actual practice of ballet'.[8]

After arriving in Europe in January 1933, he stayed for ten days in Paris, going to classes with the famous expatriate Russian ballet teachers and, unforgettably, seeing Josephine Baker on stage. He reached London in February. Hard classwork in Paris had left him undecided whether or not he really wanted to devote himself to ballet, and in London he began by acting two bit-parts in a play, *I Hate Men*, with Rawlings, at the Gate Theatre. Writing a decade later, the actor Esmond Knight remembered a meeting with him backstage at Drury Lane Theatre during a run of *Wild Violets*. Knight shared a dressing room with an Australian, Fred Conyngham, who was visited one day by a young stranger, 'an unusual personality, who made them laugh'. Conyngham gave him names of London managers to contact. Afterwards,

> Freddy said 'Amazing chap, that. I'm willing to bet you that within three months he'll have established himself over here in some way or another'. The visitor's name was Robert Helpmann, and in three months he was well in with the Old Vic Ballet Company. [9]

Rawlings had given Helpmann an introduction to Ninette de Valois, the young director of a new ballet company, the Vic-Wells Ballet, at Sadler's Wells. He found his way there (unimpressed that it was in the London suburbs) and saw a programme that included two ballets by de Valois – the avant-garde *The Scorpions of Ysit* and a new choral ballet, *The Birthday of Oberon* (which he described to Salter as absolutely horrible) – and Alicia Markova (who enchanted him) with Stanley Judson in *Le Lac des cygnes, Act II*. The next day, 8 February, he had a momentous interview with de Valois. A widely quoted story records that de Valois, on seeing him, said, 'I can do something with that face'. Telling it later, Helpmann suggested that it was not said in any flattering tone but meant that something would *have* to be done about it. De Valois herself wrote of their meeting:

> Portrait of a young man, very pale, with large eyes; he is wearing a huge camel-hair coat. I am struck by a resemblance in some strange way to Massine. He comes forward and speaks to me very politely – it appears that he has been waiting downstairs for some time. Instinctively I know that this is Margaret Rawlings' Australian find. Everything about him proclaims the artist born.[10]

The next day he was part of the company, and working harder than he really liked at the company barre. 'She would have welcomed anything male on two legs', he told Salter. A week later, de Valois was summing him up astutely in her logbook:

> On the credit side: talented, enthusiastic, extremely intelligent, great facility and vitality, witty, cute as a monkey, quick as a squirrel, a sense of theatre and his own possible achievements therein. On the debit side: academically backward, technically weak, lacking in concentration; too fond of a good time and too busy having a good time ... By a series of leaps and bounds he set about making short work of my curriculum.[11]

The Vic-Wells Ballet, at this point, was still very new. The organisation on which it depended comprised the Old Vic Theatre and Sadler's Wells Theatre, jointly managed by Lilian Baylis. Ninette de Valois's small group of dancers which, until then, had mainly contributed to plays and operas, had given its first full evening of ballet at the Old Vic on 5 May 1931, and was gradually building up a repertoire of short ballets, largely choreographed by de Valois herself. By 1933 they were appearing regularly at both the Vic and the Wells, south and north, respectively, of the Thames, in ballet programmes and in operas and plays.

Money was extremely tight, but when Helpmann was recruited in February there was a major production in view – a staging of *Coppélia* by Nicholas Sergeyev, who had been *régisseur* of the Imperial Russian Ballet in St Petersburg until 1917, and who had reconstructed *The Sleeping Princess* for the Diaghilev Ballet and *Giselle* for the Camargo Society in London. Although this first version of *Coppélia* (premiered on 21 March 1933) was in two acts only, it was a considerable undertaking for the young company. The role of Swanilda was initially danced by Lydia Lopokova as guest artist, Stanley Judson was cast as Franz, and Hedley Briggs as Dr Coppelius. Helpmann, as a newcomer, danced in the corps de ballet mazurka and czardas – the subject of another famous anecdote, recorded by de Valois:

> 'Lilian Baylis had begun to pick him out. 'I like that boy, dear, who puts too much brilliantine on his hair. Do stop him, his head's rather large anyway, and it makes one keep looking at him.' 'Perhaps,' I suggested, 'that is what he means you to do, perhaps he thinks the brilliantine just another good idea.'[12]

According to Helpmann it was not brilliantine – he had polished it up with vaseline topped by paraffin – but it was certainly a good idea.

Meanwhile, in class, canteen and dressing rooms, he was getting to know his fellow dancers. He was very different from them. He was alone in being Australian and in having had so much experience of commercial musical shows. He knew nothing of the British ballet world. Typically, he did not slip unobtrusively into the scene. Leslie Edwards recalled [13] a first glimpse of him backstage at the Wells (wearing the camel-hair coat and brown trilby hat) and being told by Claude Newman that he 'was de Valois' new colonial wonder'. However, he quickly conquered any resentment that was felt, and by force of his ability to amuse them became 'the leader of the pack'. He was not, of course, cannoned into stardom – that was not de Valois's way. The other young men in the group of village dancers were Travis Kemp, Antony Tudor, Guy Massey, Toni Repetto, Leslie Edwards, Patrick Hall and Pat McGrath. Helpmann was programmed as Bobby Helpmann, and although that was quickly changed to Robert, it was as 'Bobby' that he became known to the profession and to the audience – if never to his family, who always called him Bob. The young women who partnered these young men in *Coppélia* were all from de Valois's Academy of Choregraphic Art (sic), out of which the Vic-Wells Ballet had grown: Beatrice Appleyard, Hermione Darnborough, Sheila McCarthy, Nadina Newhouse, Freda Bamford, Ailne Phillips, Joy Newton and Gwyneth Mathews. Helpmann's only other listing on a programme that season was as one of the trio named War, Pestilence and Famine in *Job* – and it is not now possible to know which of the three he danced.

Early May saw the end of the winter season at both the Old Vic and Sadler's Wells. There would be no performances until September. De Valois got Helpmann a month's engagement from 21 June, to appear as one of six dancers in *The Fantasticks*, for which she had arranged the dances, at the Lyric Theatre, Hammersmith, transferring to the recently opened Open Air Theatre in Regent's Park. Otherwise, the summer was an opportunity for him to take the measure of the London social and theatrical worlds, and to widen his circle of acquaintances. He lived very centrally. Initially he took digs in Half Moon Street, deliberately chosen because he was a reader of the Bulldog Drummond books, and then he was offered a share in an apartment owned by the actress Bertha Belmore. He discovered that there was a remarkable network of the arts in Britain: music, design, literature and all branches of the theatre were closely linked. In addition, above the arts and extremely influential in every way, there was an important crust of moneyed upper-class and aristocratic interest and patronage with which all artists had to establish some *modus vivendi*.

Balletically, it was an exciting period. In June, the Camargo Society brought its activities to an end with galas at Covent Garden, at which the Vic-Wells Ballet danced *Coppélia* and *Le Lac des cygnes, Act II*. At the Savoy Theatre, three companies appeared: Edward James's Les Ballets 1933 (choreographer Balanchine, dancers Tilly Losch and Tamara Toumanova); a group headed by Serge Lifar, Felia Dubrovska and Alice Nikitina; and the Ballets Jooss, with their recent great success, *The Green Table*. Starting in July at the Alhambra Theatre, the de Basil–Blum Ballets Russes de Monte-Carlo, with Leonide Massine, Alexandra Danilova and the 'baby ballerinas' Toumanova, Irina Baronova and Tatiana Riabouchinska, was the talk of the town.

The range of styles and techniques was a revelation. Helpmann was acutely aware that, as an outsider, he was sadly ignorant of who was who and what all of them did. Dancers he met were working all over London, in stage shows and cabarets and music hall programmes as well as with Marie Rambert at the tiny Mercury Theatre. He needed to know how people were related to each other, either through training, nationality or marital and sexual partnerships. He set about learning everything he could of this new milieu. He realised that he would have to build on useful contacts and find a place in the social as well as the theatrical scene; but, as a freethinking, no-nonsense Australian, he was naturally determined to do this on his own terms, regardless of English conventions and taboos. Constant Lambert – music director of the Vic-Wells Ballet, composer and conductor, *bon viveur* and man of the world – knew everyone and had all the qualifications needed to tutor him in this vital sphere. He was only four years older than Helpmann, and his father, George, who had grown up in Australia, was well known there as an artist. Lambert and Helpmann found they had much in common, and Helpmann soon applied to him to supplement his general artistic knowledge. Would he perhaps draw up some guidelines: what should I read, what should I listen to, what should I look at? And what are the backgrounds of all these people I am meeting? Lambert, amused and liking him, made him lists and found that he applied himself assiduously to his self-imposed task. This thoroughness was a typical family trait.

Meanwhile the company prepared for their September season. The two theatres opened roughly at the same time. At the Vic, operas and plays were staged in repertory along with ballet; the Wells concentrated mainly on opera and ballet. Many operas, of course, had a dance element, sometimes a substantial one. Helpmann knew that de Valois was planning opportunities for him, and he had to work hard to measure up to them technically. The first, great, chance came on the ballet's opening night at the Wells on 26 September 1933. *Job*, a masque for dancing, had been choreographed in 1931 by de Valois for the Camargo Society to a score by Ralph Vaughan Williams. It was a major work, based on Blake's illustrations to the Book of Job, with a dominant leading role of Satan that had been created by Anton Dolin and so far danced only by him. Dolin, however, was due to act in a West End play, *Ballerina.* As his replacement, de Valois chose the unknown corps de ballet boy from Australia, convinced that he could make it work, knowing that if he did, it would also to a considerable extent make his name. During the summer break, she gave him the musical score to study and lent him the book of Blake's illustrations, telling him that all the choreography was developed from them.

De Valois's faith was justified. People were surprised and intrigued. It was a complete change from the towering athleticism of the experienced and widely known Dolin to the slender, Ariel-like newcomer who looked younger than his twenty-four years. All the same, Helpmann had natural magnetism, innate theatricality and a determination to prove himself, and he got away with it. In *The Dancing Times*, The Sitter Out (probably the editor, Philip Richardson) called it 'a most creditable rendering ... It was a trying ordeal for him to follow in the footsteps of Dolin, and though he still lacks "strength" in his interpretation of the part, I am sure that increased experience and consequent confidence in himself will soon enable him to remedy this defect.'[14] Jasper Howlett, writing later, recalled the occasion:

[In *Job*] Helpmann succeeded amazingly well. He did not make Satan a conception of Miltonic strength, it was a lithe figure of incarnate evil.

Eager eyes in pit and gallery had singled him out, and were watching for him. ... [They] decided that 'Bobbie was coming on'.

He certainly 'came on' with meteoric rapidity. He had 'elevation, ballon, easy movement and, above all, intellect, far rarer in dancers than one might suppose'.[15]

In accordance with company policy, Helpmann also danced small roles in the repertoire. During the 1933/34 season he was a gendarme in de Valois's *Douanes,* a comedy about a Customs post in France; he danced in the mazurka in *Fête Polonaise* and was one of the musicians (and later the Bridegroom) in *The Wise and Foolish Virgins*; he was in the Valse Noble in the revival, staged by the former Diaghilev dancer Wanda Evina, of Fokine's *Carnaval* (and soon progressed to Florestan); he was one of three Gods in de Valois's modernistic *Création du monde* and Georgie-Porgie in her *Nursery Suite.* He appeared in operas, as a tumbler in *The Snow Maiden*, as a clown in *Tsar Saltan* (its first London performance) and as a Fury in *Orpheus.* At the same time, he danced Dolin's role of Vertumnus in Ashton's *Pomona*, and the title role in his *The Lord of Burleigh.* More importantly for the future, he worked with Ashton on his new ballet for Markova, *Les Rendezvous*, creating the *pas de trois* with de Valois and Stanley Judson. This contained fast, staccato choreography, very sharp and controlled and full of directional changes, showing a woman flirting with two suitors.

Important productions were featured in the early months of 1934. *Giselle,* as revived by Sergeyev for the Camargo Society for Olga Spessiva and Markova, had been a notable success, and now it was staged for the Vic-Wells Ballet with Markova and Dolin in the leads. It was a ballet Helpmann had loved when he saw it with Pavlova, and now he was allotted the neat, meaty part of Hilarion (in those days a purely mime role) and enjoyed it. Then came the company premiere of *Casse-Noisette (The Nutcracker)*, again for Markova, and he had fun with the Danse Chinoise. He danced *Le Spectre de la rose* in January (without any particular success) and *Les Sylphides* (in which he was always excellent) in March.

However, the really exciting event came on 3 April, with his first leading-role creation – the Master of Treginnis in de Valois's *The Haunted Ballroom.* A Gothic melodrama based on a story by Edgar Allan Poe, it was set to a commissioned score by Geoffrey Toye and evocatively designed by the three-woman team of Motley. It was about a family curse – each head of the house ended up danced to death by vengeful ghosts – and de Valois made it a striking vehicle for Markova, Helpmann, and William Chappell as The Stranger Player. The chance of partnering Markova was a pleasure for

Helpmann, who greatly admired her performances. Always better liked by audiences than by critics, *The Haunted Ballroom* built up and sustained a memorable sense of otherworldliness, largely owing to Markova's ethereal lightness and Helpmann's tremendous conviction. H.B. Sibthorp wrote that

> the ingredients are extraordinarily well mixed – 'ham', but very best quality ... blending classical technique with Central European group movements most discreetly and successfully. Helpmann has his first big personal success – an impressive character study within a strict framework of classical outline. He contrives to look haunted and hag-ridden without suggesting that he is stricken in years ... it lies outside the scope of a classical dancer pure and simple – a complex character role, and his sincerity, together with his developing technical powers, have made it a truly moving performance.[16]

The critic in *The Era*, who called it 'a distinguished ballet, macabre, touching and beautiful', also praised Helpmann: 'He did not fail to achieve a high emotional and really terrifying pitch the few moments before he went through his death agony. It was an intensely interesting and realistic performance.'[17]

William Chappell had begun dancing with Marie Rambert. He had also studied art at Chelsea College of Art, where his special friends included the artist Edward Burra, and he made his career as a theatre designer as well as a dancer and stage director. Walter Gore had joined Rambert after lessons with Massine, as had Ashton. Ashton and Chappell had both danced with the Ida Rubinstein Ballet under Bronislava Nijinska as choreographer, and both had worked for the Camargo Society. It was with Ashton, Chappell and Leslie Edwards, who had reached the Vic-Wells Ballet from Marie Rambert, that Helpmann made friends, finding, as he did with de Valois and Lambert, that a shared sense of humour was an important bond. Outside ballet, especially in the dramatic theatre, he was also making contacts, one introduction leading to another. Even before *The Haunted Ballroom*, he knew the great American actors Alfred Lunt and Lynn Fontanne, and Lunt had advised him on makeup for the Master of Treginnis. He had also met Vivien Leigh, who had just made her first headlines in the play *The Mask of Virtue*; and friends, to Helpmann, were friends for life.

The season ended on 28 April and the dancers dispersed, most of them trying to find some extra money in commercial theatre. In May, Helpmann had an engagement at the Royal Opera House, Covent Garden. He was principal dancer for the operas *Schwanda the Bagpiper* (another first London performance), which introduced him to Central European modern dance as it was choreographed by Margarethe Wallmann, a former pupil of Mary Wigman; *Arabella*; and, in June, *La Cenerentola*. From his point of view, the last was the best, as he danced a charming *pas de deux* with Markova, choreographed by de Valois. Also in June he had a small part in a short-running play about a ballet company, *Precipice* (which starred Dolin), at the Savoy Theatre; this was directed by Gabriel Toyne and included a little ballet by Dolin and Wendy Toye called *La Mort*.

He then appeared regularly from June until September in a series of mostly new short ballets organised by Sydney Carroll at the Open Air Theatre, Regent's Park, partnering the young Danish ballerina Nini Theilade. There were disastrous weather conditions on the opening night of 2 June – thunder, lightning and rain. The muddy ground was hard to dance on but somehow the dancers kept their footing. Although reference books suggest that her choreographic debut was in 1936 with the Royal Danish Ballet, Theilade did in fact create *Psyche* and *During the Ball* for herself and Helpmann in 1934. *The Dancing Times* thought that, although *Acis and Galatea* (choreographed by Letty Littlewood) was too long-drawn-out and meandering, 'Robert Helpmann and Nini Theilade gave a very charming performance with the material at their disposal ... [He] is certainly the best male dancer of the younger generation. His technique improves steadily – there seems every hope of his becoming a great artiste in the near future'.[18] He and Theilade also danced in a production of *As You Like It*.

The new Sadler's Wells season began on 2 October 1934. Helpmann danced his first Albrecht in *Giselle* with Markova, and there was a new de Valois ballet, *The Jar*, in which he was the Sicilian farmer who owned an enormous jar. Sibthorp called the ballet 'artless and ingratiating' and wrote of 'much bustle, an occasional shrillness in movement and sound, but some passages of quiet contemplative beauty'. He praised Walter Gore's Tinker as 'a whole, rounded study', and continued: 'Helpmann revealed a new burlesque side to his talent as the irascible Don Lollo Zirafa'.[19]

The twentieth of November was an important date in Vic-Wells Ballet history. For the first time, they staged *Le Lac des cygnes* (as it was always then designated) in its entirety. It was, naturally, planned to display Markova in the dual role of Odette–Odile, and it was her triumph. All the same, Helpmann as Siegfried was considered impressive in his partnering, mime and dancing. There was never much love lost between Dolin and Helpmann, but where partnering was concerned there was mutual respect, and Helpmann acknowledged that he learned much about the presentation of a ballerina from Dolin. P.W. Manchester recorded that he 'partnered impeccably through three strenuous acts' and went on to say that he 'thoroughly deserved the ovation he had the opportunity of winning when he sailed round the stage in a series of *grands jetés* which displayed an elevation of which he had never previously been suspected'.[20] This elevation and his steady technical and interpretative advances were the product not only of his own hard work, but also of de Valois's zeal on his behalf. She taught him herself, but also arranged for him to have regular classes with Tamara Karsavina and, when possible, Olga Preobrajenska in Paris and other Russian teachers such as Stanislas Idzikowsky, who taught at the Vic-Wells Ballet School, and Nicholas Legat.

5

De Valois's next creation for him was intended to be *The Rake's Progress*, and they started to work on it, beginning with the final mad scene with its terrifying staccato solo. At that point, Helpmann was approached with an offer to appear in a forthcoming West End revue, *Stop Press*. He was in a quandary. The revue would give him wider experience, for which he was always eager, and considerably more money than the Vic-Wells Ballet could afford. There he was paid three pounds a week and gave back a pound of that for classes. He talked it over with de Valois, who considered it very carefully. At last she said that she felt it would be a good thing for him to do the revue – on condition that he would come back to her at the end of it. She would, of course, have to go on with the scheduled production of *Rake*, but the role would be his on his return.

Stop Press, produced and directed by Hassard Short, had its first night at the Adelphi Theatre on 21 February 1935 and ran until 1 July. It derived from a New York success of 1933 with a score by Irving Berlin, *As Thousands Cheer*, but it was presented in London by Clifford Whitley, a journalist who had worked with Lord Northcliffe. Whitley arranged for additional material, more relevant to Britain, to be written by Greatrex Newman, and in his programme note declared that it was 'an attempt to give the stage's reflection of events past, present and future, and a satire on everyday occurrences'. Each item in the revue had a newspaper connection and was based on either a column or a news item. The cast was led by Dorothy Dickson, Phyllis Monkman and Edwin Styles, and the principal dancers were the Americans Margaret Sande and Florence Chumbecos, and Helpmann. Sande had been 'one of The Girls' in the New York show. Chumbecos, a chorus dancer in *The Band Wagon* in New York in 1931, had suddenly found her break when she replaced Tilly Losch in a dance number with Fred Astaire and was so successful that she continued as his partner until the end of the run.

Helpmann appeared in four scenes: *Lonely Heart Column* and *Revolt in Cuba* with Sande; and *Book of the Month – The Beggar's Dream* and *Echo of Former Romance (You and the Night and the Music)* with Chumbecos. *The Beggar's Dream* (called *The Beggar Waltz* in *The Band Wagon*) was the number Chumbecos had danced with Astaire. A romantic scene of a beggar boy outside the Vienna Opera House who dreams of dancing on stage with the prima ballerina, it had been choreographed by Albertina Rasch; no doubt

Helpmann, always an Astaire fan, was delighted to follow in his footsteps. Rasch was not credited in the London programme, nor was Charles Weidman, who had choreographed *Lonely Heart Column* and *Revolt in Cuba*. In New York, these had been performed by his group of dancers led by Letitia Ide and Jose Limon. It was the first time Helpmann had encountered American modern dance ideas and he greatly enjoyed the experience.

He returned to the Vic-Wells Ballet for the opening of the winter season in late September 1935, and immediately took over the promised role that would become very much his own. De Valois had staged *The Rake's Progress* in May with Walter Gore dancing the lead. It was a masterly dramatic ballet with Hogarth-based designs by Rex Whistler and a commissioned score by Gavin Gordon, and Helpmann brought it to life, moving effortlessly from the ironic humour of the early scenes to the stark tragedy of the ending. Again, as with Satan, he was to build on these early performances as the years went by. In his absence, Markova and Dolin had led the company, but they had now left to form a company of their own. De Valois had recruited an excellent dancer from Rambert, Harold Turner, who had already made a mark with an effective double role as the Dancing Master and the Gentleman with a Rope in *The Rake's Progress.* He was a stimulus rather than a rival for Helpmann. They were totally dissimilar. Turner was very much the more virtuoso technician and he had a pleasing flair for the lighter range of acting roles. However, he was lacking in Helpmann's musicality, as he wrote disarmingly in the *Vic-Wells Association Magazine,* about a rehearsal of the peasant *pas de deux* in *Giselle:*

> I walked graciously to my position for the beginning [of his solo], gave an acknowledging look to the chef d'orchestre and gaily commenced my solo ... suddenly things seemed to be not quite as they should. My steps refused to synchronise with the music, there was no sympathetic understanding, no inspiration, nothing ... it dawned on me. I was dancing the variation from *Le Lac des cygnes.*[21]

It is not possible to imagine Helpmann, always acutely aware of and in sympathy with music, having this kind of aberration. He and Turner appealed very differently to audiences, and each had warm and enthusiastic supporters (banners, apparently, were displayed in the Sadler's Wells 'gods'), but Helpmann's strength lay in his versatility as well as his musical responses. Already the ballet public had discovered his range, from classical princes to comedy cameos by way of the great dramatic roles of Satan and the Rake. It was beginning to seem as though there was nothing

– apart from technical dance fireworks – that he could not provide. For the most part, de Valois was able to find appropriate opportunities for both these young men. Just as they had different slots in *The Rake's Progress*, they went on to create the Red Knight (Turner) and the Red King (Helpmann) in *Checkmate*, and the Blue Skater (Turner) and the *pas de deux* (Helpmann) in *Les Patineurs*.

As well as employing Turner, the company had gained new young women. Pearl Argyle, the eldest of them, was from Johannesburg, a notable beauty and a decorative and delightful dancer who had difficulty in enlarging her talents beyond the 'chamber ballet' style of Marie Rambert's Mercury Theatre. Mary Honer was a delicious soubrette with a formidably strong technique. Pamela May had a marvellously cool linear elegance, while June Brae had good looks, great warmth and charm to compensate for less technical security than the others had. Most important, emerging from the corps de ballet was the exceptional Margot Fonteyn. She had already made a mark in a revival of Ashton's *Rio Grande* and now she was to be gently and carefully groomed to succeed Markova as the company's prima ballerina and Ashton's special muse.

On 8 October 1935, the Vic-Wells Ballet took into its repertoire Ashton's *Façade*, which had been created for the Camargo Society in 1931. The anomaly about this ballet is that, although Walton's music is closely linked with Edith Sitwell's poems, so that as a concert piece it can be given with a spoken narrative, Ashton's ballet-divertissement really does not relate to the words, only to the music. The revival was excellently cast. Ashton danced the Tango with a clever *demi-caractère* dancer, Molly Brown, as the Debutante. Turner and Chappell made a delightfully indolent Popular Song duo, and Fonteyn successfully took over the Polka, which had been created by Markova. A new *pas de trois* called Country Dance was introduced, a burlesque of a country girl (Argyle), her yokel lover (Richard Ellis) and a lecherous squire (Helpmann in plus fours and matching hat). Later in the month *Douanes* was revived, re-dressed by Sophie Fedorovitch, and Helpmann enjoyed dancing the leading role of Cook's Man opposite de Valois as the stylish Tight-Rope Walker.

November saw an important new Ashton ballet, *Le Baiser de la fée*, based on *The Ice Maiden* by Hans Christian Andersen and set to a score by Stravinsky, in which he cast Argyle, Fonteyn and Turner as the Fairy, the Bride and the Young Man. Ashton followed this in January 1936 with a rather rarefied *pas de deux* for Argyle and Helpmann. *Siesta*, a slight 'mood' piece of summer languor and sensual grace, may well have been an ancestor of mature works such as *Monotones*. Ernest Newman described it in *The Sunday Times* on 26 January:

> On the rise of the curtain we saw Pearl Argyle and Robert Helpmann recumbent on the stage, looking so comfortable that one almost felt inclined to call out to them not to dream of disturbing themselves on our account. But slowly, as the music went on, the conscientious couple seemed to realise that rather more than this was expected of them. They rose to their feet, felt the urge of life returning to their sluggish limbs, treated us for two or three minutes to a few dance movements, and then, apparently tiring of it all quite soon, wisely lay down again and seemed to share our relief that it was all over.[22]

Siesta was repeated at the gala opening of the Arts Theatre, Cambridge. For Helpmann, it began an interesting association: from 1936 until 1939 he choreographed for the revues staged by the University Footlights Club at the Arts. George Rylands, who directed the first Footlights Revue, *Turn Over a New Leaf*, in June 1936, enlisted him as dance-arranger, and Helpmann created a cabaret scene featuring the then novel dance, the samba. His dancers were two Panamanians, Harmodio and Tito de Arias. Margot Fonteyn, as a member of the Wells company, came to see the show (she was to marry Tito de Arias in 1955). Robert Hewison recorded that for the 1937 *Full Swing* Helpmann did a potted, send-up version of *Les Sylphides* for an all-male cast, and quoted him: 'I taught them the actual steps, and Peter Eade, who was the ballerina, actually got up on points. We played it absolutely straight, but I chose all the big football boys, with great big hairy legs and hairy arms. The audience got absolutely hysterical.'[23] (Obviously it was a primitive ancestor of the Ballets Trockadero de Monte Carlo!) *Pure and Simple* followed in 1938 and the *All-Male Revue* in 1939.

Earlier in 1936 (10 January) de Valois staged an enchanting little ballet, *The Gods Go A-Begging*. As *Les Dieux Mendiants*, the story and score (Handel arranged by Beecham) had been used in 1928 by the Diaghilev Ballet, with choreography by Balanchine, but de Valois's version had great grace and style as well as charming Watteau-esque designs by Hugh Stevenson. The tale was about the appearance of gods as servants at a courtly eighteenth-century *fête champêtre*. Argyle and Chappell were the Gods, but Helpmann had an elegant and flirtatious role as the leading nobleman, partnering Ursula Moreton for historically based formal dances. There is no suggestion anywhere as to his knowledge of historical dance, but de Valois had recruited, for the Academy of Choregraphic Art, the services of Nellie

Chaplin, who had made a special study of 'ancient dances and music', and he may well have been tutored by her.

The star production of the season, however, came in February when Ashton provided Helpmann with an outstanding principal role in *Apparitions*. This was a remarkable union of Liszt music (arranged by Lambert, who also wrote the scenario), exquisite Cecil Beaton designs, and a well-known Gothic theme of a poet pursuing his ideal woman (Fonteyn) through laudanum-induced dreams. This theme, of course, was also the basis for the Massine/Berlioz *Symphonie Fantastique* and Bronislava Nijinska's *La Bien-aimée / The Beloved One*. *Apparitions* was an immense success. Ashton, Lambert and Helpmann all knew how to present emotional theatre with conviction, and audiences of the time were more than ready to accept it. From the brief opening scene in which the Poet sees the triple vision of the Hussar, the Monk and the Woman in Balldress and then falls into a trance, Helpmann was able to draw an onlooker into the troubled mental world of Romantic thought. He could sustain the mood by mimetic intensity and fluently lyrical dancing, past the successive images of a ravishingly costumed ballroom, a snowbound plain, a funeral procession and a witches' sabbath, to a poetically achieved suicide. Modern revivals cannot reproduce the impact such a ballet made in the 1930s and 1940s.

These years of 1936 and 1937 were richly creative for the Vic-Wells Ballet. In addition to *Apparitions*, Ashton choreographed *Nocturne*, a delicately atmospheric ballet to music by Delius, about a young man torn between love for a young flower-girl and a society beauty whom he eventually chooses; a scintillating, and still popular, ballet-divertissement, *Les Patineurs*; and the unique and entrancing *A Wedding Bouquet*. De Valois staged *Prometheus* and *Checkmate*.

Helpmann had leading roles in all of them. There were no problems about *Apparitions* – as well as displaying his dance strengths of lyrical and musically sensitive movement, it made full use of his natural talent as a mime, which he had improved by studying with Karsavina as well as with Ursula Moreton and de Valois, both of whom had been tutored by another great mime artist, Francesca Zanfretta. *Nocturne* had similar choreographic qualities, conjuring up a dreamlike Paris redolent of *fin de siècle* nostalgia, and the *pas de deux* in *Les Patineurs* was perfectly tailored for him and for Fonteyn, with its smoothly gliding steps and unusual lifts.

A Wedding Bouquet was entirely different. It had a text from Gertrude Stein's play *They Must. Be Wedded. To Their Wife*, freely adapted by Lord Berners (who also composed the music and designed the set and costumes) in consultation with Lambert and Ashton. Fortunately, when she finally saw the ballet, Stein was delighted with it. Everything fell naturally into place once they began to work on the idea of a French provincial wedding at which everything goes slightly wrong (which quite possibly was picked up by Stein from Brecht's 1919 play, *A Respectable Wedding*). Episodic and impressionistic, and (for those who liked it) entrancingly funny, *A Wedding Bouquet* was blessed with an ideal cast. Mary Honer was the dumb little bride, Fonteyn the demented Julia, and June Brae the disarmingly inebriated Josephine. Helpmann's Bridegroom trod a brilliant tightrope of styles – stage dancing, classical dancing and Chaplinesque mime – to create a delicately balanced portrait of a charming philanderer caught in marital toils. As Mary Clarke has written, '*A Wedding Bouquet* gave [Helpmann] a refreshing and rewarding change [from romantic and traditional roles] and established him overnight as a comic actor of the first quality.'[24] In fact, it was Helpmann's improvisations one day at rehearsal that prompted Ashton to make the ballet so amusing; and together they worked out a superb skit of a classical *pas de deux* that Honer and Helpmann danced to perfection. In a radio interview in 1971, Helpmann spoke about how *A Wedding Bouquet* brought him 'into close contact with three extraordinary people – Berners, Stein and Alice B. Toklas. When first given the text,

> [I] read the words – and thought I had gone mad. I *had* read *Four Saints in Three Acts* when Ashton had done it in America, but this seemed to be absolutely potty ... Then we set off to meet Stein and Toklas in the south of France. They were brilliant and funny, very amusing. She used words as painters use paints, to get the effects she wanted. She explained that the words that were used in *A Wedding Bouquet* were based on remarks she heard as she went across the room at a village wedding.

Berners was even more eccentric, a man who could paint cross-eyes on his ancestors' portraits, feed buttered scones to a white horse sitting on a chair by his fireside, and dye his pigeons in an assortment of colours with vegetable dyes.

> He was so enthusiastic about life, a great character ... *A Wedding Bouquet* wasn't supposed to be a particularly funny ballet, it all happened in rehearsal ... it gradually grew to be hilarious. Mary Honer, who was marvellous as the Bride, really thought it was a romantic ballet – I don't think she knew for quite a considerable time that the more romantically she looked at me the funnier it all became.[25]

Recent, over-emphasised, revivals of the work fail to achieve the light-handed witty sophistication of earlier days.

Prometheus was something of an oddity. Lambert had devised a scenario that was neither completely serious nor entirely comic. Sibthorp describes it as giving a 'tongue-in-cheek twist to a legend that refuses to be twisted'. It was never very popular, although it did have its admirers. Even Sibthorp, who did not like it, admitted that there was 'fine, taut dancing, masculine yet graceful ... full of great bounds and soaring leaps' and that Helpmann had a 'lyrical *pas seul,* all lightness and energy'.[26] A critic for *Time and Tide* was seriously impressed: 'The ballet, regarded as pure dance form, is very satisfying, thanks to Ninette de Valois' simple and unaffected choreography, faithfully interpreting the classical form of the music. Robert Helpmann sustains the troubled, other-worldly mood with admirable success.'[27] Helpmann was not very happy with it; the aspect he enjoyed was creating a character who fulfilled his task of stealing fire from heaven in spite of having to cope with a demanding wife and family, as well as having a liaison on the side with an exciting seductress (June Brae).

On 19 January 1937, when Fonteyn, at seventeen, danced her first Giselle with Helpmann as Albrecht, the Sadler's Wells public had seen a significant sign of what later became the great Fonteyn–Helpmann partnership. Both critics and audiences of today are, of course, incapable of remembering anything before the great Fonteyn–Nureyev partnership! Fonteyn and Helpmann were tremendously compatible in all their work together, and over the years perfected a remarkable dramatic and lyrical rapport. In her *Autobiography*, Fonteyn looked back:

> It was in *Apparitions* that the harmony of dancing with Robert Helpmann began taking hold. ... As a man of the theatre he was the finest mentor imaginable. Helpmann had only to walk on stage to draw all eyes to himself, for he had a magnetic stage personality. ... And yet as a partner Helpmann was easy and considerate; he must have shown a good deal of patience with me, as I was so inexperienced. ... I had complete confidence dancing with him. ... The fourteen years of our felicitous partnership gave me time to develop, albeit unconsciously, my own presence and style.[28]

Throughout the mid-1930s, besides putting in a very full programme of ballet and other theatre performances, Helpmann lived an intensive social life. Apart from his own contacts with leading stage personalities and Lambert's special friends in the world of music and art, he was introduced into the large circle of titled and internationally important people that Ashton had steadily built up since the days when he was an impoverished student of Marie Rambert. Ashton had a talent for spontaneous entertaining at house parties, and Helpmann was a clever adjunct in impromptu acts and charades. He made close friends of the Sitwells, particularly of Edith, who thoroughly enjoyed his quick wit. He in turn relished her style and eccentricity, found beauty in her unusual appearance, and became deeply fond of her. Great ladies of histrionic quality would always appeal to him, whether they were grand-manner actresses such as Edith Evans or irresistible comics such as Margaret Rutherford. Sitwell wrote to Geoffrey Gorer about how Helpmann had entertained her with a hilarious mime of a story told him by Arnold Haskell (this is quoted in Haskell's *Balletomane at Large*). Haskell had been sought out by an aunt of Aldous Huxley's ('an imposing woman of a certain age'), entertained to dinner, and then 'she snuggled closer to me on the sofa, fixed me with her large, unblinking eyes and said, "Do you like kissing? It's all right, I've sent the maid away." I made a bolt for the door, slammed it and ran down five flights of stairs, a bearded heroine of a Victorian railway novel.'[29]

This high-society milieu was a completely amoral world of every form of sexuality and constantly changing extramarital attachments, in which young men and women spent their emotional energy on all kinds of amorous liaisons. It was far removed from most middle-class professional or business standards, and it was made exciting and enticing to young people by the wealth, the extravagance and the opulent lifestyles of the people who drew them in, just as they, as professional working artists, amused and excited the spoilt darlings who were willing to pamper them. In his brilliantly edited book of Edward Burra's letters, *Well, Dearie!*, William Chappell wrote of it: 'Sexual ambiguity was the rule. Sexual promiscuity and sexual aberration was the mode'; and, additionally, he points out that 'In the 1920s and 1930s it was practically a point of honour [for young artists] to send everyone and everything sky high'.[30]

Ashton and Helpmann were entirely divergent in their reaction to this stratum of society. Ashton, by temperament and upbringing, passionately desired to be accepted as part of it. Because of the riches, titles and social standing of these people, he was willing to play court jester to entertain them, but only within limits; he would always be careful not to offend them in any way because he intended to join them. Helpmann, with his inborn Australian independence, looked on them from a different viewpoint. He was delighted to test them out as an audience on which to sharpen his perceptions and flex his inventive muscle, but had no inferiority complex about them as people. He was not going to grovel to them because others were impressed by their power and their money – and, as an incorrigible taker of any stage, he was frequently tempted to challenge them with flamboyant and provocative behaviour. In her Ashton biography, *Secret Muses*, Julie Kavanagh makes an interesting comment to the effect that Ashton 'fitted in' with upper-class people, 'unlike the hilarious but socially hazardous Bobby Helpmann'.[31] Helpmann was 'socially hazardous' because he did not give a damn about any of them – unless, as with Edith Sitwell, he found something he valued in a personality.

The saving grace, however, for all the young dancers who were lured into the parties and house-parties of the powerful rich was that they were sincerely dedicated to their demanding careers. Whatever shenanigans they got up to in summer vacations or weekend relaxation, they were primarily bound to the disciplines of dance theatre, to classes and teachers, rehearsals and performances, and the steady enlarging of their artistic horizons.

6

In those days the social calendar was packed full of events, many linked with the summer season: parties, charity galas and costume balls (which often included dance engagements, such as a Silver Rose Ball in aid of the National Society of Day Nurseries in December 1935 for which Ashton arranged a tango-like *pas de deux* for Helpmann to dance with Lady Plunkett). There were the various royal courts at which debutantes 'came out', annual fixtures such as Wimbledon tennis, the Henley regatta or the Theatrical Garden Party. Helpmann, gregarious, amusing, immensely energetic, popular, and – as in Sydney in the 1920s – quick to take every opportunity for irreverent action, packed his free time full of diversions.

In 1937 everything was particularly glamorous because it was Coronation Year for George VI, and Helpmann had a special interest in royal activities because his sister Sheila was being presented at court. She came over with her mother and brother Max, and Bob had the job of escorting her from the Dorchester Hotel to Buckingham Palace. On the great day, therefore, a large hired car laden with two elegantly turned-out Helpmanns (Sheila in an exquisite court dress and traditional feathered headdress) joined the long, crawling line inching up the Mall. They played cards on their laps to while away the time until Sheila made her curtsey to the King and Queen.

In June the entire family went to Paris for a short ballet season arranged by the British Council to coincide with the great International Exhibition. Performances were given at the Théâtre des Champs-Elysées, and de Valois's *Checkmate* saw the light there initially as *Echec et mat*. Magnificently unified, with music by Arthur Bliss and striking designs by E. McKnight Kauffer, it also had four entirely admirable dancers in the leading roles. Brae was the magnetic and ruthless Black Queen, Turner the Red Knight who fell in love with her, May the tender and quickly defeated Red Queen. Helpmann was metamorphosed, at age twenty-eight, into the senile and poignant Red King who is finally checkmated. Annabel Farjeon, recalling the creation of the ballet, stressed that de Valois usually prepared her ballets beforehand and this time her 'private imaginings had been pretty accurate':

But as the Red King, Robert Helpmann took the character entirely into his own hands. He became a dithering, senile old man, pushed in every direction by his Queen and his Knights [she means the Black Queen and her Knights]. Unable to make up his mind, with arms shaking, he tottered from square to square as though blown by a violent storm, to be ultimately hoisted prostrate on the staves of the Black Pawns.[32]

P.W. Manchester wrote:

Helpmann and Pamela May were able to give performances which were in the great tradition of ballet mime. May in particular was a revelation. Not that Helpmann's portrayal fell behind hers, but by then we had come to take almost for granted his infinite variety, and though he could continue to delight, he could no longer astonish us.[33]

For Maytie and Sheila, it was a thrill to see Bob in works such as *The Rake's Progress, Apparitions* and the new *Checkmate.* Maytie wrote:

The horse chestnuts were all in flower, and we stayed at a dear little hotel called the Hotel Galilee. Ninette was with us, and Margot, Constant Lambert, Freddy Ashton and Leslie Edwards. Sheila and I poked about on our own during the day and went to the ballet at night, and afterwards picked up the others and went on to night clubs and low dives with some other friends. We never once got home before seven a.m.[34]

While Markova and Dolin were with the company in 1935, a successful summer provincial tour had been arranged, taking in Blackpool, Bournemouth, Glasgow, Edinburgh, Manchester, Birmingham and Leeds. Helpmann had been away with *Stop Press,* but the pattern was established, and from his return to the company he was involved in touring each summer. Audiences in the regions took the dancers to their hearts, enjoying them in programmes of mixed bills that included the latest London successes, such as *Apparitions* and *The Rake's Progress.* Well-established local newspapers such as the *Manchester Guardian* and *Yorkshire Post* produced informed notices. Very different from the high-society events of London, it was a life full of high spirits, good companionship and elaborate jokes (not by any means all of them outrageous or salacious), based on a vast selection of theatrical 'digs' and meals ranging from tremendous 'high teas' to deplorable porridge. There were other provincial events. Among a number of active ballet clubs, a particularly lively performing society was established in Liverpool, and each year, when it staged a programme, de Valois lent leading dancers and ballets. In January 1937 Helpmann and Fonteyn appeared there in Act II of *Le Lac des cygnes* and the Aurora *pas de deux*; in May 1938 he danced with Honer in *Casse-Noisette* Act III and de Valois's *Hommage aux belles viennoises*, and in December 1938 he and Fonteyn danced *Giselle*, with Ashton as Hilarion.

Another extramural activity came with the Vic-Wells Ballet's appearances on BBC television, an interesting new medium. As early as 1934 Helpmann had been televised in the Danse Chinoise from *Casse-Noisette* for a divertissement programme. The company as a whole was involved in regular television performances, beginning in November 1936 with excerpts from *Job*, with Helpmann as Satan. Few people could view the transmissions, and they were unrecorded and distinctly experimental, but the dancers found it all stimulating as well as welcome for the extra cash it brought. They presented several popular ballets, such as *Les Patineurs, Carnaval*, Act II of *Le Lac des cygnes* and, ambitiously, *Checkmate*, that could work reasonably well in the very restricted conditions of the time. Helpmann was in most of them. (All their appearances have been splendidly documented by Janet Rowson Davis in a series *of Dance Chronicle* articles.[35])

Helpmann, in addition, appeared with Dinah Sheridan in a play, *The Maker of Dreams*, in 1938 and with Maude Lloyd in Ferruccio Busoni's *Arlecchino* (termed a 'theatrical capriccio') in 1939. In 1936 Fokine was in Europe working with Rene Blum's Ballets de Monte-Carlo and later with de Basil's Ballets Russes de Monte-Carlo. Helpmann had already danced the lead in *Les Sylphides*, but Fokine now rehearsed him both in that and in the title role of *Petrushka*, with a view to his appearing as guest artist with one of the Russian companies. This never came about, but Helpmann found it fascinating to work on these ballets with their choreographer.

The first British performances of *Checkmate* were given during the regional tour in September 1937 and at Sadler's Wells on 5 October. There were no other new works that involved Helpmann, because he had leave of absence to act in *A Midsummer Night's Dream* at the Old Vic. Eager to gain experience in the spoken theatre, he had made a bargain with Lilian Baylis, a remarkable lady of whom he became very fond. Knowing her constant need for economy, he suggested that, instead of receiving the pay rise due to him, he should be allowed to audition with Tyrone Guthrie, the director, for the role of Oberon. When she agreed, he took great care over his dealings with Guthrie and the drama company, well aware that there might be some resentment over the use of a ballet dancer as an actor. Possessed of a naturally fine speaking voice, which he had regularly exercised in mimicry, he sought Margaret Rawlings's advice about a coach and benefited from working with Beatrice Wilson, who eradicated the last traces of an Australian accent as well as helping with voice production. In his audition he relied on the poetry of the role, eschewing all balletic movements or gestures. He was accepted by the rest of the cast and, in fact, caused flutters among the young women students who were taking part.

In her charming book *Dramatic School*, Patricia Don Young makes the point that they were all in the habit of going regularly to watch the Vic-Wells Ballet and were thrilled to be rehearsing with him:

Seeing him in practice clothes we had been prepared for disillusionment. But we soon discovered that there was something infinitely more arresting about this lithe figure in black tights than there had been in any blonde-wigged Prince. The general effect, the black hair bound back with a band and the slightly olive complexion, was most exciting – rather Spanish. We sighed with relief. And, leaning forward to catch some of the conversation, noted with satisfaction the musical cadence of the well-modulated voice.[36]

Baylis's action about Helpmann's request was, sadly, one of the last contributions she made to the history of the Old Vic. On 24 November 1937, she collapsed with shock at hearing the news that one of her much-loved dogs had been run over and killed, and she died on the following day. Helpmann admired her greatly, and never forgot what he owed to her. She had taken the keenest interest in him from the first, encouraged him in every way, and also forged a firm friendship with his mother when she visited London. It seemed tragic that Baylis was not there for the opening night of *A Midsummer Night's Dream* on 26 December.

The production, exquisitely designed by Oliver Messel and with dances arranged by de Valois to the Mendelssohn music, was acclaimed. Don Young and her friends were taught to fly, and loved it:

We zoomed our way up and down through the painted gauze forest screens without mishap and just regained *terra firma* in time to escort Titania [Vivien Leigh] on to the stage for her first rencontre with Oberon. How fantastically lovely they both looked. He, in a gleaming, scaly, insect-like costume, with a sharply-branched headdress and a glittering, iridescent makeup; she, in a silver and white ground-length ballet dress strung with garlands of leaves.

She describes the final scene:

We carried wands with lighted torches stuck in the tops, and when Oberon called out from the darkened stage: 'Through the house give glimmering light', on we would rush from four different points. This was the part we loved. In and out among the trees we weaved our various ways, waving the lighted wands and looking – so we were told – like white moths fluttering after a stream of flying glow-worms ... the air seemed heady with enchantment. It seemed to float down from the overhanging branches of the trees ... and above all else, it generated from the lean, green figure of Oberon who, standing motionless in the centre of the stage, used to be the focal point of our torchlight gyrations.[37]

The critics liked it too. Horace Horsnell opined in the *Observer*:

In Mr Robert Helpmann and Miss Vivien Leigh, Fairyland has a King and Queen who look their parts and move adroitly. The speech of this Oberon has clarity and fire. He wears his unearthly trappings with the airy confidence of a master dancer, and when he leaps or pirouettes the effort is not apparent.[38]

James Agate in *The Sunday Times* commented, 'Hardly any of the players in the present revival, with the exception of Mr Robert Helpmann, who is the Oberon, appears to have the faintest notion that he or she is speaking verse.' He went on to mention 'three outstanding performances' – Vivien Leigh, Gordon Miller as Puck, and 'Mr Helpmann's Oberon, the best I have ever seen or ever shall see in this line'.[39]

The gorgeous Messel costumes were the cause of one of the happiest anecdotes about the production. Helpmann and Leigh were presented to the Queen and the two young princesses, Elizabeth and Margaret Rose; during their bows their crowns became inextricably entangled and they had to back out firmly interlocked, and more than slightly hysterical.

In Helpmann's absence Ashton had staged the now lost but never forgotten *Horoscope*, which starred Fonteyn and the young Michael Somes. It was set to a score by Lambert and had designs of great simplicity and purity by Sophie Fedorovitch. It was a far greater success than the production de Valois created for Helpmann and Pearl Argyle in April, *Le Roi nu*, which had music by Jean Françaix and elaborate designs by Hedley Briggs that linked it to seventeenth-century court ballets. Horsnell in the *Observer* was reasonably kind to it:

De Valois has taken the scenario and composed new and ingeniously detailed dances for it. ... As the ballet proceeds, one begins to suspect that its decoration is better than its choreographic foundation. Individual dances look good, but the composition as a whole lacks progressive form ... The outstanding figure is Mr Robert Helpmann as the Emperor. He dominates all his scenes, and shares miming honours with the three tailors who are brilliantly made up and acted by Frederick Ashton, William Chappell and Claude Newman.[40]

Soon after, Helpmann was again on acting leave. He had been asked by the director Nancy Price to take three roles – Felix the Butterfly, Mr Cricket, and the Chief of the Yellow Ants – in a short-running production of *The Insect Play* at her Playhouse Theatre. It opened on 27 April, but on 10 May he was creating the role of Paris in a new and distinctly unmemorable Ashton ballet, *The Judgment of Paris*. This was staged for a gala to raise funds for enlarging the Sadler's Wells stage, and had music by Lennox Berkeley and designs by Chappell. The enlargement of the stage was part of an immensely ambitious project planned for February 1939: the production of Petipa's *The Sleeping Beauty (Princess)* in its entirety. Because of this, there were no new ballets during the rest of 1938. There was one excellent addition, however, to Helpmann's personal repertoire: he was lent to Marie Rambert to take over for half a dozen performances the leading role of A Personage in Ashton's 1933 ballet *Les Masques*. In it he partnered Maude Lloyd, and was admirably suited to the brittle, sophisticated comedy of flirtations and cross-purposes that so perfectly matched the Poulenc music.

Reviving *The Sleeping Princess* was a tremendous task. It was staged by Sergeyev and de Valois, in consultation with others who remembered the Diaghilev Ballet version of 1921, and with Lambert as music director. Relatively little money could be spent, so that Nadia Benois was commissioned to design, within a narrow budget, sets and costumes that came in for a great deal of criticism. Technically, the ballet made enormous demands on all the dancers, and extra dancers had to be recruited to swell the corps de ballet. Fonteyn, of course, was to be Princess Aurora – a frightening challenge. Helpmann would partner her as Prince Charming (and in the first weeks of 1939 he was once more acting Oberon at the Old Vic). Honer and Turner would dance the Bluebird *pas de deux*, Brae would be the Lilac Fairy. Mimes from Sadler's Wells Opera were enlisted for Carabosse and Catalabutte. There was more than enough work in store to occupy everyone's energies in the run-up to the first night, 2 February 1939.

P.W. Manchester hated the designs intensely, and commented,

> To me, the depressing effect of the whole decor permeates the production throughout. Fonteyn's Princess Aurora has the authentic dazzle and charm, allied to the classical brilliance which puts her high amongst present-day ballerinas. She and Helpmann have brought the famous adagio to a degree of perfection which is unsurpassed anywhere. But there is very little in the rest of the ballet which can truthfully be said to satisfy.[41]

In spite of this, the production won its public, and its performance steadily improved as the rest of the cast gained increased confidence and skill. The BBC televised Acts I and III, and a special accolade came in March, when the company were asked to dance those acts at the Royal Opera House, Covent Garden, at a Royal Gala for the state visit of the French President, M. Lebrun, and his wife. Leslie Edwards described this as

> a great and glorious night. Nobody minded the long wait [for curtain up], entertained as we were by Helpmann's impersonations of various members of His Majesty's Government, who he depicted as having just one last brandy at the French Embassy ... Our laughter, the grandeur of the setting and the occasion ... all this we thought back upon when, in a matter of months, we were at war.[42]

In March, too, Helpmann was acting again at the Old Vic, this time as a trio of characters in *The Taming of the Shrew* – Gremio, Nicholas and The Tailor. For the season, the company had several actors he would later know well – Laurence Olivier, Ralph Richardson, Anthony Quayle, Pamela Brown, Martita Hunt – and the designers, Oliver Messel and Roger Furse, would later design ballets for him.

There was another significant point: a small role in *Shrew* was played by Michael Benthall, a 19-year-old Oxford University student determined to make a career in the theatre. Benthall had been seriously involved with acting at Eton. Later he would be associated professionally with two plays in which he appeared there, Shakespeare's *King John* and *Hamlet* (he played the title role); and he had gone on to work with OUDS (the Oxford University Dramatic Society). He met Helpmann a few months earlier, when Sadler's Wells Ballet appeared at the New Theatre in Oxford. He had gone along to see *The Rake's Progress*, but as he had been to a party the night before, he fell fast asleep in the theatre. Meeting Helpmann later at an OUDS party, he had tried to tell him how marvellous he was, not having seen a step. Now they met again at the Old Vic during the run of *Shrew* and discovered that they were both Shakespeare enthusiasts. They even began talking about a possible production of *Hamlet* – a play that enthralled them both – for which Benthall might be associate director to Tyrone Guthrie and in which Helpmann would play the lead. This apparently pipe-dream idea was fulfilled in 1944. The Helpmann–Benthall friendship grew into a lifelong personal partnership that resulted in many distinguished theatrical collaborations.

The *Shrew* was again directed by Guthrie, and starred Ursula Jeans and Roger Livesey. Philip Page in the *Daily Mail* found it all 'the greatest possible fun', and declared that 'the virtuoso performance of the evening was that of Mr Robert Helpmann, who doubled the parts of the senile Gremio and the epicene tailor. And Mr Helpmann is a Sadler's Wells ballet dancer!'[43] Helpmann had also agreed to choreograph a piece, *La Danse*, for the Royal Academy of Dancing Production Club, set to Ravel's *La Valse*; but when he had no time to finish it, Wendy Toye generously did this for him. *The Dancing Times* felt that 'we saw enough of Helpmann's work to make us want to see a good deal more. The use he made of his dancers moving down the stage in straight lines and the general groupings of his *corps de ballet* (the Black girls with the occasional incursions of the Purple girls) was most effective, and formed a most attractive setting for the work of the two principals, Travis Kemp and Sadie Jacobs'[44] (Jacobs was later well known as Sara Luzita). It would be three years before any more of Helpmann's choreography would be on show.

7

The Vic-Wells Ballet's winter season of 1938/39 ended on 18 May and the summer passed in a provincial tour. The company appeared at the Princes Theatre, Manchester, from 21 to 26 August, and there Richard Buckle saw a mixed bag of repertoire. He later wrote very unenthusiastically about most of it, but ended:

> *Job* is now an English classic. It is a noble conception, nobly carried out. The music of Vaughan Williams and the paintings of Blake, adapted by Gwendolen Raverat, have a ripe biblical splendour. Ninette de Valois' groupings for the angels above and the children of Job below are simple and inevitable, while her dances for Satan form a daring contrast. John Nicholson was a patriarchal Job, Stanley Hall a statuesque God; and Helpmann, leaping, posturing, pointing, climbing the steps of Heaven, rolling down helterskelter to Hell, was Satan himself. More than any of our dancers, Helpmann is surely the rock upon which the Vic-Wells church is built.[45]

The company went on to Liverpool and gave its last peacetime performance there on 2 September at the Royal Court Theatre. It travelled to Leeds, where it was due to open at the Grand Theatre on 4 September; but on 3 September World War II was declared and everyone's lives and plans were thrown into total chaos. The company was disbanded the next day, and as London theatres were closed, the Sadler's Wells season that should have begun on 18 September was cancelled. Helpmann, along with Ashton and William Chappell, went to the Isle of Wight to stay at Quarr Hill with his father's sister Jean, who had married her English cousin Colonel Robert Rudyerd-Helpman.

Alternative arrangements were soon made for the company – and there are various views about who was responsible for the plans. What can be factually proved is that contractual details were, as usual, negotiated by the Old Vic–Sadler's Wells management. It was decided to tour on strictly economical lines. Ballets were to be accompanied by two pianos (played by Constant Lambert and Hilda Gaunt) instead of an orchestra, and everyone was asked to accept a cooperative basis for salaries, calculated on takings. Lambert and Ashton met the company on 18 September in Cardiff, as de Valois was staying in London to look after the Sadler's Wells Ballet School and help her doctor husband, Arthur Connell, with his short-staffed practice.

The tour was hard work. The company usually gave six evening performances and three matinees, with programmes chosen from a repertoire of eight widely varied, short ballets. The first date was Leicester on 2 October. By 26 December, however, as London had settled down to the 'phoney war' period, it proved possible to get back to Sadler's Wells, where the first new production, on 23 January 1940, was Ashton's immensely impressive *Dante Sonata*. This unforgettable confrontation of the Children of Light and the Children of Darkness, set to Liszt and exquisitely designed by Fedorovitch, matched the mood of the moment to perfection. Fonteyn, Somes and May were the tranquil personifications of Light, while Brae and Helpmann were magnificently strong exponents of Darkness. P.W. Manchester described it as 'a terrific emotional experience'. Writing in 1942, with the war still very much present, she said:

> Most of us feel at times, and particularly in these days, that the world is too much with us, and we would give anything to be able to roll on the floor and tear our hair and scream. *Dante Sonata* does it for us. Ten, even five, years ago such a ballet would have been unthinkable. Ten years hence it may be, we hope it will be, a museum piece of significance only as a symbol of a past world from which all hope had fled. Today it has a dreadful relevance which finds an echo in all our hearts.[46]

That 'dreadful relevance' meant that dancers and audiences were deeply involved with each performance of the ballet. It was a strong attraction during the next regional tour, which preceded a spring season that opened on 1 April at the Wells. The three-act version of *Coppélia* was then produced, with charming designs by Chappell that linked together blues, greens and whites, or fuchsia purples and reds, to marvellous effect. Honer and Helpmann made delightful partners as Swanilda and Franz, and Claude Newman was an excellent Dr Coppelius.

May 1940 brought a great adventure, now widely chronicled. As part of a national policy about cultural propaganda to neutral countries, a Vic-Wells Ballet tour had been set up by the British Council to Holland and Belgium, while ENSA (Entertainments National Services Association) had arranged for the company to continue to France to entertain the troops. They left England on 4 May for The Hague and opened on 6 May at the Theatre Royal to a packed and enthusiastic house, many women in full evening dress with tiaras and long white kid gloves. At the end, the stage was deluged with tulip petals. They went on by bus to perform at Hengelo, near the German border, and the next day continued to Eindhoven to dance at Philips's factory theatre. Their last performance was at Arnhem, and then they were bussed back to The Hague on 10 May – the day of the German invasion of Holland.

Annabel Farjeon, then a dancer with the company, has recounted what followed.[47] She remembered each detail and stage of the company's four-day ordeal of uncertainty and waiting, while de Valois argued with military authorities about how her dancers could be repatriated. They had to leave company properties such as music, sets and costumes for their ballets, and could take with them only small quantities of personal possessions. Where Helpmann's story is concerned, all accounts agree on how his spirit and sense of humour kept hearts from despair. In her *Autobiography*, Fonteyn affectionately calls him 'the court jester', saying that he 'wrapped truth in humour in order to break the tension he perhaps felt more than anyone else. He made a joke out of everything so that even de Valois, who felt personally responsible for the whole troupe, relaxed and laughed.'[48] Farjeon recalls him ad-libbing in the character of a well-known ballet fan, with invented telephone conversations commiserating with dancers' mothers about the Dutch debacle, and then entertaining the company with a spontaneous performance of highlights from *Miss Hook of Holland* that included songs and an impromptu clog dance. The company eventually reached Ijmuiden and were able to board a cargo ship for England. On 14 May all were safely home.

Maytie Helpman in Melbourne read a banner headline in the newspaper, 'Robert Helpmann caught in the invasion of Holland'. She tried desperately to get more information, and then on 14 May he cabled her himself: 'Arrived safely from Holland tonight, everything all right, do not worry, writing.' Some days later she had a long and dramatic account of it all from her son, who began, 'One hour ahead of the invading Germans, and after missing death by gunfire by inches, we escaped from Holland to England. I shall never forget the hell of Holland's invasion, which I saw at first hand.' He wrote of going onto the hotel roof in The Hague with Lambert and watching the German planes coming over and men tumbling from them, 'their parachutes billowing out behind them, floating gracefully down; they were a beautiful sight against the clear blue cloudless sky; it was hard to believe that their calm descent was the forerunner of destruction, terror and death.'[49]

Back in London, where German air raids were to become a part of daily and nightly life, the show went on with a remarkable example of British reaction to disaster: de Valois's new ballet, *The Prospect Before Us.* This was not only a comedy but a comedy about rival theatre managers in London in the late eighteenth century. One might ask what kind of relevance to a capital city in dire trouble there could be in such a production. There was, of course, none; but de Valois, taking a leaf out of Helpmann's Dutch behaviour, knew that a court jester could do a very great deal for public morale. The ballet was another work of the greatest unity. The music of William Boyce was arranged by Lambert, and the designs by Roger Furse were based on Thomas Rowlandson. The scenario was adapted by de Valois from John Ebers's book *Seven Years of the King's Theatre.* The choreography offered a stylish impression of the period and had delightful roles for Pamela May as Mlle Theodore, Alan Carter and John Hart as Didelot and Vestris, and Claude Newman as Mr Taylor. Helpmann was allotted the prize role of Mr O'Reilly. In a radio interview in Australia in 1971, he said that de Valois told him that

> O'Reilly 'was 'an outrageous character and it would be perfect for you' ... She always was very cut and dried in her mind over choreography ... but this was a comic character and she left a lot to me, saying every now and then 'I want you to invent something funny here ... I have left you lots of gaps, and you can really go to town with it.'.[50]

He did indeed do this, creating an incomparable comic study, and ending with a never-to-be-forgotten, by those who saw it, drunk dance. Horsnell, in the *Observer,* liked the ballet very much, and wrote that 'Pamela May, who leads the ladies, has never danced better; and Robert Helpmann, one feels, has seldom had the chance to dance so well. His bibulous defiance of managerial catastrophe is a cadenza worthy of Massine. This irresistible frolic crowns a season that has been as brilliant as adventurous.'[51] De Valois later wrote, 'In *The Prospect Before Us* I created in Mr O'Reilly a role that was deliberately inspired by Helpmann. He has made of this fantastic Rowlandson figure an endearing and entrancing character study of a balletic clown – culminating in the now famous inebriated dance'.[52]

Helpmann became a talking point in London for a different kind of comedy only a few days after his return from Holland. On 22 May a revue, *Swinging the Gate,* had its premiere at the Ambassadors Theatre. Everything about it was right: it was presented and produced by Norman Marshall; designed by Chappell and Hedley Briggs; and there was a bright battery of theatre stars on stage headed by Hermione Gingold, Madge Elliott, Peter Ustinov and Hedley Briggs. Helpmann, dashing over from Sadler's Wells in taxis after appearing in ballet, contributed a number of impressions of leading actors and actresses. *The Bystander* commented:

Robert Helpmann made his debut as an impersonator a week or two back when *Swinging the Gate* went on at the Ambassadors; his friends already knew his witty, malicious mimicries. Herbert Farjeon ranked his imitations thus: Isabel Jeans and Margaret Rawlings, superb; John Gielgud, fair; Laurence Olivier, very good; Margaret Rutherford, very good indeed. That Mr Helpmann is a fine actor is appreciated by anyone who has seen him in such Vic-Wells ballet roles as the Red King in *Checkmate* and [in] *The Rake's Progress.* From these to his burlesque bridegroom in *A Wedding Bouquet,* his Oberon in *The Dream,* and his turn at the Ambassadors is an astonishing range of versatility.[53]

The *Observer* said:

I have often felt of late that there should be a six months close season for imitations of famous players. Then Robert Helpmann arrives, and persuades one, so brilliant is his mimicry, that there is life in the old game yet. He fails only with Mr Gielgud. His ladies, Miss Isabel Jeans, Miss Margaret Rawlings and Miss Margaret Rutherford, are incredibly exact in aspect as well as intonation.[54]

His disguises were minimal. He wore a neat lounge suit and used only a hat, a wig or a boa to support his characterisation. Female impersonation, of course, went back to the *Sylvia* pizzicato in 1920; and in a later revue at the Tivoli Theatre, Melbourne, he had been an outstanding success in an impersonation of the American star Stephanie Deste as Wanda in *Rose Marie.*

The phoney war was over. No one had any doubt but that World War II was now properly under way. Air raids on London, at this point, were in the first stage of 'sticks of bombs' (five or six at a time, like a string of firecrackers) and incendiary bombs. These would be succeeded by V1 flying bombs and V2 rockets. People were setting up wartime routines for responding to constant alerts. Theatre performances continued, for the most part at earlier hours, often matinees. Warning signs were shown in the auditorium when alerts were on, but audiences stayed in their seats. If it was in the evening, we went home through blacked-out streets to houses whose windows had for the most part been replaced by weatherproofed material. We slept in Anderson shelters in our gardens, or Morrison shelters inside our rooms, or on underground railway platforms. Often we lacked hot food because gas and electricity supplies had been damaged. Those at work could be faced, at the end of the day, by barricades and a home and family destroyed.

To Helpmann, going home by underground to a mews flat near Victoria Station that he had taken over from Benthall, who was now serving as an army officer, the mass of people who spent every night in bunks or mattresses on the platforms were particularly memorable. He told Elizabeth Salter how he and Fonteyn would watch 'the community life of families, greeting each other as they settled down for the night in the places reserved for them; children bedded down beside couples making love under their blankets, and old people snoring as they slept.' He saw it as 'a return to the tribal instinct, a subterranean life that reached back through the centuries to man the cave dweller, with its own clearly defined rules'. The wide range of Helpmann's friends (throughout his life) is illustrated by the fact that it was he who suggested to the sculptor Henry Moore that he 'go down and look at them. Go and see, just for the shapes. Hundreds of them, shapes of people sleeping, people turning over, people stretching.' Moore did, and has left us a magnificent record of such scenes.[55]

As well as being short of sleep and home comforts, Londoners, like all Britons, were on short food rations. The dancers of Sadler's Wells Ballet (as it had begun to be called) were subject to the same dangers, privations and problems as the balletgoers who watched them. De Valois wrote,

> The company was now suffering badly from lack of sleep; I could sense a very real fatigue, due mostly to bad nights, disturbed days and lack of proper nourishment ... it was taking toll of everyone's reserves and even the reserves of youth [she had a number of teenage dancers to consider] were fully taxed.[56]

They were regularly losing men to the armed forces. Gradually Chappell, Richard Ellis, Leslie Edwards, Michael Somes, Alan Carter and Ashton were taken. The younger John Hart and John Field continued for some time, but went in the end. Helpmann, as an Australian, was not liable to the call-up; Gordon Hamilton, another Australian, and Alexis Rassine, a South African, were recruited, as was David Paltenghi, who was Swiss. Unlike World War I, when white feathers were sent to men who did not serve, this second world war put everyone in the front line. Sadler's Wells was no longer available for performances. It had been taken over as a refuge for bombed-out families, although the school continued for some time in the large rehearsal room. Provincial tours went on, as did ENSA tours to various camps. Punitive air raids were not confined to London but were encountered in Birmingham, for example, and in Bath.

8

The next London season, given at the New Theatre (later the Albery and now the Noël Coward) in St Martin's Lane, opened on 14 January 1941. The 27th saw the premiere of another remarkable ballet by Ashton, *The Wanderer*. Rehearsals for this had begun in the peaceful country setting of Dartington Hall, a residential college in Devon where the company had spent Christmas. Set to Schubert's *Wanderer Fantasia* and hauntingly designed by Graham Sutherland, it was a plotless ballet with a strong central role for Helpmann. The action symbolised phases and moods of a man's life: May and Somes represented young love, Margaret Dale and Deryk Mendel were the epitome of butterfly childhood, and Fonteyn had an unusual part to play, which became known, although never so programmed, as Worldly Glitter. The choreography was passionate, poetic, athletic and gymnastic. It was a controversial piece, slightly ahead of its time. *The Times*, as always then unsigned, found it all perplexing:

> The one thing which Mr Robert Helpmann and his colleagues never do is to wander. They dance, they run, they perform callisthenics of a vigorous kind; they fall in heaps on the stage, writhe over one another, and pile themselves in strange figures and shapes. ... Are we justified in assuming that any symbolism is intended? The printed programme gives us no clue, for the dancers are named but no characters are assigned to them. ... It is a brilliant exhibition of all the arts and antics of ballet technique. Perhaps that is enough, and it is merely oldfashioned to ask what it is all about.[57]

Horsnell liked it more:

> The choreography is ingenious, and some of the movements – particularly the pas de deux – beautifully danced by Pamela May and Michael Somes – are delightful. Robert Helpmann's histrionic fire lights up the somewhat posed part of the hero and his style is excellent ... In short, a spirited, original composition more likely to enliven contemporary programmes than crystallise into a classic.[58]

A different style of journalism in the *Evening Standard* anticipated tabloids to come:

Freudian fantasy in which a tortured soul is manhandled by brown and black inhibitions and clawed by green neuroses ... Central emotion-torn figure throughout was danced by Robert Helpmann; tattooed lads in blue football shorts and yellow shirts dragged him round before the inhibitions got him. But he had his lighter moments with delightful Margot Fonteyn, clad as a circus acrobat to represent World-Glitter. The Wanderer's travels are in his own mind. What a labyrinth![59]

Provincial tours continued to alternate with London seasons, and the regions appreciated them. C.F.D. in the *Yorkshire Post* wrote of a visit to Harrogate:

It is proper that in wartime such beauty as belongs to our national culture should be shared as widely as possible, not merely for the value of its contrast but because it is ours, is one of the things for which the war is being fought ... for beauty is surely the common ground on which all people meet in this matter of ballet. We may not understand all the technical subtleties which go to make its artistry. It may not even be always intelligible as a mimed narrative. But nobody could deny that this is human movement carried to a climax of conscious beauty, a kind of dream fantasy from which all heaviness has been refined away.[60]

The programme under review was *The Gods Go A-Begging*, *The Wise Virgins* (Ashton's biblical ballet set to J.S. Bach and designed by Rex Whistler) and *Les Sylphides* (danced by Fonteyn, Helpmann, May and Brae). The same critic reviewed the second programme:

It is a mistake to suppose ... that the ballet is always profoundly solemn. The Sadler's Wells Ballet ... is showing how cunningly a joke may be pointed with a toe-shoe ... In *Façade* ... it is the heart of the matter ... the whole company threw themselves into this brilliant clowning with terrific glee.[61]

The next new production, in May, was in complete contrast to *The Wanderer.* De Valois had planned to produce Gluck's *Orpheus* in 1940, using both opera and ballet companies, and Fedorovitch had completed a set of exquisite designs for this. Now, de Valois adapted it as a ballet with singers in the orchestra pit. This was a limpid and lovely work, featuring Helpmann as Orpheus, May as Eurydice and Fonteyn as Amor. These two productions

– *The Wanderer* and *Orpheus* – exemplify Helpmann's rewardingly accurate responses to all kinds of music. In every ballet he danced, and in every ballet he choreographed, music was the commanding officer and he the obedient serving man. In *The Wanderer* he had expressed many emotions reflected in Schubert's score through Ashton's vigorous and exciting choreography, while in *Orpheus* he personified the marvellous restraint and intense feeling of Gluck's opera (the tragic ending was used). His unforced versatility as a dancer was proved by his interpretation of music that ranged from Berners to Liszt, from Adolphe Adam to Richard Strauss, from Tchaikovsky to Roberto Gerhard.

In August and September 1941 he took over two of his greatest comic roles – Ashton's double of the Nocturne Peruvienne solo and the Tango in *Façade*, and Dr Coppelius in *Coppélia*. He was to become closely identified with both the Dago and Coppelius and, by virtue of his inventive and perfectly timed comedy, both were to give delight to countless audiences over the years. As a comedian of genius, he was endlessly entertaining. P.W. Manchester wrote:

> He has both humour and wit, and the two are exquisitely combined in what is probably to date his greatest triumph, the glorious, ridiculous, preposterous Mr O'Reilly in *The Prospect Before Us*. Leslie Henson [a fine English musical-stage comedian] himself has never made me laugh harder, and I am perfectly content to go on rocking for as long as he cares to sit on the floor and accept the applause [for his drunk dance] with that nicely adjusted mixture of drunken gravity and innocent, if breathless, pleasure at successful accomplishment.[62]

De Valois wrote:

> I am guilty of encouraging Helpmann's interpretation of Dr Coppelius up to the height of its utmost humour. Great clowns are rare, and Helpmann clowned Dr Coppelius with genius – sharply outlining the old man's stupefying senility with nonsensical detail. He laid bare those flashes of guile shown by wicked, frustrated old men who call on their wiles to offset their loneliness in a world they have set against them.[63]

These descriptions emphasise a vital element in all Helpmann's acting: its keen observation of, and sympathy for, human nature. Some dancers, tackling either Coppelius or the Red King, have produced clever puppet characterisations. Helpmann contributed real people with depth and background behind the surface portrait, and added to their memorability by apt and effective makeup. It was easy to fill in the daily life of Coppelius or O'Reilly or the Stepsister in *Cinderella* and even of the *Wedding Bouquet* Bridegroom, and discover a person conceived in the round.

The end of 1941 saw him making another tiny dance arrangement, a pretty little scene called 'The Old Shoemaker' staged for the actor Richard Hearne in the revue *Fun and Games*. He was also involved in a new medium, acting the small part of a Dutch quisling in the film *One of Our Aircraft is Missing*. This gave him the experience he wanted, to learn something about cinema at first hand; it featured him among actors such as Eric Portman, Alec Clunes and Peter Ustinov; it gave him some welcome extra cash; and, significantly for the future, it was written, produced and directed by Michael Powell and Emeric Pressburger, for whom he would eventually work on *The Red Shoes* and *The Tales of Hoffmann*.

Meanwhile, as a result of Ashton's call-up to the RAF, Helpmann was preparing his first ballet choreographed for Sadler's Wells Ballet. This was scheduled for 14 January 1942, and its subject, Milton's *Comus*, had been suggested by Benthall. Lambert, a master arranger of music for ballets, contributed and orchestrated a score taken from seven of Purcell's theatrical works, and Oliver Messel (in a week's leave from the army) enriched the production with eloquent Stuart-inspired designs. Two evocative excerpts from Milton's masque were spoken by Helpmann. *Comus* was warmly received. Horsnell wrote in the *Observer*:

> Milton's sweet sedate verse did not oppress the choreographic invention of Robert Helpmann or temper the artistic fire of his performance as Comus. This lovely little ballet is no mere routine addition to the repertory. It vindicates the brilliant talents of the artists concerned; shows that the modern stage can still establish contact with its illustrious past, and should enchant all beholders.[64]

Dyneley Hussey in *The Spectator* made the point that the 'choreography is well devised and shows imagination without ever becoming far-fetched, as so often happens when the desire to devise something new is not held in check by good judgment. ... *Comus* must be numbered among the best things Sadler's Wells has given us.'[65] Herbert Farjeon in *The Tatler* found Messel 'the presiding genius of this lovely fragment' and went on:

> Choreographically Mr Helpmann, whose first ballet this is, emerges if not startlingly at least well – and well is well! The sword dance of the

Brothers, the feast of the Rout, the whipping by the Attendant Spirit, the flowing entrance of Sabrina and her nymphs, are fresh mint and of fine stamp. Mr Helpmann's own performance as Comus is vivid, vital, electric, and worthy of the finest mime (I have said it before and shall probably say it again) since Nijinsky.[66]

The Dancing Times made an interesting point:

Robert Helpmann has followed the theme so closely that the dancers' movements immediately bring to the mind of the audience Milton's own words [It is typical of the time that the critic could imagine the audience knew its Milton!]. Thus, though the words are lost to the ear, their significance presented through the dance is made clear before the eyes of the spectators. That is the task of a 'literary ballet', and never hitherto has this choreographic problem been so brilliantly and perfectly solved in English ballet ... The actual steps are simple and do not call for a display of virtuosity. This is in keeping with the poem and is noteworthy because a choreographer, in his first ballet, is usually too interested in the actual technique of the dance to worry about characterisation. [67]

A.H. Franks, who wrote with great perception about all Helpmann's early ballets, later commented:

The stage spectacle ... was wholly exciting. The enactment of the Lady's adventures by means of solo movement punctuated by a series of highly inventive and beautiful tableaux, plus the quotations to which Helpmann gave perfect utterance, formed a work so satisfying that I was unconcerned as to whether it should be called a ballet or a masque. Checking my memory now ... I am struck again by the composition of the groups, the slow majestic development of the action, the delicate hints of characterisation ... and the abundant invention in all the elements.[68]

The ballet began with the Attendant Spirit (Margaret Dale), the guardian of virtue and chastity, alone in a wooded glade. Her slow solo – a kind of invocation – was entirely a matter of line and balance in arabesque, as she indicated in turn the paths of evil and of good. As she left, the Rout appeared, human beings altered into beasts by Comus (the son of Bacchus and Circe). They were dressed in satins, feathers and lace, rollicking and jigging in drunken good humour and driven on by their delighted master.

Here was recited the opening speech, the passage that begins, 'The star that bids the shepherd fold / Now the top of heaven doth hold' and ends, 'Come, knit hands and beat the ground / in a light fantastic round.' The ensemble that followed formed an amorous and mock-courtly circle as background for a leaping and turning solo from Comus, but ended when he drove off his beastly retinue on the approach of the Lady – Fonteyn, dressed in white, and the embodiment of beauty and chastity. Separated from her accompanying brothers, she expressed her anxiety and exhaustion in delicate *pointe* work and wandering floor patterns. Comus returned, disguised in manner as a simple and subservient shepherd, offering to guide her to her escorts. She was hesitant, unsure at first of trusting him, so he used his magic powers to persuade her. As soon as they left, the Brothers (John Hart and David Paltenghi) appeared, searching for their sister, and established their characters as soldierly young men in a vigorous sword duet. The Attendant Spirit appeared, warned them of the Lady's danger, and began to guide them to Comus's palace.

Where the first scene was an exquisite landscape of a wooded glen, the second was a high arched hall, in front of whose open windows stood a low garlanded table set with wine and fruit and a central candelabra. Surrounded by the Rout, Comus (now resplendent in regal scarlet) led in the Lady. Waking her from her bemused state, he wooed her in a *pas de deux*, but she continued to shrink from him. Lifting her to the table and setting a crown on her head, he continued to dance in front of her, and then poured enchanted wine into a goblet. He raised it to her lips and, with the second speech, tempted her to drink. That speech began, 'Why are you vex'd, lady? Why do you frown?' and, after describing the delights that the potion would bring her, ended, 'One sip of this / will bathe the drooping spirits in delight / beyond the bliss of dreams. Be wise, and taste'. At this point the Attendant Spirit and the Brothers arrived and dashed the cup from Comus's hand. He fled. To free the Lady from his lingering spell, the Spirit conjured up the river nymph Sabrina (Moyra Fraser) with her attendants, and their rippling dances, in which long gauzy scarves gradually winding over Sabrina's arms symbolised the unwinding of the threads of evil magic, restored the Lady to a joyous reunion with her brothers. The Spirit, brandishing a long whip, drove off the Rout in disarray, and in an apotheosis the frustrated Comus was contrasted with the happy and united family group.

The unity of inspiration among choreographer, designer, the Purcell/Lambert music and Milton's poetry made *Comus* a lasting pleasure. But how was Helpmann to follow that beginning? He had already made the decision. He had always been captivated by the play *Hamlet*. He had grown up with a keen appreciation of Shakespearean drama and poetry, and was now also familiar with literary commentaries, ideas and differences. Authorities such as Nevill Coghill, John Dover Wilson and G.B. Harrison had ensured that, where *Hamlet* was concerned, every pro and con was aired and debated with exciting daring, and every psychological nuance suggested. Like so many others in the theatre, Helpmann wanted to act the part. He hoped that someday Tyrone Guthrie would let him do so.

Meanwhile, he could work on a ballet. Talking the project over with Lambert as well as with Benthall, he came to a vital decision. Not for him the blow-by-blow translation of play scenes into dance episodes spun out at great length. Instead, he envisaged a very short work (to Tchaikovsky's *'Hamlet' Fantasy Overture*) into which, with cinematic fluency, he could distil the essence of the play, rather than parallel its text. As he listened to the music, he found all the clues he required for an impressionistic action. Taking as his text the chilling phrase 'For in that sleep of death what dreams may come', he considered characters and actions as Hamlet's dying memories, fragmentary, confused and full of ambivalence. He needed a designer, someone with a striking personal vision, and in one of his regular sweeps around the Bond Street area art galleries he found exactly the right one.

Leslie Hurry was Helpmann's age; a birth date of 10 February 1909 made him almost exactly two months older. A delicate, imaginative child, he had struggled throughout the 1930s towards an artistic style of his own, becoming more and more isolated and introspective. By November 1941, however, when Helpmann saw his work at the Redfern Gallery, he had reached a stage where, to quote C.W. Beaumont, he 'sought to give expressive form to his scattered thoughts and combine them into a subjective composition: anatomical details, sectional drawings, and chosen symbols were knitted into a planned pattern'.[69] Helpmann was immediately drawn to these pictures, especially, perhaps, to a dramatic and moving portrait of Hurry's dying friend Grace Douglas, which Raymond Ingram has described as 'a combination of representation and surrealist fantasy' that attempted 'to portray the imaginative world of the sitter'.[70] This married perfectly with Helpmann's vision of his ballet *Hamlet* – according to Beaumont, 'he felt that Hurry was endeavouring to express in painting what he himself hoped to convey in terms of mime and dance' – and he immediately invited Hurry to discuss a collaboration. They listened to the music together, Helpmann told him what he was planning to do, and Hurry agreed to the proposal. Jack Lindsay writes, 'Helpmann's idea of the ballet as a fitful flaring leap of imagery through Hamlet's mind at the point of death was something to which Hurry could unreservedly respond; and his design and costumes powerfully uttered this crisis-moment in the drama'.[71] The result was a triumph, as was discovered when the ballet (or, as Beaumont terms it, the 'mimodrama with dances') had its premiere at the New Theatre on 19 May 1942. For Hurry, it was the beginning of a fruitful career in the theatre; as Lindsay says, 'because of it, Hurry found the solid ground for which he hungered'.

An enthusiastic audience for a first night is no guarantee of critical approval, and with a creation as powerful and unusual as Helpmann's *Hamlet* there was bound to be controversy. Writing quickly, some critics inevitably took the easy way out of describing what they had seen. First of the admirers was Elspeth Grant in the *Daily Sketch*: 'This dynamic, enthralling ballet opens and ends with the carrying away of Hamlet's corpse ... The dream-distortion of the incidents of the play, the confusion of Gertrude and Ophelia, or Yorick and the gravedigger, is brilliantly conceived and executed'.[72] Horsnell in the *Observer* called it 'a firstrate piece of imaginative theatre, excitingly assembled, brilliantly decorated, and appropriately tuned ... A striking virtue of this new work is the theatrical mastery and reconciliation of its prime elements – drama, music and decoration. It has a passionate homogeneity.'[73]

Dyneley Hussey in *The Spectator* was one of those who was bothered about the lack of dancing and found the music unhelpful, its 'unrelieved shadows' meaning that 'the potential man of action that Hamlet is cannot be emphasised'. However, he allowed that the ballet 'has the peculiar fluidity and inner logic of a dream. Mr Helpmann has made an imaginative re-creation in another medium of Shakespeare's poetic idea ... [It] is in the nature of a stimulating essay upon his theme. It would puzzle exceedingly an audience ignorant of the original'.[74] This last was certainly a valid point, but Helpmann was not in the business of catering to 'popular' taste or knowledge. The London theatre audience at the time knew its classics. Critics could assume that their readers would pick up all kind of references in a way that is now impossible, and a choreographer could assume the same type of education in his viewers.

Herbert Farjeon felt that Helpmann's ballet 'should be as eagerly discussed as widely enjoyed'. He put his finger on a salient point:

[The ballet] presents, as it were, the play's rarefied essence, not its narrative counterpart. Ballet, pure and simple, it is an independent work of art of a rare and lovely order; and to attempt closely to collate its action with that of the play would be to pursue elusive analogies. The blending of its prime elements – dancing, decoration and music – is close and congenial. They are equal and happy partners. The emotional effect aimed at is quickly achieved and brilliantly sustained. It has the throbbing, irrational intensity of a dream. Mr Helpmann's keen sense of the theatre is shown by the coordination between the ballet's technical and aesthetic features, his skill in the economy with which he makes each point without interrupting its mood ... the heart of the tragedy is there, epitomised and presented from Hamlet's point of view.[75]

There were remarkably few dissenting voices, although there was, of course, a core of balletgoers who could not accept such a 'mimodrama' without set dances in the ballet repertoire. Oddly enough, one of them was A.V. Coton, who wrote very disparagingly of 'long mime episodes linked by multiple chorus entrances and exits'.[76] Yet Coton was a foremost admirer of Kurt Jooss's *The Green Table* and *Big City*, which had as little formal dancing as *Hamlet*. Helpmann made it clear in a speech to the Royal Academy of Dancing in July that he had made very positive decisions about the content of *Hamlet*:

To have attempted to treat [it] in terms of *fouettés* and *entrechats* would have been completely wrong, both dramatically and musically, but to exclude a choreographic dramatic rendering of such subjects because they demand a larger element of mime than pure dancing seems to me to be dangerously limiting the scope of the ballet as a whole. I therefore tried to adjust the conventional mime of the classical school and combine it with the movement, thereby evolving a type of mimetic-movement which should be more understandable to a modern audience.

The question of the general audience was always to be of prime importance to Helpmann, and in this address he insisted that

ballet is essentially a theatrical art; its function is in the theatre, so that its appeal must be theatrical, and therefore to me ... the first and foremost thing is to appeal to the theatregoing public and not to a specialised few. No artist likes to imagine that his art appeals only to a specialised few. And I feel convinced that if ballet is to take its place in the public's heart beside the cinema and the other forms of theatre in this modern age of action, its appeal must be theatrical as well as purely technical.

He could not resist the comic ending, and quoted a letter he had received: 'I want you to know how very much I enjoyed your new ballet. As I have many times said to my husband, *Hamlet* always has been ruined by the words.'[77]

The ballet opened with Hamlet's body being carried offstage by four cowled and robed pallbearers, rather than the play's soldiers. After a very brief blackout, the action began. It has to be stressed that from beginning to end it was a matter of swift cinematic images, economical in movement but rich in significance; each one translated visually some key passage in Shakespeare's text. The Gravedigger appeared first, rolling Yorick's skull downstage and, as Hamlet entered, holding it up to him. Hamlet was drawn back by the Ghost, turned to face him, and was told of his father's murder. Court ladies appeared, dancing, and were followed by Polonius and Laertes, Claudius and Gertrude. Ophelia and Gertrude moved alternately before Hamlet, stressing his ambivalent feelings for both. The stage cleared. Laertes returned to bid goodbye to Ophelia in a brief duet. Polonius interrupted this to send Laertes away, and then directed Ophelia to Hamlet. They, too, danced a duet, tender and lyrical until Hamlet became aware of Claudius and Polonius watching them, when the mood abruptly changed. The court returned, and the Page (as Prelude) gathered everyone round for the play-within-a-play, in which the characters were projections of Hamlet's imagination: the Ghost identified with the Player King, Ophelia with the Player Queen. Hamlet forced Claudius and Gertrude to watch the murder. Ophelia took the orb from the Ghost's hand, Claudius moved forward to pour the poison into the Ghost's ear, and Hamlet pointed to him accusingly. Hamlet embraced Ophelia–Gertrude, the court dispersed in dismay. Claudius knelt; Hamlet drew his dagger to kill him but instantly stopped, seeing him at prayer. Polonius appeared and Hamlet rushed to stab him. Gertrude entered, passing Polonius's body, followed by the Ghost, who forced Hamlet slowly across the stage, where he collapsed on the steps.

He therefore saw nothing of the next section. Claudius and Laertes entered, struggling, but were disturbed by the mad Ophelia. There were flowers in her hair and in her hands. She wrung her hands as she danced, and gave flowers to Laertes, to Claudius and to Gertrude. She embraced Laertes passionately, and then left, followed by him in sorrow. Hamlet rose as a funeral cortege approached him, led by a woman mourner. As she reached him, she opened her veil to reveal herself as Ophelia and not the Queen. Bewildered, Hamlet pulled aside the shroud from the bier and found that the body was his mother's. He sank to his knees and the bier was hurried over him and offstage. Laertes, about to kill Hamlet, was restrained by Claudius. Hand-clasped as plotters, they left together. The court assembled, carrying goblets; the Page (now identified with Osric) brought the foils; Claudius, Laertes and Gertrude greeted Hamlet. The tragedy happened with the greatest rapidity. Gertrude drank the poisoned wine, Hamlet and Laertes took up their foils, Laertes stabbed Hamlet in the back. Hamlet, turning, stabbed Laertes, Laertes accused Claudius of poisoning the sword-tip, and Hamlet, knowing he was dying, fought with Claudius. Then, seeing that Gertrude had been poisoned by the wine, he forced Claudius to drink its dregs. Surrounded by the dead, he watched the Gravedigger enter tipsily, holding the skull as a cup, which he offered to Hamlet. About to take the skull, Hamlet was arrested by the pains of death. The four pallbearers entered and lifted his body, so that the end of the ballet matched the beginning – as does the Tchaikovsky score; at every point in the entire action. in fact, the already existing music had been perfectly allied with the dramatic action.

Hamlet was stamped with a tremendous application and vision. Helpmann had steeped himself in the play, its characters, its atmosphere and its puzzles, and applied his acute imagination to its every facet. The correspondence between action and play-text was endlessly fascinating for any student of Shakespeare, and appealed considerably to everyone interested, or working, in the dramatic theatre. Once the cue of contrasts and identifications was grasped, the wealth of subtle nuances made it a stimulating exercise for a literary mind. Details, such as the complex tenor of Ophelia's behaviour in madness, were all traceable in movement and expression; for example, her bawdy songs were recalled in the way she wantonly fondled the legs of Claudius and Laertes.

9

The ballet made Helpmann even more the talk of the town in London, although he had already become well known through his performances and his personality. It was difficult for Ashton – unhappy in his service life in the RAF, temperamentally subject to feelings of insecurity about his own work, and jealous of admiration given to other artists – to accept his popularity and his success. It was inevitably galling, for example, to hear how audiences delighted in Helpmann's Nocturne Peruvienne and Tango in *Façade*, when these had been Ashton's much-admired creations. It was worse to hear him praised as a choreographer. Ashton, indeed, felt that he had to rally all his friends and supporters to ensure that his own importance to Sadler's Wells Ballet would never be jeopardised. From that time on, his resentment against Helpmann never lessened, however much they might later tussle happily on stage as the Stepsisters in *Cinderella*.

In 1942, however, Helpmann, whose character did not tend to feelings of martyrdom, continued to make the most of any chances that came his way. That summer he composed dances for two musical shows, the revue *Fine and Dandy* and the Jessie Matthews musical *Wild Rose*. When people realised he could speak as well as dance, the BBC invited him to give poetry readings, take part in comedy shows such as Arthur Marshall's 'Nurse Dugdale' spots, and talk on various services, including the Forces Programme.

ENSA had found that the Services accepted ballet, and men on leave were frequently going to performances at the New Theatre or in tour cities. They were impressed, and carried the memories into their wartime lives. In July 1944 *The Dancing Times* printed a short piece, 'A Balletomane in a German Prison', by Lieutenant David James, RNVR: 'Fortunately I had had a week's leave of eight visits to the Wells [Sadler's Wells Ballet] just before capture and was actually sitting in Germany within a fortnight of sitting in the New Theatre. My ballet memory was therefore fresher than usual.' He got phonograph records of ballet music and produced two recitals with a running commentary: 'I attempted to finish the second programme with as close a reconstruction of a ballet as I could. For this purpose I selected *Comus*, both because I regard it as one of the finest of modern ballets and also because its structure and the relationship of music to action is such as to render it easy of analysis by the non-expert.' He goes on to describe how he made a backcloth with the characters drawn in pastel chalk and

Cinderella – A Stepsister, with Frederick Ashton.   (*Anthony Crickmay*)

Job – Satan's dance.
(*Gordon Anthony*)

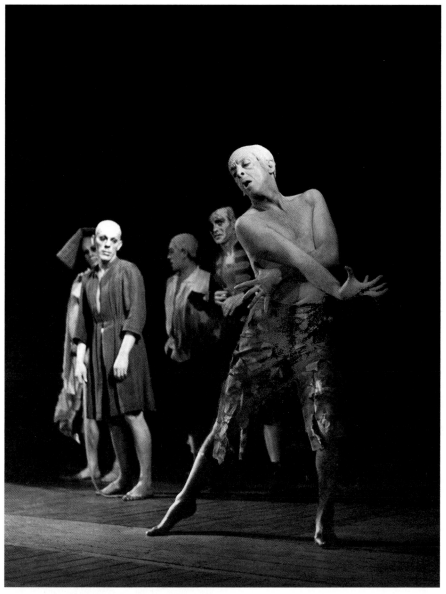

The Rake's Progress – The Rake. The mad scene, with Ray Powell as the Man with a Rope. *(Roy Round)*

The Prospect Before Us – Mr O'Reilly. The drunk dance. (*Gordon Anthony*)

Coppelia – Dr Coppelius.   (*Gordon Anthony*)

Hamlet (the ballet) – Hamlet.   (*Gordon Anthony*)

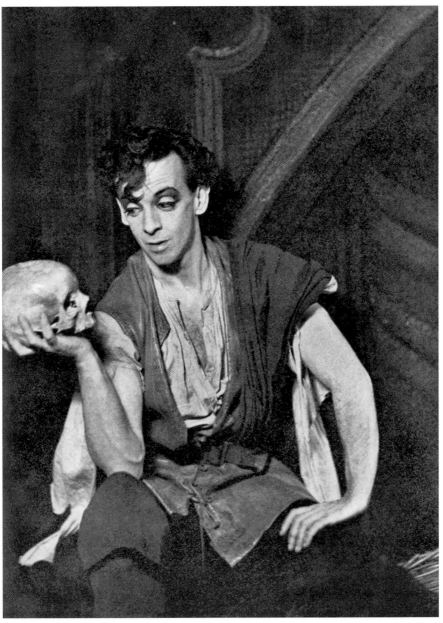

Hamlet (the play, 1944) – Hamlet.　　　　　　　　　　　　(*Gordon Anthony*)

Miracle in the Gorbals – The Stranger. With Pauline Clayden as the Suicide. (*Gordon Anthony*)

then talked about the different types of movement of the Attendant Spirit, Comus, the Lady, her Brothers, the Rout and Sabrina before playing through the music. The prisoners also compiled a weekly home-news bulletin of non-personal information from private letters, and Lieutenant James comments: 'Since relatives were continually going to the ballet in all parts of the country, hardly a week passed without some mention of Sadler's Wells Ballet's activities in London or the provinces.'[78]

In a Forces broadcast, Helpmann talked of dancing for troops in garrison theatres and for audiences of munition and other war workers in the provinces. With the company, he was touring extensively and working hard. Week after week he was alternating Franz and Dr Coppelius, dancing *Les Sylphides, Swan Lake, Giselle,* and the Dago in *Façade* as well as his own two ballets. Ballet, for these audiences, was 'something they had read about and perhaps dismissed as vaguely highbrow and "West End", yet they took to it like ducks to water and flocked in. And it wasn't the comic ballets with their broader appeal that rang the loudest bell, but the old ones like *Les Sylphides* and *Swan Lake.*'[79]

One of the tour dates, in June 1942, was at the open-air theatre in Victoria Park, Hackney. Pleasantly situated, seating, on slatted iron chairs, about 250 people, with a nearby kiosk for teas and ice creams, this was an agreeable way of watching *Les Sylphides, Casse-Noisette Act III* and *Façade*. When rain fell (but it was rather a good-weather week) the performance had to stop because the unprotected musicians could not risk instruments getting wet. The audience put up its umbrellas and stayed in place until the shower was over. *Façade* began, and Helpmann as the Dago leant out from the covered stage and mimed to the public that the rain was past and the sun was shining again ... There were other open-air seasons in later years; and even after the company transferred to Covent Garden after the war, touring dates could be unusual: regular balletgoers found themselves in the large Davis Theatre, Croydon, at the Woolwich Granada, at the Gaumont State Theatre, Kilburn, or the sizeable but long-gone King's Theatre in Hammersmith.

In autumn 1942 de Valois revived *The Rake's Progress* for the first time since Holland, restoring to Helpmann one of his greatest roles. It was a particularly good staging, admirably cast with a mixture of older and newer talent. Set against Joy Newton's adorably common Ballad-singer and Honer's wide-eyed and warm-hearted Betrayed Girl were delicious cameos of ladies of the town from Celia Franca and Palma Nye. Gordon Hamilton was memorably fine in a double of the Dancing Master (very delicate) and the Gentleman with the Rope (starkly realistic). Helpmann himself was absolutely in command throughout: in the witty burlesque of the opening scene; in the rollicking ribaldry of the orgy (he was alone in making a link, at the end of that scene, by a fractional turn of the head and change of expression, with the beginning of true decadence that the Rake shows when he allows the Girl to pay off his debtors); in the desperation of the gambling den; and in the deep pathos of the madhouse. This final scene was painful in its intensity. In the long passage where he was merely present on stage, his emotional reactions were conveyed through his eyes and never at any point over-stressed. All shades of feeling were encompassed – horror, peace, comprehension struggling with uncomprehending misery, memories of civilised behaviour and impulses toward primitive violence – and all were aptly linked to the music and the choreographic action.

In November Helpmann staged his third ballet, *The Birds,* to Respighi's *Gli uccelli.* Obviously, pressure was put on him to prove that he could invent orthodox dance *enchaînements* and deal with a typically balletic subject in terms of classical dancing. The choreography he composed was original and attractive; the ballet itself was neither a success nor a flop. It was mounted on the younger dancers, with Moyra Fraser starring as the delightful Hen and Beryl Grey creating the lyrical Nightingale. It might have had a very different fate if it had been cast with more experienced artists, who could have given its dance technicalities with a greater sense of excitement. Undoubtedly, however, it was a contradiction of Helpmann's true creative talent and a disappointment to those who felt he should have been encouraged to stage a powerfully theatrical successor to *Comus* and *Hamlet.* Its strongest suit was in design; Helpmann, again looking around art galleries, chose a Chinese artist, Chiang Yee, who was making a name at the time with his illustrated books as 'The Silent Traveller' and who produced a ravishing garden setting and charming costumes.

It was not fiercely criticised. Horsnell in the *Observer* termed it 'a pretty piece of animated chinoiserie'.[80] Elspeth Grant in the *Daily Sketch* called it 'light, sweet, delicious';[81] and James Redfern in *The Spectator* found it 'an entrancing ballet' with 'just the right touch of sentiment' in the comedy and a rewardingly 'complete unity of style in music, choreography and decor'.[82] *The Dancing Times* made the point that 'the choreography is full of invention and clever parody. If anything, in some instances it is too complicated, and although one admires the freshness and charm of the young dancers of this company, one has to admit that some of the *pas* are still beyond their technical powers. It seems that occasionally the choreographer has become too interested in the technicalities of movement'.[83] *The Birds* was hampered by an overenthusiastic reception from fans, something that was beginning to be a problem in Helpmann's career. Unwise adulation, in the audiences and sometimes in print, inevitably pushed some people into an equally unbalanced state of animosity toward him and his undoubted versatility.

January 1943 saw Fonteyn's debut in the comedy role of Swanilda in *Coppélia,* with Helpmann now firmly entrenched as Dr Coppelius, which gave him rather more fun than Franz. Fonteyn was an instant success (although she became more effective still when she had settled in to the style and possibilities of the role). What was not instantly apparent was the brilliant teamwork that she and Helpmann would gradually set up in Act II, so that no Franz could make very much impression when they were around; but it soon was noticed that they were engaged in a fruitful battle of wits, a grand rivalry in which on every occasion they enjoyably did their best to cap each other's ideas. Helpmann's Coppelius drew critical plaudits. In *Time and Tide* Edwin Evans called him 'a resourceful mime with more than a dancer's dramatic imagination. His choreographic regulation of senility was a feat of virtuosity, a Pantaloon of deftly contrived steps and gestures'.[84] *The Times* commented, 'The way that shuffling gait with which he enters develops into an ingenious dance of the most rapid movement, without ever dropping the character of the old necromancer, is one of his most brilliant creations'.[85] *Apparitions* was revived in March, and Helpmann also arranged the dances for a delightful production of *The Merry Widow,* starring old friends of his, Cyril Ritchard and Madge Elliott.

At this point Ashton got leave from the RAF to create a new ballet. It was perhaps not a particularly good idea, after *Comus* and *Hamlet,* to go to a literary source for a subject, but the new production was *The Quest,* based on Spenser's *The Faerie Queene,* which had been adapted by Doris Langley Moore some five years earlier. With a commissioned score by William Walton and designs by John Piper, it had many choreographic felicities but also many longueurs – particularly, unfortunately, in the final scene in the House of Holiness. Helpmann was provided (probably intentionally) with an exceedingly dreary role as St George. It came slightly alive only when he fought and killed the three Saracen knights. The curly brown wig, heavy tunic, voluminous cloak and large red banner with which he was initially saddled fairly rapidly disappeared. In *Time and Tide* Edwin Evans overlooked any choreographic weaknesses, saying

Frederick Ashton has made of it a true dancing ballet. Not only are there dances, but the action itself is danced as well as mimed. As there has been in some preceding ballets a tendency to stress the action at the expense of the dance, this production was feted by the audience as the return of the prodigal.[86]

Taking a different view, at a later visit *The Times* considered it

essentially a dramatic piece, theatrically effective, and relying for its tension more on its construction than on its actual dancing. ... A good deal of the choreography lacks distinction. Mr Ashton is too experienced and too resourceful ever to be at a loss for an appropriate movement, but it is only in the grouping of the last act and in the dances of combat that he has struck off anything with the mark of inevitability on it.[87]

If St George was a deadly bore, the return of two joyous character-isations, Mr O'Reilly and the Bridegroom in *A Wedding Bouquet*, compensated Helpmann for its tedium. *A Wedding Bouquet* was new to most current balletgoers, as it had been out of the repertoire for some time. It completed the tally of comedy ballets, in total contrast but delightfully complementary to *Coppélia*, *Façade*, and *The Prospect Before Us*. It was extremely well cast and staged, and was given extra point by Lambert's joyous narration in place of the original chorus. The delectable mixture of Fonteyn's mournful Julia, Moyra Fraser's bibulous Josephine, Palma Nye's brisk Webster, and Margaret Dale's silly, sentimental bride made a perfect setting for Helpmann's immensely clever Bridegroom. This was not a credible character like O'Reilly or Coppelius, but a subtle composite observed from Astaire, Chaplin, French farce and English music hall. As in *Façade*, he contrived both to act and comment on the choreography, creating a fine liaison between the work and the watching audience.

In that autumn of 1943 Helpmann also put in some time, and earned some money, filming the tiny comic cameo of the Bishop of Ely in Laurence Olivier's *Henry V.* Then, in September, the company had an important date when they restaged *Le Lac des cygnes* with brilliant new designs by Leslie Hurry, infinitely better than the revised versions he came up with later at Covent Garden. It would be wrong to overlook Helpmann's performance in this ballet. Although he talked of 'cardboard princes', they never appeared so when he performed them. They were valid and interesting characters. His impeccable partnering of any ballerina, but in particular of Fonteyn, raised the two great *pas de deux* in Acts II and III to an exciting perfection of style and timing, as well as establishing them as part of the narrative flow and structure through the dancers' emotional shading. Their collaboration in Act IV was in keeping with the old Sergeyev version and the elegiac music. In those days, only one solo and a coda in Act III were allotted to the prince, and they were within Helpmann's technical range.

Arnold Haskell wrote, 'It is another proof of his acting ability that he makes one believe in his own classical dancing. I do not in fact know how good a dancer he is, his technique is so absolutely the servant of his acting. There are probably a score or more male dancers who are far finer classical technicians, yet who produce only half the effect.'[88] William Chappell endorsed this: 'Helpmann is an actor first, a dancer second, but definitely a dancer. He has rarely given an awkward performance in the most exacting technical role, because any discrepancies in his technique are more than compensated for by his ease of movement and his uncanny sense of performance.'[89] Leo Kersley, writing an obituary in *Equity News* observed:

Helpmann was never a virtuoso dancer using technique for technique's sake; he was only interested in what technique could be used to convey. He was a dancer with a technique which allowed him to do what he wanted with sureness, precision and smoothness. His dancing looked as easy as cutting butter, whether he was jumping, turning, showing a position – or doing all these things at once.[90]

10

Toward the end of 1943, Robert Helpmann had two important projects in view. He had got his way with the theatre director Tyrone Guthrie, who had arranged for him to act Hamlet with the Old Vic Drama Company in February 1944, and he was planning a ballet on Oscar Wilde's *The Picture of Dorian Gray*. The latter is one of the tantalising losses that occur in the theatre. It should have been the desired return, after *The Birds*, to the proper course of Helpmann's choreographic career. Atmospheric designs were completed by Sophie Fedorovitch, and Helpmann had commissioned new music from Clifton Parker. Parker, however, failed to finish the assignment, and because of this the ballet never materialised.

A final date in December before quitting ballet temporarily for drama brought Helpmann back to his beginnings with the Vic-Wells Ballet when Ninette de Valois revived *Job*. The critic of *The Times* commented on the fact that it had been so long out of the repertoire that there were signs of inexperience in the cast. He continued:

> There is no reason why the present company should not … achieve the polish of their predecessors, especially as they have Mr Robert Helpmann still in the role of Satan, acting it with a concentration of insidious malevolence such as neither Dolin, his predecessor, nor he himself, in his less experienced days, has previously put into it.[91]

Job was given a number of performances that winter, culminating with three in a row in early February 1944. These were astonishing. What had seemed like a definitive account of Satan by Helpmann was amazingly surpassed on the second night, and surpassed yet again on the final Saturday, which was the last night of the ballet season. The role of Satan has not been well preserved in contemporary revivals of *Job*. The strongly athletic dancing has been coarsened to the point of caricature, with clutching, clawlike fingers and emphasised joint angles. As Helpmann danced it, muscular power and control were subordinated to linear poetry – fortunately there is a series of photographs by Gordon Anthony perpetuating the sculptural grace that underlined Satan's state as a fallen angel of supernatural beauty rather than a grotesque demon. His portrayal was subtle and imaginative, encompassing challenge and triumph, malice and mischief. He ascended the throne of God with assurance, but found no lasting satisfaction there.

February 1944 is a good moment to write briefly of my personal reactions to Helpmann in ballet up to that time. I had always been fascinated by versatility in the arts, and he was the first dancer I found who matched up to my demands. One afternoon in 1939, as a schoolgirl, I saw him as Albrecht in *Giselle* and the Red King in *Checkmate*, and marked him down as someone special. A theatre observer, trained by my mother from earliest childhood, I had cut my teeth on stage arts from grand opera and D'Oyly Carte, via famous musicals, to classic and contemporary drama and, later, to Ballets Russes companies, and was in the habit of considering critically everything and everyone I saw on stage. Between then and 5 February 1944, there lay years of Sadler's Wells Ballet-going.

By the beginning of 1944, I had seen him in an interesting selection of roles, ranging from the classical princes to Satan and Mr O'Reilly. They were so widely differentiated, in choreography and music, in period style, and in tragedy and comedy, that they made an absorbing course of study for anyone who delighted in the skills of the performing artist. I discovered, among other things, that he was constantly creative. Sometimes the creativity was so delicate that it was barely apparent; at other times, as with Dr Coppelius, it was a matter of substantial invention over the years. Even now, dancers are reproducing ideas of his in the belief that they are part of that role's choreography. He was undoubtedly an attention-commander, but his respect for a ballet's structure and for the other dancers involved meant that comic byplay was inserted into pauses and gaps in the action. While his technical range was limited, his line, carriage and placement were a constant pleasure. His *port de bras* were of copybook perfection and his musicality deeply satisfying. Immensely important was the fact that he always came to a performance with a fresh approach. However bored he might be at the thought of yet another *Coppélia* or *Façade*, when he stepped on stage in costume and makeup (and he was a supreme makeup artist) histrionic impulses began to circulate in his veins, and audiences responded with keen enjoyment.

The qualities he brought to his acted Hamlet in 1944 were his knowledge in depth of the play; his understanding of the dynamics of Shakespeare's dramatic poetry; his inborn onstage ease; and his ability to create character and relationships with conviction. He had a musical and flexible voice which, however, had never before had to discover the full power and stamina of the experienced player, and on the first (press) night this disadvantage was accentuated by an attack of influenza. From the audience's point of view, however, his vitality, clarity of diction and intelligent variety of pace made his performance intensely interesting. Physically, he was slighter in build than most dramatic actors and he played Hamlet as maturing from indecision and youthful weakness to a princely command of thought. The first test came with the battlement scenes, where tempest and calm were admirably united; and this authority was matched with humour in the bitter-sweet exchanges with Polonius or Rosencrantz and Guildenstern – poisoned candies, proffered with courtesy. Each point with the players was well delineated and the 'Rogue and peasant slave' soliloquy was delivered with passion and a dramatically well-contrived close. 'To be or not to be' was the least effective speech; the nunnery scene had little tenderness, but the closet scene was a deftly changing variety of moods. 'How all occasions' was deeply thoughtful and sombre. There was irony in his exchanges with the Gravedigger over Yorick's skull and a courteous wit towards Osric, an exciting fight and a poignant death. And on the first night, to remind everyone of things present, the anti-aircraft guns of London opened fire as Fortinbras spoke, 'Go, bid the soldiers shoot ...' By the end of the run in April, Helpmann had left that first-night Hamlet far behind. Day-by-day knowledge of this first major role in spoken drama had strengthened an interpretation conceived with thoroughness and passion.

He was surrounded by an excellent cast. Margot Grahame was Gertrude; Basil Sydney, Claudius; Pamela Browne, Ophelia; Lawrence Hanray, Polonius. Dennis Price was the Horatio and Geoffrey Toone, Laertes. Charles Hickman was Osric and Gus McNaughton the Gravedigger. Naturally, notices were mixed (this happens with all Hamlets!) but it is interesting to re-read them. Most were from the first night, but some critics went back as well later in the run. W.A. Darlington in the *Daily Telegraph* decided that Helpmann's Hamlet 'has intelligence, speed and humanity. It is clearly spoken. It has wit and balance. But it lacks weight, power and drive'.[92] *The Times* also found it 'much too light', but commented, 'he speaks the soliloquies with a quiet grace which misses none of their significant points'.[93] Desmond McCarthy in the *New Statesman* wrote:

Light, small and nimble, there are moments when Mr Helpmann is physically at a disadvantage. But Hamlet's uncontrollable excitement, his affectionate friendliness, his sudden transitions from ferocity to love (subtly graded in his great scene with his mother) ... [he] conveyed most admirably. It was characteristic of his interpretation that he spoke the rhyming couplet 'O cursed spite' not with ringing bitterness, but faintingly; and that other famous curtain couplet (this was an original reading) 'The play's the thing', not triumphantly, but with deliberate meditative certainty.[94]

Horace Horsnell in *Tatler* drew perceptively on his knowledge of Helpmann as a dancer: 'His equipment is, in the best sense, theatrical. He is a superb mime, and has a flair for the grotesque. Satire, one suspects, enters freely, if dispassionately, into his artistic attack. His theatre sense is acute, possibly ruthless, and he is obviously ambitious ... Attack, rather than defence, would seem to be the mainspring of his professional strategy.' Horsnell goes on: 'Other items in this ingenious artist's equipment include a clear, if light, speaking voice, sense and sensibility, possibly pride and prejudice, and certainly persuasion.'[95]

There were other critics who were enticed by the performance. James Redfern in *The Spectator* wrote boldly that it 'was the best Hamlet I have ever seen, and I have seen most in our day'. He accepted that Helpmann 'is slightly built ... and his voice is light in quality. In spite of these apparent handicaps, he is tremendously impressive.' The chief reason for his success, Redfern felt, was 'not merely his intelligence ... but the truth and sincerity of his conception ... The result is that we feel everything that Hamlet says could not be said otherwise, and this reality makes the performance intensely exciting.'[96] One nameless critic writing in *John o' London's Weekly* declared, 'This was not an actor playing the Prince of Denmark...this was the Hamlet of any time and any place; the thought-ridden weakling who yet, having at length in bitter pain decided, is stronger than them all. This was the living Hamlet.'[97]

The production, and Helpmann's performance, was very much a talking point of the time, and Hermione Gingold, one of his special theatre friends (they first met in *I Hate Men* at the Gate Theatre in 1933), recognised this in the 'little revue', *Sweeter and Lower*, in which she was appearing at the Ambassadors Theatre. The *News Chronicle* wrote it up, with appropriate photographs of Helpmann as Hamlet and Gingold as Helpmann as Hamlet. Her item was described as a 'brilliantly malicious lampoon'. The reporter spoke to her

before the performance ... She was feeling very nervous. 'I told Bobby all about our ideas for the sketch', she told me, 'and he said "Say what you like", but the critics gave me the impression that perhaps I had gone a bit far'. However, all was well. 'No sooner was the curtain down than

Robert Helpmann was in her dressing-room. He gave her a resounding kiss, invited her out to supper, and they left arm in arm.[98]

Presumably it was all a splendid piece of publicity jointly planned by them both ...

11

Helpmann rejoined Sadler's Wells Ballet at the King's Theatre, Hammersmith, and the company's New Theatre season began on 30 May 1944. It opened with *Le Lac des cygnes* danced by Beryl Grey and David Paltenghi (Grey had made her debut as Odette–Odile on her fifteenth birthday the year before, partnered by Helpmann), but although alternative dancers were now being given plenty of chances, the most substantial ballets still depended considerably on Fonteyn and Helpmann. The only new work of the season was Andrée Howard's *Le Festin de l'araignée*, which, in spite of splendid designs by Michael Ayrton, failed to win balletgoers' hearts. It was still wartime, and in July the V1 flying bombs seriously affected London theatregoing. Although twenty houses closed, fourteen stayed open and did good business, including the New Theatre with Sadler's Wells Ballet. I remember one occasion when, during *The Gods Go A-Begging*, a bomb fell in nearby New Row. The theatre chandelier rocked fiercely, displacing dust that fell like a gauze curtain over the auditorium. Neither the dancers nor the orchestra missed a beat and no one left from the audience.

Meanwhile, the playwright Rodney Ackland was adapting *Crime and Punishment*, in which Helpmann was to play Raskolnikov. He had worked assiduously on vocal technique, and by his last night as Hamlet there was every reason to think that he could make a dual career of acting and dancing. His first loyalty, however, was to Sadler's Wells Ballet, and they needed a premiere for their next London season. This was to be at a larger theatre, the Princes (now known as the Shaftesbury), in October. One of the earliest announcements about the new production appeared in the *Manchester Daily Mail* of 31 August. H..R. Jeans opened by saying that 'Glasgow's traditional razor slashers, with blades stuck in the peaks of their caps, and addicts of the notorious "red biddy" [a lethal mixture of rough alcohol and methylated spirits] are to figure in a fashionable West End ballet.' Helpmann, appearing in Manchester with the company, had told the paper that they were rehearsing it already, and it would be called *Miracle in the Gorbals.* He was quoted as saying:

> The music by Arthur Bliss is very modern indeed and contains all sorts of rhythms, like the rumba and the palais glide. The settings by Edward Burra show the city's tenements. I play the part of a mystical stranger

who restores to life a girl who has apparently committed suicide. The stranger wins the admiration of the people living in the street to such an extent that it arouses the jealousy of the razor gang, who then murder him.[99]

The scenario was by his partner, Michael Benthall, currently a captain with the army in France, whose earlier posting had been to an anti-aircraft gun battery in the Gorbals.

The news horrified Glasgow's Lord Provost, James Welsh. He immediately leapt to his city's defence, maintaining that 'the traditional razor slashers of Glasgow are a pure fiction as applied to the city today'. He was supported by statements from Glasgow police, who could not 'recall a single instance of razor-slashing in the Gorbals throughout the five years of war', and the local Church of Scotland minister (surely overprotected!) who had 'never once come into contact with an act of serious violence'. The director of Glasgow's Welfare Department said, 'I should place any attempt to depict Glasgow as gang-ridden on about the same par as mythical sea-serpents of pre-war days', and a town councillor severely opined, 'If this ballet is aimed at rousing public opinion against such [slum] conditions it has my approval. But if it is designed merely to tickle the sensation-seeking appetites of fashionable West End audiences I can only regard it as in very bad taste.'[100] A reporter for another paper, *The Leader,* gleefully entered the lists. He maintained that 'the case these gentlemen make out for a reformed Glasgow is, as they might put it, not proven', [an allusion to the famous Scottish legal verdict that supplements 'guilty' or 'not guilty']:

On the page [of the paper] in which their remarks are quoted there appeared accounts of various court cases in which eight Glasgow men were charged with violently assaulting their fellow citizens. Razors certainly seem to have gone out of fashion. One man strangled a woman to death with his hands, and another beat a policeman with an iron bar. Knives, broken glasses and bottles were said to have been used in other instances.[101]

All this was excellent publicity. Helpmann had, of course, no intention of arousing public opinion against slum conditions or of tickling fashionable London's 'sensation-seeking appetites'. Such flurries in civic teacups, however, could only sell tickets at the Princes. Before the first night of *Miracle* on 24 October , various other things happened. Helpmann choreographed, to admirable effect, the movement and dances in the Troll scenes of a notable Old Vic production of *Peer Gynt* that starred Ralph Richardson. Sadler's Wells Ballet opened their Princes Theatre season on 27 September, and in the third week staged a charming revival of Fokine's *Carnaval.* This had a delectable Columbine in Fonteyn, a marvellously musical Chiarina in Pamela May, and a spirited Papillon in Pauline Clayden. Alexis Rassine was an excellent Harlequin. About Helpmann's Pierrot *The Dancing Times* waxed eloquent:

> It is by Robert Helpmann's portrayal of Pierrot that these fine threads [of Fokine's choreography] are held together and the story prevented from developing into a series of divertissements ... it is by his tactful handling of this most difficult role that the audience is made aware of the pathos as well as the love and gaiety of the ballet.[102]

There was no insincerity in the performance. Like most stage artists, however, Helpmann could operate on various levels of consciousness and, unknown to his audiences, in the section where Pierrot collapses near the footlights, he found that he could whisper into the backstage intercom and convulse waiting dancers with irreverent comments.

Meanwhile, the elements making up *Miracle in the Gorbals* were fitting together with the smoothness of a good jigsaw puzzle. Burra's designs had been completed before Bliss's score was written. Burra was the perfect choice of artist. His admirably controlled personal idiom of realism and surrealism matched the scenario's blend of mysticism and daily life. In 1931 he had designed an Ashton ballet, *A Day in a Southern Port* (later known as *Rio Grande*), for the Camargo Society. He was very much part of the wickedly amusing artistic world of the time, the highly talented young people who were capable of great artistic endeavour but who revelled, in their personal lives, in anarchic, offbeat humour at everyone's expense, including their own. Burra and Helpmann, not particular friends, were alike in balancing the grave and sensitive side of their natures with madcap wit. Both laid aside levity where *Miracle* was concerned, and collaborated with extreme taste and seriousness.

Haskell, in his monograph *Miracle in the Gorbals,* tells how Bliss worked with Benthall's full scenario, with Helpmann and with Burra's designs when he came to compose the music. A study of El Greco's paintings had given Helpmann the idea of basing the hand movements of the Stranger on El Greco positions, and he mentioned this to Bliss to explain the kind of music needed on the entrance of the Stranger. [103] Haskell reported:

Helpmann assembled his company on the usual bare stage and went over his story in detail, acting every role, as I saw Fokine do in *Petrouchka*. A choreographer with this rare gift of mimicry can save endless rehearsals in carrying his company with him. From the very first, the company responded with enthusiasm as they built up the ballet ... the long work went through from rehearsal to production without a change, a remarkable feat that shows Helpmann's extraordinary gifts as choreographer-producer, and the two are by no means always linked together in so harmonious a fashion.[104]

Miracle was so clearly constructed that it never needed a programme synopsis. It was rich in characterisations, providing a cross-section of Gorbals types from a mixed variety of older and younger women, working men, urchins and a beggar (a wonderful cameo by Leslie Edwards), to the toughs who kill the Stranger. The scene was set almost casually: children played with a car tyre; young couples, flirting and teasing, met at the fish-and-chip shop; a more lyrical pair of lovers (Shearer and Rassine) had thoughts only for each other; older women, respectable and tidy or happily inebriated, gossiped at their tenement doors; the beggar scrounged in dustbins; a group of young men gathered around a pub; and a prostitute (Celia Franca) looked to them for trade. It was a robust and varied community, with two outsiders – the man who was tactfully programmed as The Official (David Paltenghi) but was obviously a spiritual leader, and a thin young girl (Pauline Clayden) who expressed her hopelessness and despair in an eloquent solo.

Out of these typical strands of slum life emerged the central action. The girl went slowly offstage, presumably towards the river, and very soon a street boy (an interesting character who bridged the gap between the urchins and the toughs, too adult for the children but not man enough for the gang) rushed on with the news that she had drowned herself. The crowd assembled, disturbed and curious, and the Official took charge as two of the young men carried on the lifeless body. This was the moment for the miracle, when the Stranger entered, took his place by the dead girl, and restored her to life. The economy and power of this short section was impressive, and then music and choreography together opened out to a mass celebration that never lost touch with the characters involved in it or the sordid street setting. The story did not, of course, end there. There was blackness ahead. The Official's jealousy of the Stranger's influence on the community led him to turn a blind eye to the gang's fear of the Stranger, whom they beat to death with broken bottles and a razor slash.

The first night of *Miracle* was acclaimed by the audience. No one, I think, was unmoved by its controlled theatricality and committed performance. Afterwards, critics contradicted each other with the kind of emotional fervour that is bound to help theatre business. Some of the writers who had so far praised Helpmann ballets became surprisingly lukewarm. Herbert Farjeon in the *Sunday Graphic* wrote:

> Although I am not a conventionally religious man myself, I was not happy about *Miracle in the Gorbals.* However sincere the intention, in practice the theme seemed to have been used for its sensational possibilities. I will even go so far as to say that it is people who enjoy art of the type of *No Orchids for Miss Blandish* who will most enjoy the slices of low life and thuggism that dominate the action.[105]

In *The Times,* the critic took a curious view: 'From the first notes of Bliss's powerful score it is plain that ballet has once more set itself the task of enlarging its subject matter, deepening its dramatic appeal and aspiring to the rank of tragedy. But it will not do. Ballet has not yet grown up to the magnitude of such a task.' He went on to instance other ballets that failed in the 'pursuit of this mistaken ideal': Massine's *Seventh Symphony,* Balanchine's *Le Fils prodigue,* Jooss's *The Prodigal Son.* However, he did allow that 'the new ballet is not lacking in dramatic power. Its massed movements and the groupings are well contrived', and he praised the choreography for the Suicide and the Lovers, Helpmann's 'reverence as the worker of the miracle', and 'the excellent piece of psychological acting by Mr David Paltenghi' as the Official.[106] Edwin Evans in *Time and Tide* felt that it 'might be classified as a melodramatic morality play'. He went on:

> The whole point is: Has Robert Helpmann justified his choice? I maintain that he has. A gargoyle on a cathedral is a work of art, and that, in sum, is what he has produced. There is reverence in the miracle, and ecstasy in the revival-like scene which follows it, and the gargoyle has a like intensity of expression. What is called 'natural acting' is one stage convention, and Helpmann has used another, that of choreography, and in doing so he has attained to a very high level of achievement. There was no mistaking the genuineness of the audience's reaction ... I shall be surprised if this novel ballet does not turn out to be both a popular success and a landmark in the development of the art.[107]

W. McNaught in the *Manchester Guardian* made a valid and interesting point: 'Soon after the curtain was up ... organised loveliness of movement began to weave spells and the cosmopolitan audience were prepared to shift the scene from Clydeside to the banks of the Thames, the Seine or the Hudson River. Any slum district should be glad of such a mirror.'[108] The Sitter Out in *The Dancing Times* contributed a long, ably considered and entirely enthusiastic review. While admitting that 'this is not for the fastidious balletgoer looking for the niceties of classical technique and the dainty subtleties of porcelain dancers', the critic declared that 'This is strong meat for an audience who understands that if ballet is to progress and maintain its rightful place in the theatre of ideas, it must take into account and reflect contemporary events.'[109] A balanced estimate was given by A.H. Franks (*Twentieth Century Ballet*), who stressed the expressive qualities of the choreography and the evocation of atmosphere, and pointed out that 'each of the thirty characters on the stage is the essence of a type, but holds our interest and sympathy as an individual ... Contained within a short ballet, the intensity of the drama is tremendous, yet it is all contrived by a composition of dance and highly stylised movement.' He speaks of photographs of the ballet:

Every one ... particularly those of the groups, makes a powerful impact for, in an essentially balletic manner, and in the most economic terms possible, are expressed the qualities and fundamental outlook of each character. Here is the character of the Stranger ... the majestic movement of the hands and arms suggesting an authority endowed by a power beyond this world; the relationship of the community one with another ... and the ironical conclusion, with the beggar, the attempted suicide and the prostitute as the only ones who mourn the death of the Stranger.

His summation is a considered response to the controversy:

It has been condemned on the ground that ballet is not a suitable medium for the preaching of a moral. It is equally obvious that Helpmann did not aim consciously at such preaching; but as the ballet achieves its purely theatrical end, in treating such a theme with magnificent theatrical effects ... it should be judged purely on its merits as a theatrical production – and viewed in that light it is as significant a work as any dance-drama yet created, marking a definite advance in the form itself.[110]

After *Miracle* and its ongoing controversies came a calm and charming revival of Frederick Ashton's *Nocturne,* which had long lapsed from the repertoire. The exquisite Fedorovitch designs were slightly recast and differently coloured, but the nostalgic attraction of the piece made itself clearly felt, and Ashton, who had used a week's leave from the RAF to rehearse it, was warmly welcomed in the small, static role of the Spectator.

12

In the wake of the Normandy landings, ENSA and the British Council decided in 1945 that Sadler's Wells Ballet could be sent to Belgium and France to entertain the Forces and to appear for civilian audiences in Brussels and Paris. The company was kitted out in khaki, and left in early January. They opened at the huge Garrison Variety Theatre in Brussels. A special correspondent to *The Times* wrote about the Channel trip delayed through gales and how the company arrived

> at a time of intense cold, and had to rehearse and later to dance in a theatre totally unheated (through lack of coal) where they and those who watched them shivered in sympathy. And with the thaw a main water pipe burst and put the auditorium under water for most of a day. Then, when coal arrived and the central heating became effective, clouds of steam arose from the sodden carpet and seats. But our English dancers, it seems, have a cheerful sense of discipline and responsibility of their own which in no wise allowed these initial unavoidable discomforts to alter their resolve to bring the best of their art to the greatest possible number of men and women on active service.[111]

Much has been written about the impact that companies like Les Ballets des Champs-Elysées and American Ballet Theatre had on London just after the war, but in 1945 the Sadler's Wells Ballet repertoire, particularly the dramatic works such as *The Rake's Progress* and *Hamlet*, made an equally great impact on Brussels and Paris. In Brussels the critic of *La Dernière Heure* commented on 'deux remarquables ballets':

> Dans le premier *[Rake]*, Mme Ninette de Valois ... fait preuve de dons d'observation inouïs, car le caractère de chaque personnage y est rendu avec une verité hallucinante. Dans *Hamlet*, qui suit fidèlement les étapes de la tragedie, d'admirable trouvailles de Robert Helpmann, comme le balancement d'Ophélie et de la Reine autour de Hamlet, nous montrent à quel point cet art est expressif et capable de traduire les nuances psychologiques les plus subtiles. De tout çela, il ne faudrait pas conclure qu'il s'agit de sortes de mimodrames. La danse n'y perd jamais des droits.[112]

The critic of *La Libre Belgique*, the newspaper of the Resistance, also praised *Hamlet*, terming it 'un drame en raccourci dont l'évocation puissante et par des moyens purement chorégraphique est saisissant et poignant'.[113] In Paris they gave eight performances at the Théâtre des Champs-Elysées of programmes that included *Dante Sonata* and *Les Patineurs* as well as bringing in *Miracle in the Gorbals*, and were entertained at receptions full of notable names. Those who had been in Paris in 1937 were thrilled to be back, even though they discovered its grave condition, lacking petrol (no taxis or buses), heat and light, and (apart from black-market supplies) food. For de Valois it was a time to meet with old friends such as Boris Kochno. In a talk she later gave to the Vic-Wells Association, she mentioned how ballet enthusiasts in Paris from the 'old Diaghilev public were outspoken in praise, particularly of *Miracle in the Gorbals*'. She instanced especially Kochno and Christian Bérard, both of whom made a point of coming round afterwards and telling them how impressed they were by *Gorbals*, which seemed to them an entirely new and individual contribution to ballet. She mentioned that performances were also given at the Théâtre Marigny, where the audience was full of American service personnel who insisted that the company 'had only to come to New York and they would be acclaimed'.[114] Other ENSA dates included Ghent, Bruges and Ostend.

By this time Helpmann was being termed by the popular press a 'three-careers man, as a star of ballet, drama and film'[115] and, although he was never a 'star of film', he was filming (in Wales) as a comically villainous eighteenth-century valet with Dennis Price, Stewart Granger and Jean Kent in *Caravan*. He was still, however, deeply involved in ballet, as he would always remain. Typically, he was thinking and speaking about the way the performing arts could cooperate and complement each other. In an article in the magazine *Bandwagon*, he declared, 'I believe that everything in life and art is a potential ballet subject. Any theme suitable for a play could be a ballet ... If anything can be commented on in writing or music, it can also be commented on in dance.' He instanced as possible themes for ballets Maxwell Anderson's *Winterset* and *High Tor*, Thornton Wilder's *Our Town*, and Jean-Paul Sartre's *Huis clos* (Bejart later staged the last-named as *Sonate à trois.*) He felt that

> these are particularly interesting times in that they are bringing an increasing affinity between ballet and drama – a highly desirable development, because the two mediums can give useful assistance one to the other. I believe that all dancers should train to be actors and all

actors as dancers. Dancers should know how to play a scene as well as how to dance it, and actors should know how to move a scene as well as how to follow its basic script requirements.[116]

It was, of course, an aim of perfection – there will always be a preponderance of dancers who have no idea how to act and of actors whose movement is at best merely that of the school gymnasium.

Meanwhile, the war in Europe was coming to an end. The company opened a season at the New Theatre on 17 April, and on Monday 7 May 1945, at the end of the performance, Helpmann (as Comus) announced that the next day was to be VE Day, and the programme would be changed from *Lac Act II, Le Festin de l'araignée* and *Comus* to *Coppélia*.

Those lucky enough to have tickets for the next night were happily in their places and in the mood for fun when the curtain went up on the familiar village setting, with Helpmann as Dr Coppelius perched on a ladder adding a Union Jack to a display of Allied flags, and a V for Victory hanging over his front door. After that, Acts I and II were played straight, but there was a red-white-and-blue bag of money for Coppelius in Act III, and he joined the dancers in the finale with a series of quickfire circling pirouettes, ending in character with a little intentionally unsteady dithering.

It was the last season at the by now dearly loved New Theatre. On 24 July Sadler's Wells Ballet was once more at Sadler's Wells Theatre for a hail-and-farewell season, as the coming February would see them translated to the Royal Opera House, Covent Garden. In its post-war state the Wells was, perhaps not surprisingly, lacking in atmosphere, and the company did not fit in quite comfortably there, although press and public were enthusiastic. Ashton's *The Wanderer* was revived and Mary Clarke wrote in *Dance*:

The choreography is exceptionally virile and matches the hard rhythms of Schubert's music, while there is inspired patterning and grouping in the slow movement ... The theme ... is an involved one about the workings of a man's mind and his reactions when confronted by material achievements, doubts and depressions, love and compassion. Helpmann has the difficult task of remaining on stage throughout, watching other dancers suggest these phenomena, and by his responses providing a connecting link to hold the ballet together. It is the kind of part which Helpmann does perfectly – and it is a part that needs Helpmann in it if it is going to 'come over' at all.

She speaks of Fonteyn's role as having 'clever choreography which does not actually need a virtuoso technique but creates an impression of spectacular brilliance', and comments that 'she has much near-acrobatic work with Helpmann which demands perfection of timing – and gets it, because for sheer timing and correlation of movement the Fonteyn–Helpmann partnership is ideal.'[117]

The year that had begun in Belgium and France ended with an ENSA tour of Germany: Hamburg Garrison Theatre, RAF Station Buchenburg, Hanover Herrenhausen, Theater des Westens Berlin and Düsseldorf Opernhaus. It was a grim assignment, although at one point it was enlivened for the dancers by an unexpected one-off activity. One garrison theatre had an arrangement with the Forces Radio Network to have part of each programme broadcast, and the radio controller commented that it was a pity nothing could be done with a ballet company. Typically, Helpmann replied that, of course, they could cope; they would rehearse and broadcast a couple of scenes from *A Midsummer Night's Dream*. Rounding up dancers who could speak – Leslie Edwards, Joan Sheldon, and others – he directed the scenes and acted Oberon.

Always determined to absorb all he could of local atmosphere, during this tour Helpmann looked around him at the devastation and horror of defeated Germany. He even persuaded the military authorities to let him visit a bunker where displaced persons were crowded in fearful conditions, and he was given a disinfected cloth to hold to his nose against the stench. He later told Elizabeth Salter:

> In the city itself it was just as though somebody had taken a scythe and mowed down the buildings. A black cross marked ruins where there was any chance of people still being alive. I used to feel hysterical as I walked at night past these buildings, imagining the thoughts and sufferings of people buried alive.[118]

He paid dearly for this experience. In spite of immunisation, amateurish as it was, he contracted a serious viral infection, difficult to identify and to cure. He was physically more exhausted by the wartime years of constant work than anyone realised, and his resistance was low. He was brought back to England on a stretcher, and although with a course of treatment he was able to get back to the company fairly quickly, he was far from well. Nothing, however, could have stopped him from appearing in *The Sleeping Beauty* when Sadler's Wells Ballet reopened the Royal Opera House, Covent Garden.

13

Much has been written about Sadler's Wells Ballet and the first night of *The Sleeping Beauty* on 20 February 1946 at Covent Garden, and there is no point in covering it all in detail. It was a high-society gala evening, with King George VI, Queen Elizabeth and the Princesses Elizabeth and Margaret Rose in the royal box; and the production, its performance and Oliver Messel's delicious designs were the perfect way of celebrating both the end of the war and the restoration of the Royal Opera House to its proper functions. Where Helpmann was concerned it was a busy evening – he was doubling as Carabosse and Prince Florimund. An elegant dowager-witch endowed with great power but no comic capering, his Carabosse was unforgettable. As Florimund he was a stylish eighteenth-century prince and a superb partner for Fonteyn in the Vision scene and the Aurora *pas de deux*. But his health was still giving him serious trouble. Medical treatment for his viral infection had severe side effects (including spinal abscesses), yet through March he not only continued with *Beauty* but also danced *The Rake's Progress, Nocturne, Miracle in the Gorbals* and *Dante Sonata* when these ballets were staged. In addition, when it came into London on 7 March he also had to oversee the Emile Littler production of the musical *Song of Norway*, for which he had composed two ballets at the end of 1945; and for Sadler's Wells Ballet he was rehearsing the largest and most complicated production he had yet choreographed, *Adam Zero*, in which he had a long and arduous leading role. With typical tenacity he shirked nothing, until finally on 8 May he was forced to withdraw to the London Clinic, where he was based until late June.

Adam Zero had its premiere on 10 April. The scenario was by Benthall, the score by Bliss and designs by Roger Furse. The first suggestion that Benthall had submitted to Helpmann, in 1945, was for an abstract ballet about a man's life cycle, to be set against scenery that would represent creation, achievement and decay. Helpmann liked this, as did de Valois when she was told about it. At that point the composer and designer were approached. After thinking it over, Helpmann began to feel that the idea was too much like the symphonic ballets Massine had staged so historically in the 1930s. He felt he would prefer to work with a more realistic scenario. Because it would be the first post-war work created at the Opera House, both he and Benthall also wanted to use to the fullest the array of stage machinery and lighting, and the extensive stage space.

Benthall's second scenario extended the original to introduce symbols linked with current affairs. These included political, social and religious allusions as well as thoughts about the devastation of liberated Europe and Germany, where he had himself served as an Army captain and which Helpmann had glimpsed the previous November. From this more complex proposal Helpmann drew the central plan *of Adam Zero:* a life-cycle theme, from birth to death, seen in terms of the composition of a ballet. There would be one leading male role, combining Adam and The Principal Dancer, and a multiple female role symbolising the creator/choreographer, the wife/mistress/ballerina, and eventually death. Other characters would also be multi-faceted; for example, the three Fates would be identified in ballet terms with the designer, wardrobe mistress and dresser. The additional ingredients proposed by Benthall were not, therefore, integral to Helpmann's overall concept, although he tried to fit all of them into the developing framework; and he would have been wise to discard them. He might indeed have done so had he been less physically weakened and less pressured over the ballet's preparation. Ashton, whose *Symphonic Variations* had been postponed because of an injury to Michael Somes, was fortunate in that he had extra time to consider, and forego, his more elaborate thoughts. As it was, it took every ounce of Helpmann's energy to complete the work at all.

Certain points were inherent in its creation. Helpmann always intended to reflect the theme both visually and musically. He planned to vary the type of dancing he used, from primitive movement and dance preparation to simple classical dance and then formal Petipa-style choreography. After that it would move into jazz and jive and end with a form of modern lyrical classicism for the great *pas de deux* in which Death would claim Adam. He had also suggested to Bliss – with whom he worked closely, staying in his country house – that the music might fall into a four-seasonal pattern, building from spring through summer and autumn to winter. His staging ideas, which incorporated changing costumes, makeup and scenery in view of the audience so that the action would be continuous, had grown out of a study of Japanese Noh plays as well as from the stimulus of Cocteau films and Thornton Wilder's *The Skin of Our Teeth*.[119] This play had been staged in London in May 1945 by the Oliviers (who were by now close friends of his), and the designer had been Roger Furse. Now Helpmann and Furse together planned the scenic development *of Adam Zero,* employing stage lifts, sectional and very mobile settings (not the commonplace they now are), and opening out the imposing cyclorama for the final scene.

The production opened on a bare stage with dancers in practice clothes limbering up for a rehearsal and the choreographer trying out steps and ideas. The designer was turning over materials and sketches, and the stage director talking to lighting men and stagehands. The principal dancer arrived and, in rehearsal, was born as Adam. (Birth scenes were not usual in 1946; Balanchine's *Apollo* was unfamiliar to London audiences of the time, and it was only later that labour pains would become the choreographic cliché they now are.) His early life was symbolised by the gradual elevation of stage lifts, culminating in a swallow dive onto the linked arms of the male corps de ballet. Dancers dressed in simple peasant-style clothes surrounded him, and brought with them his first love. The stage then cleared for an enchanting duet of interested encounter, courtship, and increasing depth of feeling. In this, the lighting and music created a strong illusion of a fine summer's day in the country. The ensemble returned, and the lyrical mood continued as the lovers were married. Here the change of tempo was over-abrupt, moving into a short and pithy 'political' section, briefly humorous, in which Adam stood with his smiling wife on a podium, miming campaign speeches.

The next section seemed a non sequitur but was linked to the ballet world of the beginning. It offered a different kind of worldly achievement – a Petipa-style classical ballet scene with a grand *pas de deux*. From this, Adam was wrenched by the approach of middle age and replaced by a new generation. As he desperately tried to compete with the young, the world began to disintegrate around him, with frenetic nightclub dancing and later images of war and brutality. He sought religious comfort in vain and was left, as an old man, to face death. Up to this point, constant demands had been made on a large ensemble, and the contrast between the succession of crowded scenes and the isolation of the two principals within the half-circle of the cyclorama was deeply moving. This last eloquent duet, which Helpmann danced with the scarlet-cloaked June Brae (who had superbly played all the women in Adam's life), moved through fear and resistance to a hypnotic tranquillity that led to acceptance and peace. As it ended, the first moments of the ballet were repeated: another birth, another life cycle began.

Adam Zero was a strange and arresting title. Adam equalled Everyman, of course, and this was easy for everyone to grasp. Zero was awkward. Many people took it as a declaration of despair, but this was not a Helpmann characteristic. His temperament, like de Valois's, was a well-balanced mixture of vision and practicality. Enormously energetic, constantly intrigued by new challenges, he was not prey to introspective neuroses, morbidity or any tendency to brood on dark thoughts. The word 'Zero' was not a confession of pessimism, merely an acceptance of universal human experience. Helpmann did not create ballets to explore his own or anyone else's psychological problems; he was concerned entirely with expressing character and situation through theatre dance and mime.

There is a curious anomaly between the immediate press (and, of course, the audience reaction) and the build-up of denigration on which, in the long run, this ballet was to founder. One or two points must be made. Helpmann's war years of artistic success and growing popularity had upset some people for a variety of reasons. Praise lavished on him, either by overly vociferous fans in the theatre or unwise paeans in print, had been both injudicious and injurious. Ashton's mounting jealousy of him and also of de Valois's increased post-war reputation as the company's founder-director was reflected in the attitude of his particular circle. This affected de Valois's choreography (she staged only one more ballet for the company, *Don Quixote*, in spite of mentioning two other projects) and it was violently operative against Helpmann. He staged only one more ballet for the company, *Elektra*, given at Covent Garden in 1963, in spite of suggesting at least two earlier productions. Obviously, there should have been room for everyone – and there was certainly never any fear that Ashton's choreographic career might be adversely affected by new ballets from de Valois or Helpmann. Ashton's return to the company had been generally welcomed, including by Helpmann, who never claimed to be a choreographic genius and admired Ashton's enormous talent without reservation. However, two distinct affiliations became apparent, rather more among critics than with the balletgoing public. The situation was largely resolved by Helpmann's increasing links with and opportunities in the dramatic theatre, which meant that he did not continue to be anyone's rival where choreography was concerned.

Looking at the press for *Adam Zero*, it is illuminating to find that it was not particularly bad. *The Times*, after saying that it 'is the expression of a pessimistic philosophy', went on:

But, given the premises, Mr Helpmann has achieved a remarkable poetic creation, to which the ingenious use of the mechanism of the theatre ... makes an effective contribution. Such pieces too often lapse into triviality or pretentiousness but Mr Helpmann never allows the mechanism to usurp the interest due to the protagonists, nor the philosophy to become a sermon. The action is swift and taut, and there are no longueurs, unless one counts as such the irrelevant passage which satirises politics [and this section was in fact later deleted].[120]

Later in the year, Philip Hope-Wallace in *Time and Tide* wrote:

Much in the presentation of this bold and poetic idea is effective, much also moving, and it is sustained by Arthur Bliss's score which, like life, is unexpected, full of good and bad patches and a medley of styles ... As so often in Helpmann ballets the main dramatic idea is strongly and cleverly put over, with many memorable and arresting *coups d'oeil* of suddenly congealed motion or mime whittled down to its simplest and most expressive factors.[121]

The Dancing Times wrote about 'a vivid and dramatic work' and emphasised how harmonious collaboration, not only among choreographer, composer and designer but also right through to the dancers, musicians and stage technicians, had resulted in 'a masterpiece of stagecraft. At no time did any discordant note or hitch take place which might upset the smooth working of this difficult production.'[122] In the May issue of *Our Time*, Janet Leeper found the theme depressing, as some other critics did, but praised the way it was developed:

The score is brilliant, the handling of crowds masterly and the eye remembers unforgettable moments of rare beauty ... We could go night after night to see the great cyclorama sweep slowly across the stage ... [for] the final dance of Death in her vast blood-red cloak of many folds, her flying figure diminishing in sharp perspective on the deep, empty stage, against a luminous background of moving clouds. That was pure poetry, the simplicity, the splendour and the economy of great designing.[123]

The photographer Merlyn Severn included *Adam Zero* in her book *Sadler's Wells Ballet at Covent Garden*, and in a later book, *Double Exposure*, she wrote of her reactions to it:

People said this was a bad ballet – perhaps it was, I don't know, I only knew that I found it strangely and deeply moving, more full of 'secret patterns' than any ballet I had seen since the war, the tender lyrical love-scenes; the awful moments of the falling bombs; the final scene of desolation in front of the great cyclorama, when Death in her red cloak sweeps over the figure of the broken old man and passes on, leaving some discarded clothes on the ground. My heart beats faster even now as I look at the pictures.[124]

14

Illness and convalescence kept Helpmann out of performance from early May until October. He had already been planning another ballet. This time it was to be set to John Antill's score *Corroboree*, which he had heard at a concert the previous November. He wrote in *New Theatre,*

> I felt an instinctive emotional response to the aboriginal rhythms ... and in my early years watched the corroboree; I have a vivid memory of the atmosphere of the native dances ... and I intend to study them in greater detail in films at Australia House. It will then be my task to adapt them to stage and choreographic terms.[125]

Designs were to be by an eminent Australian artist, William Constable. This project foundered, and Helpmann also had to withdraw from the play version of *Crime and Punishment,* which was taken over by John Gielgud. One gratifying balletic consequence of his absence was that, wherever the company showed *Hamlet* with David Paltenghi in the lead and *Miracle* with Michael Somes as the Stranger, there were critical compliments on how well the choreography of the two works emerged with different principals. Definitive as Helpmann's own performances were, the ballets were in no way dependent on him for their success. But no one at the time had the range and charisma to take over the role of Adam Zero.

Helpmann returned for the winter ballet season, which brought the premiere of Ashton's *Les Sirènes,* a frivolous follow-up to the pure-dance masterpiece he had staged in April, *Symphonic Variations. Les Sirènes,* with a score by Lord Berners, was a rather laboured joke that lacked the style or wit of *A Wedding Bouquet,* but the dancers had a good time cavorting on the Riviera in Edwardian costumes. Ashton played an Oriental potentate who arrived by balloon; but on the first night this made him queasy, so the balloon descent was transferred to Helpmann's entrance as an outrageous Australian tenor, Adelino Canberra, who sang (literally) a brief bel canto aria and later stood on his head wearing a striped bathing suit. In addition, there was a bravura *pas de deux* with Fonteyn as La Bolero, a Spanish ballerina.

The next new production at Covent Garden was not purely balletic; it was a joint venture with singers, dancers (choreographed by Ashton) and actors of Purcell's *The Fairy Queen*, and in it the stately acted parts of Oberon and Titania were taken by Helpmann and Margaret Rawlings. He was very much back in business, and talking of another ballet project (again aborted) based on the tragedy of Inez de Castro. More solidly, he and Benthall were going ahead with plans for a drama company and productions in 1947. This materialised at the Duchess Theatre in London in March with an historic production of John Webster's *The White Devil*, in which Rawlings and Helpmann led an admirably starry cast that included Andrew Cruickshank, Hugh Griffiths and Martita Hunt. Benthall's production was masterly as to pace and understanding; and it was designed by Paul Sheriff (sets) and Audrey Cruddas (costumes) in unforgettable colour combinations of various reds, yellows and whites against black backgrounds – Helpmann's black costume as Flamineo was a talking-point, as it included a bare midriff.

It was immediately apparent that he had gained greatly in vocal range and power. The characterisation was robust, bawdy, amusing and properly melodramatic, and through it flashed the splendour of Webster's words. The performance was incisive, persuasive, mockingly humorous, delightedly lecherous; and at the last Helpmann brought a wild music to the great lines 'We cease to grieve, cease to be fortune's slaves, nay, cease to die, by dying ...' James Agate was moved to write in the *Sunday Times* that 'his whole performance was marked by a virtuosity, a virility, and a quality of sheer verbal passion that are rare things on our stage today'.[126] Peter Ustinov in *New Theatre* was enthusiastic: 'Let it be said from the outset that Mr Robert Helpmann is excellent in this play. He speaks the lines for all they are worth, not a penny less and a few pennies more, and does not seek to explain anything away.'[127] Clifford Bax in *Theatre Newsletter* declared: 'When Robert Helpmann no longer dances, our dramatic critics may discover that he is a notable actor who speaks poetry as though it were his daily idiom.'[128]

The second play of the season was a problem piece, uneven and tantalising, but in its way exquisite. Leonid Andreyev's *He Who Gets Slapped*, in an English version by Judith Guthrie and directed by Tyrone Guthrie, was withdrawn much too quickly after only fifteen performances. It was a tangled, difficult play; but the colourful confusion of action and ideas threw into relief some scenes of great theatrical conviction. The leading role was that of an aristocrat who became a clown, fell in love in vain with a beautiful circus girl and eventually poisoned them both. In it Helpmann linked visionary power to bitter sarcasm, while great tenderness emerged in the scenes where the clown strove to 'stir the sleeping diamond' of the girl's soul. The critics were very hard on the play's obscurities and its production, but on the whole spoke generously of the player. This was encouraging, for Helpmann, deeply disappointed at the brief run, was soon accepting an offer to go to Stratford-on-Avon the following year and play King John, Hamlet and Shylock at the Shakespeare Memorial Theatre.

While he was away from Sadler's Wells Ballet, the company was busy with revivals by Massine (who was equally resented as a rival by Ashton) of *Le Tricorne* and *La Boutique fantasque.* By July 1947 Helpmann had begun work on the film of *The Red Shoes,* in which he had a small part as a principal dancer with the 'Lermontov Ballet' but also choreographed and danced in the central *Red Shoes* ballet – contrary to some statements, only the role of the Shoemaker was composed by Massine for himself. This assignment proved that temperamentally Helpmann was an ideal collaborator. Each key contributor to the film – directors Michael Powell and Emeric Pressburger, composer Brian Easdale and designer Hein Heckroth – testified to this. Although his experience of films had previously been as a bit-part actor, he fully absorbed the technical aspects of filming and was both creative and adaptable at every stage of the work. As Michael Powell put it,

> screen ballet is always in a process of growth ... That is where Helpmann was so good. Even in the planning stage he always saw it as a film. And, because he saw it like that, he could plan for it even though he had not the faintest idea how his plan would be put into execution. We got on excellently. It was largely a question of realising each other's aims.[129]

After eight days of discussion about the creation of the ballet in detail with Helpmann, Heckroth described him as 'a 100 per cent theatre man'. He reported on how he, Easdale and Helpmann worked out a length of twenty minutes and then found this had to be cut to twelve-and-a-half:

> The musician worries about his music. I worry about my colour continuity ... Only Bobby Helpmann remains calm and does not claim any time for his steps. Instead he makes concrete suggestions to us two where we should cut ... in the end we are allowed to cut to fourteen and a half minutes.[130]

Easdale was equally pleased at working with Helpmann. When he had finished his piano score, the general feeling was that it was just the thing but that certain passages were in symphonic form rather than ballet form ... I had this one general discussion and then three further discussions with Helpmann alone. He is wonderful to collaborate with, never forcing his own point of view or ignoring yours. He only asked for one direct change.[131]

Talking to Monk Gibbon, Helpmann himself analysed the task of choreographing a screen ballet. He termed it

partly a matter of significant omission. There is no possibility of orchestrating choreographically on the screen. On the stage you can give your soloist one movement and orchestrate it with the corps de ballet because they are all in the audience's eye ... On the screen that is impossible; the camera has already done the work of selection ... I realised this before I ever began. I realised that it would be useless and a waste of time to choreograph the parts that were not visible.

Gibbon asked if doing it piecemeal might not lose the sense of continuity. Helpmann replied that he

always bore in mind what *would* be happening elsewhere, even if it *wasn't* happening ... Throughout the whole ballet I had three things in mind – choreographic pattern, a balletic version of the story, and a symbolic vision of the theme of ambition.[132]

In an interview, Helpmann talked freely about his life in the performing arts. He began by sketching his current activities: 'keeping up ballet practice, planning a new ballet, rehearsing a new play, spending most of the day in a film studio, consulting with artists and directors about costumes, scenery and so on ... people in the theatre just don't have time for an easygoing life'. 'The theatre', he said, 'is my life and my work, and it always has been, from my earliest years.' He then paid tribute to his mother, who had come to Britain for the first time in nearly ten years:

[She] helped and encouraged whatever aptitude I had in my extreme youth. It was no mere theatre infatuation on her part; she knew what she was talking about, and still does, and her constructive criticism was, when I was starting, just as valuable to me as her encouragement.
I want to continue acting. I want to learn more and more about how to use the magnificent resources of the film; but I hope it will be a long time before I desert ballet.[133]

15

Maytie Helpman and Sheila had arrived in the UK in May 1947 for an open-ended stay (which only came to an end in December 1948). They settled into a flat in London. They were met by both Bob and the remaining member of the family, Max. Before the war, Max had been in England, attending Elsie Fogerty's Central School of Dramatic Art, studying production and stage management, occasionally working as an extra in Pinewood Film Studios and living with his widowed aunt, Jean Rudyerd-Helpman, at Iver Heath. When war was declared he was acting with York Repertory Theatre, but in 1940 he enlisted in the Royal Navy (following the long-ago tradition of the Helpmans) and started as a stoker on minesweepers. He was recommended for officers' training and later was on escort duties in the Western Approaches, taking part in Operation Overlord in 1944. He wrote to his mother about 'the never-to-be-forgotten knowledge that one was a tiny part of the most colossal combined operation ... the trick was, not to be stuck at a desk once the invasion started; I managed this by wangling an appointment as navigator of a lead ship to a bunch of Tank Landing Craft.' That did not end his service. In 1945, after a staff course at the Royal Naval College, he was appointed Staff Officer Operations at Trincomalee in what was then Ceylon. He returned to England after his discharge in 1947.

In England that year Sheila joined a company run by Cyril Ritchard and Madge Elliott in an enjoyable production of *The Relapse*, and went on to act with Hal Thompson in a production of *Separate Rooms*. Her acting career in Australia had been continuous. After leaving school in Adelaide, she had joined the Melbourne Rep run by Gregory McMahon. Then she acted at the Minerva Theatre in Sydney with a well-known actor, Edwin Styles – in one play, *The Night of January 16th*, a co-actor was a very young Peter Finch. An association with the J.C. Williamson management came in 1945 when she acted with Ritchard and Elliott in a season of Noël Coward plays.

In England in 1947 Max also got work as an actor in various plays, including *Dark Eyes* starring Edwin Styles, where also in the cast was an unknown Yul Brynner, and a Canadian actress Barbara Chilcott, whom Max would marry in 1952. Christmas 1947 was therefore a complete family affair, with a performance of *The Sleeping Beauty* at Covent Garden on Christmas Eve followed by supper at the Caprice. Helpmann had returned to Sadler's Wells Ballet for the season that began on 12 November, but had no new roles. He was of course engaged to appear in Stratford from April to October 1948. This might well have meant that he would not be seen in ballet for many months. However, the Stratford plays were given in repertory, and Helpmann appeared regularly at Covent Garden in his usual roles. There was a splendid revival of *Job*, with new designs by John Piper, in which he danced Satan. When the ballet went to the Edinburgh Festival, programmes were arranged so that he appeared there for four days, spent the next three in Stratford, and was back in Edinburgh for the following three.

The Stratford season opened on 15 April with *King John*. It was the third season to have as its overall director Sir Barry Jackson, whose theatre life had included Malvern Festivals and Birmingham Repertory Theatre. He had, since 1946, been a challenging and enterprising force at the Shakespeare Memorial Theatre – too much so, for the Board of Governors had just decided not to renew his contract. As usual, he had chosen the plays for 1948, and assembled a notable company. The plays were to be directed by Benthall or Anthony Quayle; Helpmann and Quayle, as leading actors, were joined by a young product of Jackson's Birmingham Rep, Paul Scofield. The women were led by Diana Wynyard and Ena Burrill, with the beauteous young Claire Bloom and the very talented and intelligent young Heather Stannard for good measure. There was an extremely experienced and satisfactory list of subsidiary actors. Designers included Sophie Fedorovitch, James Bailey, Audrey Cruddas and Motley.

Throughout the long season from April to October, Shakespeare was well served. Productions and acting were of the highest quality and full of interesting details. Jackson's choice of plays was ideal, both in terms of literary balance and in suitability for his assembled company. *King John* was followed in due course (and played in repertoire) by *The Taming of the Shrew, The Merchant of Venice, Hamlet, The Winter's Tale* and *Troilus and Cressida*.

The opening play, *King John*, came very much to life in Benthall's production – he had, of course, been familiar with it from his Eton days, when he acted the Bastard in a school performance. It was marked by a great fluidity of action, moving tidally between England and France (countries differentiated by colour schemes: shades of red for England and of blue for France). Helpmann as John (red-haired and bearded) was petulant, flamboyant, meeting the great moments with controlled and exciting fire. There were great contrasts of pace, and whipflicks of comedy; and he played the death scene with a passionate restraint and a rich poetic sadness. Harold Hobson in *The Sunday Times* wrote of 'Mr Helpmann's pale and haunting performance [in which] a febrile flame licks lasciviously at its edges'.[134] Ivor Brown in the *Observer* described it as 'a sly, slim, rufous fox ... beautifully spoken; the voice of kingly craft carries, subtle and precise; the small features are sharply expressive'.[135] Alan Dent in the *News Chronicle* described 'a pale, evil-purposed, red-haired fox, with minatory hands, crafty eyelids'.[136] Philip Hope-Wallace in *Time & Tide* commented: 'Understanding the vital importance of gesture timed to a split second and held for the exact length of time, this vastly improved and clever player, time and again, does the essential in catching the visual attention.'[137]

The Merchant of Venice was given on 19 April and Helpmann was Shylock. For this he had mixed notices. His characterisation was developed from a study of the Habima players in accent, intonation and makeup (some critics felt this was overdone), and was a strong portrayal of a fiercely proud and inflexible man, contemptuous of pleasure-seeking Gentiles, almost too dominant for Benthall's distinctly light-hearted treatment of the play. *The New Statesman*'s critic, however, loved the production, and wrote of 'the sultry pathos of Mr Helpmann's beautifully moving Shylock ... [which] seems to me a masterpiece. In the high Renaissance glare, his black villain, perfectly accented, exalts and cringes and wails with a wonderful conviction.'[138]

The third play was *Hamlet*, in which Helpmann and the young and charismatic Paul Scofield alternated; and it was given in a controversial early Victorian setting, reactions to which were on the whole, understandably, adverse. The quality of the production and performance were lost in the impact of the visual incompatibility, and the two Hamlets suffered from this. Court dress, uniform, dressing gowns all helped the other actors, but Helpmann and Scofield had to contend with a frock-coated opening scene, only later reaching the comparative ease of an open-necked shirt. Nor did the period suit Helpmann's approach, his command of poetic speech, his speed of movement, eloquent mime and rapier intelligence; and he had considerable difficulty coming to terms with this. Alan Dent in the *News Chronicle* praised his 'clarity and control' and wrote: '[His performance] has a good share and showing of intellect, fire, daemonism, subtlety and philosophy'; but found little pathos in his death scene and an overall lack of charm.[139] *The Times*'s critic found 'his movements are always good to see, and he is always good to hear ... but for all that Hamlet's imaginative life remains somewhat remote'.[140] Harold Hobson in *The Sunday Times* summed up his reactions to the two casts: '[Helpmann] is a Hamlet of electricity and energy, the man of action; [Scofield] is Hamlet the thinker'.[141]

Throughout the Stratford season, Helpmann pursued his double career, driving between Warwickshire and Covent Garden, flying between London and the Edinburgh Festival where Sadler's Wells Ballet were appearing, acting Hamlet and dancing Albrecht in *Giselle*, often on consecutive evenings. When the Shakespeare season ended, he went back to ballet.

The summer, however, had shown a product of his third career, when *The Red Shoes* was premiered in July. As far as his small acting role as the dancer Ivan Boleslavsky was concerned, it was unimportant, but his contribution as choreographer certainly mattered. It was as stimulating a dance sequence as had appeared on screen. The film got immense publicity and has, of course, become a cult movie. Moira Shearer made an international reputation from it. Reviews of the film had to discuss all kinds of points about the story, the setting, the acting and of course the Powell–Pressburger direction, but some of them also mentioned the core ballet. Fred Majdalany in the *Daily Mail* wrote: 'This is not merely a new ballet but a ballet conceived in terms of cinema and brilliantly using cinema mechanics to switch between fantasy and reality in a manner impossible on the stage.'[142] C.A.Lejeune in the *Observer* wrote: 'The highspot of the film is unquestionably the "Red Shoes" ballet, especially devised for the film ... to my mind the wedding of movement and colour here is almost perfect'.[143] Dilys Powell in *The Sunday Times* gave it some space:

> In *The Red Shoes* we enjoy for once a ballet written and composed for the cinema in the first place. For this pleasure – and it is an extreme pleasure – we must thank Brian Easdale, whose music brings so sharp an excitement to the film; Robert Helpmann, the choreographer as well as dancer and actor throughout the piece; and Hein Heckroth, to whom we owe the designing of the whole production but whose composition in form and colour is naturally most free and most beautiful in the limitless world of cinema ballet.[144]

At the end of 1948 two new roles waited for Helpmann, both in Ashton ballets. *Don Juan*, set to the Richard Strauss tone poem and designed by Burra, has perhaps been underrated. It was an able piece of choreography, in spite of the fact that David Vaughan reports that Ashton himself felt he did not 'fully bring it off'. Vaughan (and presumably Ashton) puts most of the blame on Helpmann for this failure, pointing out that he 'was by now severely limited technically and also failed to generate the personal magnetism that would have enabled him to be the dominant figure in the ballet'.[145] Given the amount of time Helpmann had been spending as an actor in plays, it was certainly no surprise that his dance technique had suffered, but the other accusation is not quite fair. Because of the brevity of the score this was an unusually compressed work – in fact, none of the dancers was at all stretched technically – and there was little possibility of characterising any of the roles.

On the other hand, *Cinderella,* Ashton's first three-act production, has survived many design and cast changes and, in spite of a good many choreographic weaknesses, still holds its place. What is overlooked now is that in 1948 ballet audiences did not expect new works to last an entire evening; only the classics did that. The Diaghilev influence was still paramount, and *Cinderella* was therefore a novelty. Not too strong, either dramatically or choreographically, and bound to its very uneven Prokofiev score, it owed an enormous debt, which most writers acknowledged, to the inimitable duo of Stepsisters (they were not programmed as Ugly Sisters) created by Ashton and Helpmann *en travestie.* The *Manchester Guardian* critic (signed only J.H.M.) wrote of 'the wonderfully comic business of the two ugly sisters (played by Robert Helpmann and Mr Ashton himself); the antics of this gorgeous pair are at least as relevant as anything in a pantomime – and few pantomimes contain anything so funny'.[146] *The Times* said,

> Brilliant too was the comedy of the ugly sisters, who were played by Mr Ashton himself as the repressed elder and by Mr Robert Helpmann as the uninhibited younger of the pair, who played up to each other with a pretty sense of caricature of female behaviour and a gaiety that avoided the grossness of farce.[147]

The New Statesman contributed:

> [But] oh, the ugly sisters! There is a timid one (Frederick Ashton) dressed in the sourest possible shade of greenish-yellow, who peeps apprehensively out from beneath a tall sandy wig, for all the world like a frightened mouse peering out of a haycock; while her sister (Robert Helpmann) in furious purple and a fan (used at one moment with the extreme of archness and the next like a truncheon) is of an aggressive hauteur that baffles description. These two are uproariously funny ... but they never for an instant overstep the boundary that divides wit from slapstick .[148]

Ashton and Helpmann had a hilarious time, both creating the characters and, as time went on, filling in countless extra details. It probably perplexed the 'lobby' that considered them rivals to find them enjoying each other's invention so cheerfully. They would never revert to any kind of friendship, but neither were the early shared years of Vic-Wells experience ever forgotten by either of them.

Revivals of ballets marked the early months of 1949 at Covent Garden. *A Wedding Bouquet* was staged, reverting unsuccessfully to the original chorus instead of a narrator as during the war; while *Apparitions*, with some changed costume colours, looked exquisitely romantic on the large stage. In both, Helpmann and Fonteyn had their accustomed places. They appeared with the company in Florence in May, at the Teatro Communale, dancing in *Rake, Hamlet* and *Cinderella*, and continued to Copenhagen as guest artists in June. In between, Helpmann appeared with the Royal Philharmonic Orchestra as an engaging narrator in *Peter and the Wolf*. Sitting for the most part on a high bar stool, he not only spoke the text with immaculate timing and emphasis, but illustrated it with telling comic mime. He repeated the performance frequently with different orchestras and conductors in different parts of the world during the next few years. Meanwhile, he was acting leads in radio plays for the BBC: the sinister husband in *Gaslight* and an admirably controlled account of the title role in Albert Camus's *Caligula*. In a broadcast for the BBC Forces Educational Programme, he had said: 'Ballet dancing is physically an exhausting profession; it requires the utmost of the artist in health and physical stamina.'[149] He was certainly a compulsive worker, constantly practising his two professions of dancing and acting, and stretching toward every aspect of the performing arts.

16

Sadler's Wells Ballet was now on the eve of its American debut, organised by Sol Hurok. On 29 September 1949, at Covent Garden, Helpmann created the mime-and-dance role of Mercury in Arthur Bliss's opera *The Olympians,* choreographed by Pauline Grant. He performed it only once, as he had to fly to New York with the ballet company on 1 October. The opening night of *The Sleeping Beauty* at the Metropolitan Opera House was arranged for 9 October, and the triumph of that occasion is firmly established in the annals of classical ballet. Fonteyn and Helpmann were Aurora and Florimund, and Ashton was cast as Carabosse. Fonteyn and Helpmann were new to New York, although Ashton had already made his mark as early as the winter of 1933/34, when he had a notable success with his choreography for the Virgil Thomson–Gertrude Stein *Four Saints in Three Acts.*

Nothing in the rest of the repertoire caught the American imagination as much as *The Sleeping Beauty* and Fonteyn's delectable Aurora. The other works shown in New York were *Swan Lake;* Ashton's *Cinderella, Façade, A Wedding Bouquet, Apparitions* and *Symphonic Variations;* de Valois's *The Rake's Progress, Checkmate* and *Job;* and Helpmann's *Miracle in the Gorbals* and *Hamlet.* Critical response was not particularly enthusiastic. John Martin in the *New York Times* preferred the 'theater pieces rather than pure ballets'. He praised *Rake's* 'beautifully consistent style, full of humor and comment and a high degree of subtle perception of both period and people' and found *Hamlet* 'equally vigorous in its own way ... a marvel of dramatic composition, not only ingenious in conception but completely gripping'. He enjoyed *Façade* but was 'less enthusiastic' about *Symphonic Variations.* Although it had 'fine invention' in it, 'it emerges as sentimental and without any great formal compulsion'.[150] *Cinderella* also left him cold. He admired the Fairies of the Seasons and the choreography for the Jester and for Cinderella and the Prince but declared it to be the 'least effective of the three programmes thus far shown'. He did, however, enjoy Ashton and Helpmann: 'They are not only grotesque and keyed to the lowest of low comedy clowning, but manage also to be deftly characterized and to supplement each other with a beautiful theatrical subtlety.'[151] They appealed also to Walter Terry in the *New York Herald Tribune,* who thought the ballet should have been called *The Two Ugly Sisters*

They slap their wigs on at wrong angles, they push each other about, they trip and totter, they grimace, they steal scenes and they even manage to color their travesty with moments of poignancy. There is little or no dancing involved in their activities and their major parts in the ballet obviously shift the focus from where it should be placed ... but dance and focus to the contrary, these two vouchsafed tremendous performances which will not soon be forgotten.

Like Martin, he thought little of the ballet as a whole, 'not, I fear, an example of the choreographer's art at its best'.[152]

Continuing the season, Martin loved *A Wedding Bouquet* ('a witty and wonderful bit of trivia'), disliked *Apparitions* ('Mr. Ashton treats it daintily, rarely getting deeper than the periphery'), and was disappointed in *Miracle* ('a banality play set in the slums of Glasgow').[153] Terry reacted differently. He, too, enjoyed *Wedding Bouquet* ('this light and frothy work ... was fun, attenuated in spots, but disarmingly zany') but not *Apparitions* ('the insipidness of its romantic qualities shadowed those more diverting elements of fantasy which managed to emerge from time to time'). About *Miracle*, however, he was positive:

[It is] a work of remarkable integrity, both in its conveyance of emotions and in the simplicity of its movement details. There are, it must be admitted, some artificial passages ... but in the main the passion is realized in stirring, theatrical, yet believable terms. Mr. Helpmann as the Stranger who restores the Suicide to life, who brings an air of remote gentleness to the sordid scene, is completely credible in the part. Gerd Larsen is splendid as the Prostitute and John Hart is fine as the harsh, self-righteous official who comes to deplore the wisdom of his evil actions.[154]

All in all, Ashton must have been surprised and distressed that major ballets of his should not be acclaimed. Helpmann, on the other hand, already inured to adverse reactions, was no doubt thankful for small mercies. An interesting reaction to *Miracle* came from Robert Sylvester in the *New York Daily News*:

It's almost impossible to believe that a ballet of superior beauty and superb force can be fashioned out of such ingredients as criminal violence, slum poverty and psychopathic sadism. But Robert Helpmann and the Sadler's Wells Ballet company have managed to do it with *Miracle in the Gorbals.*

He felt it was surprising to find that a technically classical dancer such as Helpmann should somehow have learned

how four hoodlums jostle, knee and slash a victim in such authentic fashion. The premiere of *Miracle*, building as it did so firmly and inexorably last night, accomplished one of those rare moments at the Met. For a long while the audience was just too stunned to applaud. And then the house fairly exploded.

He commented on something that was indeed a sign of the prevailing attitude of the Covent Garden management towards Helpmann: '*Miracle* should never be done as an opening ballet, of course, but the company doubtless can't handle the scenery changes with this particular bill unless it is put away first.'[155] There was nothing particularly complicated about the scenery of either *A Wedding Bouquet* or *Apparitions*, so presumably the order was decided on some other grounds. One interesting side effect of *Miracle*, of significance to British dance theatre, was that the young Robert Cohan, later founder-director of London Contemporary Dance Theatre, was immensely impressed by it and acknowledged it as an important influence on his career.

After New York the company went on tour to Washington DC, Richmond, Philadelphia, Chicago, East Lansing, and then to Canada (Toronto, Ottawa and Montreal). Everywhere the dancers were feted and entertained. *The Red Shoes* had proved a great success, so that Shearer and Helpmann came in for plenty of additional press attention.

When the company returned to London on 13 December, the next Covent Garden season began rather tamely with *Cinderella*, but Helpmann's mind was already on other things: he was scheduled to direct his first opera at the Garden, *Madame Butterfly*, on 17 January 1950 – although, awkwardly, the Covent Garden planners seemed to have overlooked the fact that de Valois was creating a new ballet, *Don Quixote*, starring Helpmann, to open on 20 February. Between these two dates, Fonteyn and Helpmann flew to Oslo to give two (unpaid) performances with the Ny Norsk Ballet to help them out of financial difficulties. They danced the *Nutcracker pas de deux* and the Spirits of the Air duet from *The Fairy Queen*, and apparently enjoyed themselves so much that later in the year they banded together with other company dancers for a provincial concert tour in England.

Where opera was concerned, Helpmann had background. He had seen his first performance (*Aida*) in Adelaide as a schoolboy. At both Covent Garden and Sadler's Wells he had regularly danced in operas ranging from *Schwanda the Bagpiper* to *La Cenerentola*, *Faust* or *Tsar Saltan*. He went to opera regularly in London. Since the end of the war, Covent Garden, under the general administration of David Webster, had been staging notable productions, some directed by John Gielgud or Benthall. But directing *Madame Butterfly* was definitely a new undertaking for him. He settled for restraint and a complete lack of balletic emphasis in movements and groupings. Elisabeth Schwarzkopf, who sang Butterfly, spoke of him to an interviewer from *The Stage*:

> One great advantage of Mr Helpmann's production was his knowledge and understanding of music. This is not an equipment of every opera producer ... in giving it the first right, he even went so far as to modify his grouping so that the conductor should not be obscured – a point that many producers give little thought to.

She went on:

> This in no way affected the beautiful delicacy and care of his production. He took infinite pains, always remaining calm in every difficulty, and that, I think, is why, in spite of so few rehearsals, the result, from the point of view of acting and spectacle, was so impressive.[156]

17

Don Quixote was de Valois's first ballet since 1944. She, like Helpmann, never regarded herself as being primarily a choreographer. Both had outstanding creative powers where dramatic choreography was concerned, but their lives were so filled with other interests and compulsions that they could never be equated with the kind of choreographer – for example, Ashton or MacMillan – whose entire career and reputation rests on a substantial and ongoing corpus of original ballets. This factor, of course, freed both de Valois and Helpmann from feelings of jealousy over other people's successes in this field. Also, although they naturally delighted in appreciation for their major ballets, they could ride out opposition. Nor were they interested in post-mortem analysis. They believed in going on strongly to the next phase of work, whatever that might be.

Certainly, in 1950 *Don Quixote* had no chance at all of becoming a seat-selling triumph. For the international ballet public, delighting in *The Sleeping Beauty* and *Swan Lake,* and being taught by some younger critics to value pure-dance works by Balanchine and Ashton as infinitely more important than despised 'dance-dramas', there was no understanding for the ballet that emerged at Covent Garden on 20 February. To go with music by Roberto Gerhard, which had been given its first concert performance in 1942 when it was conducted by Constant Lambert, and with distinguished designs by Burra, de Valois mapped out a treatment of Cervantes's characters that was so reticent and intellectual that it made no concessions at all to popular taste. All the same, the critic writing in *The Times* knew what it was all about:

> Miss Ninette de Valois has achieved unity with an unusual balance of the ingredients, and so produced a work of art of great distinction. The movements of the dancers are gestures writ large and there is no lack of invention in them – administration has not extinguished the artist in her. Miss Fonteyn, for instance, as the alternating personality of the slut Aldonza and the lady Dulcinea, has had devised for her movements of hair, shoulder and *pointes* that were at once dramatic and balletic. But there was no place for sustained choreography on an extended scale. Every one of the five scenes contained a concentration of action in an economy of movement that gripped the attention by virtue of its visual significance.

He went on to praise Helpmann's creation of the title role:

Don Quixote is a character who on the stage may easily become a bore. Not, however, if he is portrayed by Mr Helpmann. The slow tempo, the strained air, the sharp, decisive movements, all made him into a real person capable of evoking not only Sancho Panza's devotion but our passionate concern.[157]

To estimate Helpmann's theatrical range, this description must be related to earlier ones of the outrageous Stepsister in *Cinderella*, of Dr Coppelius, of Mr O'Reilly, of the Rake and the Dago. It has to be accepted that one actor-dancer encompassed the vast differences among such roles. His Don Quixote, in fact, was an interpretation of dignity and power, a very noble portrait. Speaking for myself, I was awed by his controlled action, his vivid quality of stillness. As in *Rake* and *Miracle*, he brought into play his ability to convey, without any sense of strain, a tremendous emotional effect. This was done by turns of the head, half-movements, the crook of a hand, a light in the eyes, a slight tremor in the muscles of the face. In contrast, a few swift moments of dancing, a wild beating at the bars of an imaginary cage, were immensely telling. De Valois's last created role for him was a proof of her understanding of and trust in his mature artistry.

Don Quixote won a good deal of critical praise from the British press. In spite of that, it did not 'take'. Relatively few performances and little interest during the next overly ambitious and overly hyped American tour at the end of the year killed it off. Increasingly, the dictates of the American (dollar-producing) market were all-powerful where repertoire and casting were concerned.

One bonus for regular British balletgoers cheered up the summer of 1950. June saw the launch of the Fonteyn–Helpmann Concert Group, which offered the ballet equivalent of a popular seaside concert party in centres such as Tunbridge Wells, Eastbourne and Brighton. The accent was on amusement for everyone, including the cast. The programme consisted largely of divertissements, although there was one ballet for the leading pair (a delightful one, Alfred Rodrigues's *Ile des sirènes*), and the dancers included Pamela May, June Brae, Harold Turner and Alexis Rassine. Helpmann narrated *Peter and the Wolf*, and the programme ended with a selection from Act III of *Coppélia*, with Helpmann back in the role of Franz. At the same time, he was contributing the choreography for John Tore's South African musical *Golden City*, which opened at the Adelphi

Theatre in June. To quote Kurt Gänzl in *The British Musical Theatre*, the production was shared between Benthall and Helpmann – 'Benthall manipulating the huge cast, Helpmann choreographing enormous set piece dance sequences which were the core of the enterprise'. These included chorus girl routines, a ballet (*The Girl in the Window*), a coon's carnival, a goldfields' saloon with a full-scale fight, and a spectacular Zulu fire ritual ... 'all of this benefited greatly from Robert Helpmann's magnificent visual sense'.[158]

The second Sadler's Wells Ballet American tour opened at the Met on 10 September with *Swan Lake*. Helpmann, still filming, did not reach New York until 24 September. This season included *Giselle, Don Quixote* and *Dante Sonata*, in all of which he appeared. At age forty-one, although he still greatly enjoyed dancing and choreographing ballets, he did not see much future in ballet; he was also deeply preoccupied with drama and films. The break, however, came unexpectedly in November when the company was playing San Francisco. Although he had not intended to leave on a sour note, he resigned after a sudden argument with de Valois. Both were no doubt stressed by the demands of the coast-to-coast tour. De Valois told the press that 'Mr. Helpmann had to make a most important film and it was impossible for him to do this and also dance with us all the time'. Helpmann said, 'I will return as guest star sometimes but I want to give all my attention to making the film of *The Sleeping Beauty* in London next autumn.' It did not take them long to get back on friendly terms, but Helpmann was never again a company member of Sadler's Wells Ballet.

The *Beauty* film, which was to be made by Alexander Korda, fell foul of a disagreement with him over how it should be done. It never materialised, although scenario details and designs by Oliver Messel are lodged in the Theatre Museum in London. The preliminary synopsis starts with an introduction in the Palace of Sans-Souci, with fireworks and monkeys dressed as pages playing musical instruments. The action is 'opened up' to show an outdoor landscape, with crowds and a procession. There follows an 'extended section of Aurora following a vision of the spinning wheel to the tower', and the Bluebird sequence is to be introduced at that point. The hunt follows a magic gazelle that turns into the Lilac Fairy as Florimund reaches it. At the wedding, the only divertissement *pas de deux* is to be that of the Cats, but the three Ivans are replaced by three chefs with a wedding cake. The Aurora *pas de deux* and variations are as usual.

A second treatment, dated 5 March 1951, by Helpmann and Benthall, begins by suggesting that, during the overture, introductory credits should be shown over backgrounds of night sky, stars whose shapes refer to the fairy godmothers' gifts, and thunder and lightning representing Carabosse. The Christening is to begin at dawn, with cinematic images of preparation: a stable yard, white horses being groomed, a supercilious cat and a white poodle walking on its hind legs, white pigeons, and borzois. Catalabutte is seen directing activities. Then, a glimpse of the wine cellar and kitchen – a christening cake with 'Aurora' on the icing – invitations being sent out by bird post, the king with his collection of clocks, the nursery with its cradle. The Princes in the birthday scene were to be Chinese, Indian, Spanish and Slavonic. In the last act, Catalabutte was to be shown opening a book of fairy tales to introduce the procession of Red Riding Hood, Goldilocks, Cinderella and Bluebeard. The traditional choreography, both dance and mime action, is not dealt with and was presumably meant to be presented as given in the Sadler's Wells Ballet production.

Before leaving Sadler's Wells Ballet, Helpmann had drawn praise in New York from both Walter Terry and John Martin for *Giselle,* in spite of the fact that he had not been dancing regularly for some months. Terry wrote in the *New York Herald Tribune*:

> If Mr. Helpmann is not a *premier danseur* in the sense of physical virtuosity, he assuredly merits the appelation through his gifts as a partner and as an actor. I do not believe that I have ever seen a better Albrecht in that aspect of the role which demands dramatic action. Not only does the English [*sic*!] star project passages of traditional pantomime with clarity of gesture and with balletic elegance, but he also invests them and augments them with dramatic qualities and tensions necessary to a detailed realization of the specific character of the hero. It is, then, a superb piece of dance-acting that Mr. Helpmann offers his audience.[159]

Martin in the *New York Times* declared that

> one would have to search long and hard to find a better Albrecht. Mr. Helpmann may not be the best dancer in the world, but he assuredly is one of its best actors. In this foolish but tender old ballet, he manages to make sense of a role which is full of foggy motivations, unaccountable reactions and emotional clichés. Fortunately, he is not afraid of a bit of ham, and he keeps the drama steadily alive when he is on stage.

Later, he stressed the collaboration with Fonteyn: 'That Mr. Helpmann is a valuable aid is unquestionable. They work together perfectly, with a

common dramatic purpose and a complete coordination of phrasing.'[160]
Some years later, Sol Hurok also defended him as a dancer:

> Technical virtuosity is not by any means all of a dancer's story. I happen
> to know of dancers who in my opinion have excelled Nijinsky and
> Pavlova in these departments but they were much lesser artists. It is the
> overall quality of a dancer that matters. Helpmann, I feel, is a dancer of
> really exceptional fluency, superb lightness, genuine musicality and
> admirable control.[161]

These observations are worth recording. The magnificent poetry and
true Romantic understanding of the Fonteyn–Helpmann pairing in *Giselle*
has been forgotten in the wake of eulogies about the Fonteyn–Nureyev
partnership. In Act II, the dreamlike fluency of the dancing, the
supernatural inevitability with which they allowed the drama to unfold,
were so absorbing that no one would have thought of disturbing the mood
by applause until the final curtain. There were neither showpiece moments
nor a sense of endeavour, merely an eloquent demonstration of skilfully
unified music, dance and mime.

The fact that there was no permanent rift between Helpmann and de
Valois was underlined in February 1951, when the smaller Sadler's Wells
Theatre Ballet, at Sadler's Wells, staged *The Prospect Before Us,* in which
for three performances Helpmann danced O'Reilly. At the end of the first,
de Valois came on stage, kissed him warmly, and keeping him firmly by the
hand thanked him publicly for 'a wonderful performance'. He also spoke.
'Somehow,' he said, 'the word "resign" has got mixed up with "retire". If
there is anyone in the house who thinks this is my last performance ....' As
the *Daily Mail* recorded, the audience 'bravoed him, and wouldn't let him
finish'.[162] On the other hand, an old promise made by de Valois that no one
else should ever dance O'Reilly was broken; for a little while, the ballet
continued in the company repertoire with Stanley Holden in the lead.

The immediate future for Helpmann was acting. He was already
rehearsing two neatly contrasted roles, Octavius Caesar in *Antony and
Cleopatra* and Apollodorus in *Caesar and Cleopatra,* which Laurence Olivier
and Vivien Leigh were putting on in London as part of the Festival of Britain
summer, productions that were later taken to New York. Meanwhile, the
Powell–Pressburger film *The Tales of Hoffmann* had its world premiere at
the Met. In this Helpmann mimed and danced the multiple role of Lindorf,
Coppelius, Dapertutto and Dr Miracle – having the not-very-easy task of
suiting his gestures and expressions to match the singing of a bass-baritone.

He later told of being presented to Queen Mary when she saw the film in London. She said 'I really must congratulate you. You have a lovely voice, Mr Helpmann.' He had answered gravely 'Thank you, Ma'am. I'm glad you think so.' Ashton did the choreography for this film, but it seems to me possible that the short, evocative solo performed by Helpmann as Dapertutto was his own contribution, growing out of his interpretation of the role and its music. In a book about the film, Monk Gibbon said something that is relevant to every aspect of Helpmann's career:

> When he acts, he mobilises his entire personality. He is not vain. His apparent hauteur is a defence rather than any desire to impress. One might say that he is saved from vanity by the conscience of the artist, which is continually urging him on to fresh efforts. No doubt he is aware of his achievement but he is incapable of being obsessed by it. With those he knows and likes he is friendly and amusing, loving nothing better than a good laugh and quite capable of burlesquing his own highest flights.[163]

In 2005 the film director George A. Romero chose to talk of *The Tales of Hoffmann* to Marc Lee in an interview for the London *Daily Telegraph*. He had been captivated by it at the age of eleven, when he was living in the Bronx. He loved the fantasy elements and the music, and was greatly impressed by Helpmann: 'Helpmann was my hero then; he was a really impressive cat, man. His eyes, his eyebrows – he beat Bela Lugosi by a mile.' His favourite scene was right at the beginning 'as he sweeps into the opera house. An overhead shot follows his progress across a red carpet, as he swishes his long cape around a scattering of gold coloured chairs. He clearly means business, and he steals the rest of the show with ease.'[164]

The two Cleopatra plays were premiered out of town and came to the St James's Theatre in London in April 1951. They made a fascinating study of play-writing styles. The role of Apollodorus presented problems that Helpmann never fully solved. The rhythm of Shaw's prose was difficult for him. While in Shakespeare or Webster his understanding of the verse structure was infallible, the Shavian dialogue was alien to him. This was a pity, as his response to Shavian wit was clear. This made for an attractive but uneven performance.

His Octavius Caesar, however, was brilliantly characterised, theatrically effective. George Rylands commented: 'Helpmann's outstanding performance conveyed Shakespeare's intention that the play be presented not only as a love story but as an imperial theme.'[165] There was much variation throughout the part, great vocal beauty, and a completely consistent portrait of leashed-in energy, steel-sharp intelligence and ruthless integrity; yet it was capable of a world of pity as he said, 'Poor Anthony!' Benthall's production of this play was on a par with his *White Devil* and *King John*, fluent, poetic, distinguishing with great clarity between Rome and Egypt.

The Cleopatras were taken to the USA and ran until April 1952. Helpmann's brother Max was also with the company as a small part actor, and while they were at the Ziegfeld Theatre in New York he married Barbara Chilcott. Helpmann was best man, Cyril Ritchard and Madge Elliott were there, as were Barbara's father and brothers. Max and Barbara went back with them to Canada. Also in New York, Helpmann broadcast with the Lunts over the NBC network in a Theatre Guild production as the Scots soldier in Barrie's play *The Old Lady Shows Her Medals*. He and Benthall saw a good deal of Katharine Hepburn, and his next acting assignment in Britain was with her as The Egyptian Doctor in a rare production of Shaw's *The Millionairess* in March. In this, of course, his problems with Shavian dialogue continued, so it was a pity that the play had a long run in London and New York. His friendship with Hepburn, however, would endure all his life.

Before the war, Helpmann had appeared a good deal on television, mainly as a dancer with the Vic-Wells Ballet. In February 1953 he made a virtuoso BBC television appearance as an actor in a half-hour one-man show, Peter Brook's suspense play *Box for One*, about a gangster on the run in a phone box receiving an unexpected call.

18

The Helpmann/Benthall relationship had firm ground in their mutual passion for the performing arts, for music and design; and had it been possible at the time, it would certainly have resulted in a Civil Partnership. Both, however, had individual careers of equal importance, which every now and then resulted in a collaboration but frequently followed divergent paths. In the post-war years Benthall directed many plays, both for the Old Vic and as a freelance director. Helpmann was continuously occupied with a variety of assignments for theatre and ballet. They shared a London home, a spacious garden flat in Eaton Square, but both travelled worldwide for their work. Benthall's parents, Sir Edward and Lady Benthall, lived in Bishopsteignton in Devon – Lady Benthall had been the Hon. Ruth Cable, daughter of the first (and only) Lord Cable. Sir Edward's career in banking was principally linked with India, but he was also a governor of the BBC from 1955 to 1960. He died in 1961, and his widow moved to London. Apart from her, Benthall's closest relations were his uncle Sir Paul Benthall and Sir Paul's sons. From his father's death he had to become closely involved, against his will, with all kinds of business responsibilities and decisions. He felt unable to accept a renewal of his Old Vic contract in 1962, and although he managed to fulfil occasional freelance productions, he became chronically stressed and gradually incurably alcoholic, dying much too early, in 1974 at the age of 55.

An important task for Helpmann came unexpectedly in March 1953. Benthall, due to direct an Old Vic revival of T.S. Eliot's *Murder in the Cathedral* starring Robert Donat, fell ill with flu, and Helpmann took over. As a director he only had to his credit *Madame Butterfly* and a farce called *The Wedding Ring*, staged in 1952, that had failed to reach London. *Murder in the Cathedral* was a much more serious matter, and his superb direction of it, with Donat's performance as Becket, was fortunately recorded. Interestingly, it was reviewed in the *New York Times* by Brooks Atkinson, who had been visiting London. He wrote of 'the great job of clarification' that Helpmann had performed, saying 'it derives basically from the clarity and the music of the speaking. Every line is delivered perfectly'. Speaking of the treatment of the chorus, he went on:

> For the most part, the chorus is in motion and clarifies the emotion of the play by huddling in casual throngs like frightened women gossiping

about Becket or by sweeping lightly across the stage like withered leaves blown around the walls of the cathedral by angry winds of fate. Although the chorus never loses its function of commenting on the theme, Mr Helpmann's imaginative staging makes it integral, vital and dramatic ... he has dramatised the script by contrasting the tones and tempos of the different story elements.[166]

W.A. Darlington in the *Daily Telegraph* was engaged by the way Helpmann staged the scene where the four knights justify their murder. They were turned into a

full blooded burlesque of a board of directors presenting a company report to shareholders. The result was an unforgettably funny scene, which yet held its place in the drama ... [Helpmann] got his special effects from this scene by calling on his actors for exceptionally good and clear speaking combined with an intelligent appreciation of the author's meaning.[167]

The production in fact was a highly emotional dramatic experience. The play, previously considered more suited to staging in a cathedral, established itself as belonging to the stage. The chorus praised by Atkinson was skilfully pieced out among the younger and older women of Canterbury, the varying voices contrasted with fine musicianship. At his disposal, Helpmann had a perfect cast – Robert Donat's magnificent Becket was supported by sound and sensitive playing from other actors. The interplay of voices remains on the recording, but the dignity of movement and the contrasts of lighting were equal to the vocal power; and the most lyrical moment was perhaps when the women moved out from the darkening cathedral, making obeisance to the altar, until one older one was left to whisper the last words, 'Blessed Thomas, pray for us',

Covent Garden got around to inviting Helpmann to appear with his old company on Coronation Night, but only in Act II of *Swan Lake*. However, Helpmann was back at Covent Garden in December, not as a ballet guest artist but as an opera director and choreographer. Rimsky-Korsakov's *Le Coq d'or* had not been staged at the Royal Opera House since 1919, and on 7 January 1954 it proved a notable success, with Mattiwilda Dobbs as the Queen of Shemakhan, Hugues Cuenod as the Astrologer, Arda Mandikian as the Golden Cockerel and Howell Glynne as King Dodon making an excellent cast. Igor Markevitch conducted, the glorious designs were by Loudon Sainthill, and Helpmann's contribution was warmly received.

There was a strong choreographic element. For *The Times* critic, he 'brought to the production both his special knowledge of movement and his sense of the comic, using both with enough restraint to prevent them getting in the way of the music'.[168] Eric Blom in the *Observer* commented:

> Robert Helpmann's production enriches it with one surprise after another. From the prologue, where the Astrologer appears somewhere on the wrong side of the sun, to the gorgeous and amusing procession in the third act, everything is twice as enchanting as and incomparably more tasteful than any pantomime.[169]

A new life had opened up for Benthall in 1953 – he had been appointed artistic director of the Old Vic, starting with the 1953–4 season. In July, supported by Bronson Albery, the chairman of the Old Vic Trust, and Alfred Francis, the Vic's administrative director, he launched a five-year plan to stage all 36 plays in the Shakespeare First Folio. He told *The Stage* that this would 'enable a whole generation of young actors and theatre-goers to see the complete works in the live theatre'. The plays would be put in repertory so that London visitors could see several each week. Although the Vic was not ideally equipped for such a system, the designer James Bailey would improve the forestage arrangement and create a new proscenium and facade.[170]

An exciting company of actors was engaged, and the great venture began on 14 September. Benthall took a considerable risk by starting with *Hamlet*, with the largely inexperienced young Richard Burton in the lead, and alternated it initially with the difficult play *All's Well That Ends Well*, with Fay Compton as the Countess of Rousillon and Michael Hordern as Parolles. Somehow the two plays managed to please audiences for some weeks, partly because they were well produced, were well designed (by Kenneth Rowell and Osbert Lancaster respectively) and showed off to good effect a company that included John Neville, Claire Bloom and Robert Hardy. *King John*, directed by George Devine and starring Hordern, came next, coupled with *Twelfth Night*, directed by Denis Carey, with Claire Bloom as Viola, Neville as Orsino and Hordern as Malvolio. Burton, directed by Benthall, made a big success with *Coriolanus* in February 1954.

Then in April Helpmann directed and choreographed *The Tempest*. Hordern was a splendid Prospero, Robert Hardy (then slim and young) was Ariel, and Burton was an unusual and excellent Caliban. Designs were by Hurry and the music by Malcolm Arnold. Ivor Brown in the *Observer* began by declaring that the play had three parts: classic majesty; wonders and music in the air; the monster and the human drolls:

Robert Helpmann, Leslie Hurry and the Old Vic Company, all at their best, have succeeded in all three elements ... the production should please all those with an eye for ballet, those with an ear for the dying fall of Shakespeare's own word-music – I have never felt the epilogue more poignant – and those who relish the rough stuff of ingenious clowning.[171]

Harold Hobson wrote in *The Sunday Times*, 'Mr Robert Helpmann has produced *The Tempest* with an exciting visual imagination, a keen sense of comedy, and here and there a glimpse of poetry. If this seems a backhanded tribute, I add that this *Tempest* is, on the whole, the most satisfying I have seen.'[172] Other critics thought differently, feeling that the production obscured the poetry, but on the whole it counted as a success.

Things were otherwise with Helpmann's next assignment, in June, when he directed Noël Coward's *After the Ball*, a musical play based on *Lady Windermere's Fan*. Plenty of critical ink was spilled on making it clear that nobody really liked anything about it, and Helpmann was probably glad that his part in the proceedings was rarely mentioned. He was in any case preoccupied with plans for acting Oberon in an Old Vic production of *A Midsummer Night's Dream* and The Devil in a Glyndebourne production of *The Soldier's Tale*, both to be launched at the Edinburgh Festival in August. This *Dream*, directed by Benthall and designed by Robin and Christopher Ironside (but with distinct links to the Messel-designed pre-war *Dream* at the Old Vic), also used Mendelssohn's music. Helpmann no doubt pressed for this, writing in *Theatre Arts Monthly*: 'Personally, and I repeat personally, I find the two [the play and the music] cannot be separated. In some curious way, in the first few bars of the overture, Mendelssohn, a German, caught the same wonderful magic that Shakespeare did in his supreme verse.' Helpmann did much of the choreography, while Ashton composed the Nocturne *pas de deux* that Helpmann danced with his ballerina Titania, Moira Shearer. About Ashton, he commented, 'Ashton, a superb example of a modern choreographer who completely understands and uses the classical ballet to its great advantage, has in his beautiful arrangement completely clarified all that I felt.'[173] Although a good deal was right about it, the 1954 *Dream* failed to achieve the overall excellence of Guthrie's 1937 staging, and certainly failed to please the American critics and public when it went on tour to the United States, where it played at the Met from 21 September through mid-October and thereafter at very large theatres across the country.

The Soldier's Tale, directed by Günther Rennert, was a very different matter; in every way this was a definitive version, and acclaimed as such. The later film was unfortunately not nearly as good, having very little in common with the Edinburgh staging, which musically, visually and dramatically was a magnificently unified whole. The *Weekly Scotsman* critic wrote that 'It is one of the delights of the Festivals that they have often thrown up, in the last week, something that completely galvanises us all. We had great hopes, certainly, about this production [of *The Soldier's Tale*] but they were easily and magnificently surpassed.' He went on to say, 'The Devil, to give him his splendid due, is, if comparisons are possible at all, the most striking performance of all. Robert Helpmann, who also devised the choreography, plays and dances the Fiend with the last degree of grotesque, leering agility and menacing grace.'[174] Felix Aprahamian pointed out in *The Sunday Times* that the company was reduced from 'the original baker's dozen ... by the versatility of Robert Helpmann, who dances Old Nick as admirably as he acts him. His unmistakable, impish features create a very intimate Devil in place of the rather impersonal one resulting from the Auberjonois masks used at the Paris and Lucerne revivals of 1946, and necessitated originally by the split role.'[175] The performance was completely in key with Stravinsky, incisive, witty and infinitely varied. Whether the Devil was wheedling the Soldier, tempting him, commanding him, playing cards with him for fabulous stakes or leading him off to hell, the characterisation was full of excitement and power.

19

The year 1955 was devoted to the drama theatre. In February, Helpmann directed *As You Like It* at the Old Vic, with Virginia McKenna and John Neville in the leads. The designs had to camouflage that season's permanent set, as Hurry had done, surprisingly well, for *The Tempest* the previous year. For *As You Like It*, Helpmann's choice of designer was Domenico Gnoli. Maurice Wiltshire in the *Daily Mail* wrote of 'a production of safe, tidy charm' and said that it was 'ably helped by the idyllic sylvan settings of Mr Domenico Gnoli, a 21-year-old Italian artist of great promise'.[176] The production was on the whole liked. Stephen Williams in the *Evening News* said 'it steps along as rhythmically and gracefully as an Elizabethan dance measure. We go to the Forest of Arden in a galliard and come home in a coranto.'[177] T.C. Worsley in the *New Statesman* described it as

> a straightforward lyric production, with touches of pure poetry in the grouping and the lighting and a really fine discretion in matching the parts; the comics, above all, are delightfully toned down ... The romantically absurd is the tone that is caught and held – and it is the right one.[178]

In May, Helpmann returned to Australia for the first time since 1932, starring with Katharine Hepburn in a long Old Vic Drama tour and playing Shylock, Angelo in *Measure for Measure* and Petruchio in *The Taming of the Shrew*. The tour did much to augment the Old Vic's finances, helping them to acquire a large building site for an annexe to house essential new workshops, wardrobe and technical office facilities. As joint stars for the tour, Helpmann and Hepburn got maximum press coverage in Australia. Marjorie Plunkett, interviewing Helpmann for the *Australian Women's Weekly*, asked him about whether Hepburn was 'a long-legged, tempestuous tomboy who is rude to the press'. He replied,

> Brusque? Rude? Nonsense! Difficult during rehearsals? Rubbish! Of course she doesn't like being interrupted during rehearsals – what good actor or actress does? ... As for her being rude to the Press, she doesn't like being asked 'Twitch up your skirt a bit, Miss Hepburn, so that we get a bit more leg into our picture.' Who would?

He had spent Christmas 1953 with the Hepburn family in America: 'Twenty-nine people sat down to Christmas dinner – every one of them a Hepburn or married to a Hepburn, except me.'[179]

The Old Vic company opened at the Tivoli Theatre in Sydney on 14 May with *The Merchant of Venice*, with Hepburn as Portia and Helpmann repeating his Stratford-on-Avon Shylock. It was an exciting, high-society evening. His mother and Sheila were in the audience. Australian papers tended to include reports about what women wore, rather as British papers once described in detail the dresses of debutantes after each royal court, so Sheila's crimson, organza, ballerina-length dress, with 'a brilliant clasp on the single velvet shoulder strap' was, to the family's amusement, duly recorded – it should be mentioned that the resemblance between Helpmann and his sister, in expressions and gestures, was uncanny. Where the critics were concerned, Hepburn's performance came in for a certain amount of carping, but Helpmann was acclaimed. The critic of the *Sydney Morning Herald* wrote: 'The wonderfully impressive Shylock ... is not one of your foully hideous hunchbacks but a proud man of distinguished bearing, a man who finds great dignity and strength of will ... in the things that make him different from Christians.'[180]

The Merchant of Venice was followed on 24 May by *The Taming of the Shrew*, in which the talking point was undoubtedly a fast, gymnastic and tightly choreographed domestic fight between Katharina and Petruchio. There had been a series of delightful rehearsal photographs of this, and the costumed reality equally delighted audiences. *The Sydney Morning Herald* found that 'the two stars were very much better balanced as partners' than they had been as Portia and Shylock. The production was praised as 'altogether fresh, nimble and heartily proud of its belly-laughs'.[181] *Measure for Measure* came in on June 1 and naturally proved less popular than the other two plays. The tour moved from Sydney to Brisbane, Melbourne, Adelaide and Perth, and offstage Hepburn and Helpmann made constant copy everywhere for Australian reporters. The last performance was in Perth on 12 November.

The Old Vic tour of Australia was considerably more for Helpmann than an acting assignment. It was a family reunion; it was an affirmation of his Australian heritage; and in typical Australian style he was inundated with requests, not only for interviews but for a vast number of extra-theatrical activities. There were appearances to be made at hospitals, colleges and department stores, as well as civic receptions in each of the cities. There were people everywhere who surged up to remind him of associations in the past. He had plenty of fun re-visiting his old school, talking to the boys of having had a record of Saturday detentions, posing for photographs wearing the school cap that he had rebelled against as a pupil, and teasing probably uncomfortable past masters by stressing how much they must have been glad to be rid of him. He had a charming reunion with his ballet teacher Nora Stewart. In addition he had to act as guide-courier to Hepburn everywhere, and match her energetic explorations on foot (or even occasionally on bicycles).

Most importantly, behind the basic demands of performances, and the desperately full timetable of public relations, lay his close and happy background with his mother and sister and their wide circle of real friends. Although they all returned with him to Mount Gambier and Adelaide, Maytie and Sheila had moved in 1938 to Melbourne, to a large house with grounds that could double as a leisure centre for young people such as the dancers of the Borovansky Ballet, and also provide kennels for Maytie's serious work of breeding, showing and later judging Pekingese dogs. They had later had a foothold in Surfers' Paradise in Queensland, and were currently living in Sydney. Sheila had continued to act – after her return to Australia in 1949, she was engaged to play Kate in *The Taming of the Shrew* with a visiting company run by Anew McMaster, something very different from the modern comedies to which she was used, but a considerable success. During the Old Vic 1955 tour, she was appearing in a 'little' revue, *Hat Trick*, at the Philip Street Theatre in Sydney, and was able to echo her brother's flair for impersonations by introducing a forthright and very funny item about a (supposed) two-way conversation (USA and Britain) between Helpmann and Hepburn, arguing about the roles they were to play in Australia. Her last stage appearance for some time was, in fact, later that year, in *The Reluctant Debutante* with Ursula Jeans and Roger Livesey. Maytie, who had had one or two serious illnesses, increasingly needed her help and comfort, so she settled for less long-term work, such as compering top fashion shows and appearing in television and films.

20

Once back in London, in 1956, Helpmann had a small role in a trivial Hepburn/Bob Hope film, *The Iron Petticoat*, and a rather larger one as a bogus clergyman in *The Big Money*. They earned him money rather than added reputation. There are, alas, no films in existence of Helpmann in a major role that can in any way be recommended as representative of his acting and dancing ability. He was better served on television, but televised plays, such as *The Ghost Sonata* or *Box for One*, are unlikely to have been preserved. He appeared as guest artist with Sadler's Wells Ballet at Covent Garden on 6 May 1956 (marking the company's twenty-fifth anniversary), in *Rake* and *Façade* (the Nocturne Peruvienne and Tango). About this, Annabel Farjeon, who had been a member of the Vic-Wells company in the late 1930s, paid tribute to him in the *New Statesman*, writing that

> the star of the anniversary was Robert Helpmann, who returned to give the most startling performance in *The Rake's Progress* I have seen. The intelligence of his present interpretation of the Rake surpasses any previous one. The disintegration of the early charm into drunken debauch, desperate gambling and finally ghastly madness, was acted with an emotional vitality that was never artificial and, at the end, painfully moving. Again, his performance in *Façade* as a Peruvian dago was inimitable. Mr Helpmann had only to walk across the back of the stage and, although there were dancers working away very prettily in front, he held the whole audience. The tango with Margot Fonteyn was rightly encored. It seems a disaster that this supreme actor-dancer is lost to the ballet – the Sadler's Wells Ballet greatly lacks a strong male personality and if only Mr Helpmann could be retrieved the balance of the company would be set right.[182]

It was indeed interesting to see these admirable performances. In spite of having been absent from ballet since February 1951 (apart from appearing on Coronation Night in *Lac* Act II, which an experienced dancer can always walk through easily) and having had little time from other commitments for rehearsal, Helpmann recreated and felt again every moment of *Rake* in a quite extraordinary manner, presenting it with power and poignancy. He danced the Peruvian with all the old ease and devilment, delighting a mixed public – some who remembered him with love, some who had no particularly warm feelings for him, many who knew him only through hearsay – and crowned the evening partnering Fonteyn in the Tango with mastery and zest. Applause forced them into an encore. At the end, de Valois gave a long talk that contained a typical comment, 'We can sit back and remember what we have achieved or we can sit up and remember what we have to do'. After Ashton had then spoken, Helpmann addressed the audience and made no secret of the fact that he had been delighted to be there:

> I really don't have to tell you what tonight means to me. I don't feel this is a company, that you are an audience. You are all friends. If I didn't feel that, I would not have stuck my neck out. If I can get my breath, I hope to be appearing at the 50th Anniversary![183]

In June, Helpmann directed *Romeo and Juliet* with Claire Bloom and John Neville at the Old Vic, and walked into a small forest of adverse criticism. Much of this grew up round Loudon Sainthill's set, planned for New York, which weighed too heavily on the small stage of the Vic. The set, and a liberal accompaniment of singing (often effective) and a largely uncut version with some slow exits and entrances were all unpopular. Cuts and an increased pace later in the season helped a great deal. There were, however, compensations: the vitality and freshness of the treatment of the lovers, the resolute sorting-out of the age groups that released nurse, friar and parents from senility to vigorous middle age, the cat-and-dog opposition of Tybalt and Mercutio. The changing temperatures from sultry midday heat to the chill of the tomb all helped to give a wider perspective to an over-familiar play.

The next December, Helpmann joined the company as an actor for the 1956/57 season. His roles were Shylock, Launce in *The Two Gentlemen of Verona* directed by Michael Langham, Saturninus in *Titus Andronicus*, and Dr Pinch in *The Comedy of Errors* (a double bill directed by Walter Hudd), and Richard III (directed by Douglas Seal). His Shylock was by now well known, but it was splendidly contrasted by his next part, Launce. Here was a disarming, endearing prattler, genially collaborating with Keith Michell's golden Labrador Duff (as Crab). The role introduced to the legitimate stage the expert timing, the easy reciprocity towards an audience, and the unfailing relish for fooling that had already captivated balletgoers.

Before tackling his other acting roles, he directed a fine production of *Antony and Cleopatra* for Margaret Whiting and Michell. In flow of movement and pictorial splendour, in which his groupings complemented Sainthill's designs, it was outstanding. There was enchantment to match the magic of the verse in the strong martial pattern of Rome contrasted with the full passions of Egypt. The problem was that Whiting and Michell failed to be convincing in the title roles. *The Times* called it 'a production which is swift, well judged and exciting ... mercifully free from "tricks". Its chief business is to give purposefulness, speed and shape to a play which is apt to make a sprawling impression'[184]; and Anthony Cookman in *The Tatler & Bystander* wrote that

> the most perceptive thing in Mr Helpmann's production is the effort made to compensate for the underlying flaw in the play [the lack of stress in its later scenes on what remains of Antony's soldierly abilities] ... he has paid great attention to the crucial scenes of the triumvirate at the council table and at the carouse on Pompey's barge.[185]

His next acting assignment was the curious double bill of *Titus Andronicus* and *The Comedy of Errors* – both, of course, in cut versions, and directed by Walter Hudd. He played an imperious Saturninus, moving through the melodrama with swift and tense malevolence, while Dr Pinch was acted with a wild abandon of flowing grey hair and beard, flapping robes, and powerfully clawlike hands. *Richard III* had an opening night that lacked pace and light, and for once, initially, Helpmann got his makeup wrong. This of course was the performance on which reviews were based. Later, changes were made, and the characterisation emerged as a very individual Richard, played with vigour, irony and a bitter honesty that could encompass the grim self-knowledge of Bosworth Eve.

In July, the Old Vic company took two plays, *The Merchant of Venice* and *Antony and Cleopatra*, to Lebanon, staging them (both, naturally, with cuts) in the magnificent setting of the ruined Temple of Bacchus at Baalbek. Then in August, a complete contrast to Richard III came for him when, at the Edinburgh Festival, he acted the lead in a production by George Devine of Sartre's *Nekrassov*. It was a good comedy role for him, a biting and hardly-exaggerated comment on the sensational press, with a theme of a swindler who poses to the French anti-Communist press as a freedom-choosing Soviet minister. It is a mixture of farce and satirical drama, and Helpmann played the part with adroit skill as to point and timing and with considerable charm. Both play and performance had an uneven reception, but it came to London for a short run at the Royal Court Theatre.

In November, he took over the lead (after Gielgud and Michael Wilding) in Coward's *Nude with Violin* at the Globe Theatre in Shaftesbury Avenue. The play had a very mixed history. It had been slated when it was first staged in London but had already had a year's run. Recently, Coward himself had taken the lead in an American production (Philadelphia and New York) and had decided to do an extensive revision, including new scenes and rewritten dialogue. These he had discussed with Helpmann; so that the role of the shady secretary Sebastien developed new character-istics. A revised production for London was jointly directed by Gielgud and Coward. Elizabeth Frank in the *News Chronicle* summed it up:

> The result brings new life to what I considered a year ago to be a slick and uninspired piece of Cowardry. Helpmann, ... resembling an extremely interesting lizard only recently disinterred from the paleolithic clay, flickers in and out of the proceedings with hooded eyes and a razor smile, in complete control of every situation.[186]

R.E.L. in *The Stage* thought that Helpmann 'is one of our most resourceful comic actors; and he has surely never been funnier than [as] the endlessly ingenious accomplice of a reputed but bogus painter'. He called it 'a beautifully timed interpretation, with its smooth variations of pace and mood'.[187]

21

Helpmann's two careers came together in 1958. Sadler's Wells Ballet (now the Royal Ballet) agreed to send its touring company to Australia and New Zealand and decided to include *The Rake's Progress* and *Hamlet* with Helpmann in his old roles. The touring company was a very separate organisation from the main company at Covent Garden. Directed by John Field, it had its own repertoire and dancers, occasionally reinforced by guest stars from Covent Garden. There was a pre-tour season in March at the Royal Opera House, when Helpmann appeared as the Rake and Hamlet, as well as in *Coppélia* and a revival of *Miracle*. Notices were totally contradictory. For every one that praised some aspect of his work there was a counterblast (often quite virulent) from another source. There was in fact no diminution in his power for putting over the Rake, Hamlet or the Stranger, and his two ballets were considerably more enjoyable than the new fare being supplied at Covent Garden in the 1950s. . This was possibly one reason why it was hard for current critics to be fair to Helpmann. There had been too many unmemorable productions. These had included Ashton's *Rinaldo and Armída*, *Variations on a theme of Purcell*, *Madame Chrysanthème* and *La Péri*. Cranko had staged the jokey *Bonne-Bouche* and *The Shadow*. Alfred Rodrigues had put on a *Miraculous Mandarin*. Additionally, two full evening works, Cranko's *Prince of the Pagodas* and Ashton's *Sylvia*, had failed to prove popular.

One new critic, Andrew Porter, wrote warmly in the *Financial Times*, starting with Coppelius on 6 March. Having commented that Nadia Nerina and David Blair 'drew inspiration from the Dr Coppelius of Helpmann', he went on:

> If anyone but Helpmann had dared to do as much with Coppelius as Helpmann did last night, we should be quick to complain of over-elaborate fussification; but Helpmann was irresistible; fantastic, but not absurdly so, pathetic at the end of the second act, but not over-dramatic. It was a brilliant assumption.

When it came to *Miracle*, his 22 March review was full of admiration:

Brilliantly constructed, brilliantly calculated, it inspires the company to a vivid, tense performance ... Some of it is sensational to the point of seeming meretricious; some of it – the moving short solo for the Suicide, the dance for the Lovers – appears to be deeply and sincerely felt, and the reel, begun by the barefoot girl who has just been raised from the dead, is perhaps one of the happiest inspirations of modern ballet. Helpmann's impassive, curiously detached performance as the latter-day Christ is still most impressive, not least for its enigmatic quality.

On 28 March he wrote, '*Hamlet* revives even better than *Miracle in the Gorbals*. Again it is superbly produced, and danced by the present company with the vividness of a new creation ... What a daring, arresting ballet it is – entirely gripping, brilliantly theatrical.'[188]

Helpmann's only new role was the one that he had learnt from its choreographer, Fokine, but never had the chance to try – Petrushka. It did not turn out to be a good idea – he did not succeed in making it his own. However, in spite of bitter comments by those critics who were now ready to attack him with the rancour of campaigners in an American presidential election, the performance was no more of a failure than most dancers' attempts have been. He could find no fruitful ground to build on because he had nothing of the puppet in his personality, and no affinity with puppet theatre. In the *Sunday Times*, C.W. Beaumont, probably the best authority on the ballet, was accurate in saying that 'in his conception of the character Helpmann presented not a puppet with fitful yearnings to be a human being but a human being aping a puppet'.[189] On 22 April Andrew Porter pinpointed the same difficulty:

He leaves out altogether that touch of crudity, of limited intellectual ability, which makes Petrushka so poignant. Helpmann was not part puppet, part man; but from the start fully sentient, quiveringly self-aware. His movements broke through the puppet convention to become too overtly expressive – and by reason of this, less affecting.[190]

Appearing as guest artist with the Royal Ballet touring company in Australia and New Zealand was not to happen until October. Meanwhile, Helpmann went there to act in and direct a locally cast production of *Nude with Violin*. After the non-Australian years, he liked the life and the climate, and greatly enjoyed the company of his family.

His brother Max and his wife Barbara were now based in Toronto, where Barbara's brothers had started the Crest Theatre. It was worthwhile and uphill work – Toronto audiences had got out of the habit of theatre-going during the war, and the Crest, with a wide and popular repertoire, did much to woo them back to an interest in live drama. In 1956, however, Max left them to join the new Festival Theatre company at Stratford, Ontario, a connection that lasted all his life. At that time they were still playing in a tent theatre, as their graceful auditorium by the river Avon was not quite ready. Max, now entirely committed to Canada, was still happy to take his holidays in Australia.

The Royal Ballet's Australasian tour was, of course, the first time Helpmann appeared in ballet in his own country, and he spent his fiftieth birthday with the company in Auckland in 1959. As on his previous visit, he engaged eagerly in the social and media life of Australia, mixing charm and wit with a judicious amount of the provocative comment and backchat that always delights the Australian press and public. An unexpected bit of publicity came when he re-visited Mount Gambier with Maytie and Sheila in January 1959 – severe forest fires swept the area, and he spent the night helping the firefighters in their risky work. He appeared on television, spoke at club and civic luncheons, gave prizes at charity balls and fetes, and spoke on radio. In one of these ABC broadcasts in August, he discussed the theatre's ability to create magic and mystery, and the modern media's desire to 'tear glamour and illusion from anybody who is trying to create that very impression':

Personally I don't want to know what age Miss So-and-So is, or what Mr So-and-So uses on his hair or how Madame X cooks her meals for her 17 children – it has no interest for me; all I'm interested in is what they do when the curtain goes up; and that should be the only interest that the press in general have in an artist ... Thinking about my life, I see that there is nothing that has not been partly or entirely influenced by the theatre. I adore it and live by it, and that is why I feel so strongly that its magic should not and must not be dispelled.

Later in the talk, he made a strong case for the theatre arts of Australia, declaring, 'It's a very important thing to remember that a country is not only judged by its butter, wool, sheep and athletes ... but by its artistic output.' Russia was a case in point, with the tours of its actors, dancers and musicians, and 'my ambition leads me to long for the day when Australia can do the same thing, which undoubtedly it can and will and must do'.[191] The importance of this statement of belief is that it formed the keystone of his later relationship as choreographer, artistic director and guest artist with the Australian Ballet.

Back in London in 1959, Helpmann staged a comedy for John Clements and Kay Hammond, *The Marriage-go-round,* and directed and choreographed the Cole Porter *Aladdin* at the Coliseum, which starred Bob Monkhouse. This was delightful. T.C. Worsley wrote in the *Financial Times*:

> The production has been entrusted to Mr Robert Helpmann. And this means much more than just excellent dancing and effective ballets – though there are plenty of these. But more than that, in close collaboration with his designer [Loudon Sainthill] he has, as it were, had a vision of what, with every resource at his hand, a really grandly magical spectacle the pantomime could be; and the vision has been grandly realised.[192]

Eric Johns pointed out in *The Stage* how this was not a traditional pantomime, in which the narrative is held up for irrelevant music-hall acts, but a magnificent treatment of the Arabian Nights story set to music:

> Exquisitely conceived is the *ballet blanc*, in which the dancers materialise through swirling mists which slowly disperse to reveal an azure sky. The great depth of the Coliseum stage is used to the full in this ballet, as delicate and fragile as a Chinese etching. Figures carrying enormous white lanterns bring the scene to an unforgettable conclusion.[193]

In November, Covent Garden had announced that in Ashton's new ballet, *La Fille mal gardée,* Helpmann would create the role of Widow Simone; but a month later (before rehearsals started) Helpmann asked to be released from the engagement, as he had commitments in America. These included, in April 1960, a staging of the Jean Giraudoux play *Duel of Angels,* for Vivien Leigh (who had first acted this play in London in 1958) and Mary Ure. Writing in the *New York Times,* Brooks Atkinson pointed out:

> Since Mr. Helpmann came into the theatre through the door of the dance, his staging emphasizes movement, proportions and tableau. It captures an unreal mood in the studied hauteur of Miss Ure, who represents purity, and the composed aggressiveness of Miss Leigh, who represents vice ... To see this stately glide of formalized figures, who are

Adam Zero – The Principal Dancer. With June Brae as Death.   (*Baron*)

Swan Lake – Prince Siegfried. With Margot Fonteyn as Odette.
(*Tunbridge Sedgwick*)

The White Devil – Flamineo. With Roderick Lovell.   (*Angus McBean*)

The Merchant of Venice, 1955 – Shylock. With Katharine Hepburn.
(*Noel Rubie*)

A Midsummer Night's Dream, 1937 – Oberon. With Gordon Miller as Puck.
(*J W Debenham*)

Façade – The Tango. With Margot Fonteyn. (*Gordon Anthony*)

Checkmate – The Red King. (*Gordon Anthony*)

Don Quixote (de Valois). With Margot Fonteyn and Alexander Grant.
(*Carl Perutz*)

also keen and amusing, is to wonder whether any American company could play them so fastidiously.[194]

Vivien Leigh, who said in a BBC broadcast in October 1960 that she 'admired him enormously' as a dancer (and as her 1937 Oberon), had asked especially for him to direct *Duel of Angels* in New York. She declared, 'He is an extraordinary person to work with, imaginative, original, endlessly patient, and he has a great facility for helping actors.'[195]

In July 1960 the Royal Academy of Dancing in London awarded Helpmann its annual Queen Elizabeth II Coronation Award. He was in New York, and wrote of his sadness that he was not able to receive it in person; de Valois accepted it on his behalf. Philip Richardson's citation acknowledged that while with the Sadler's Wells Ballet 'he set an unsurpassed example of artistry and true theatre sense which inspired all who worked with him ... He carried the success and morale of the Company on his shoulders throughout its most difficult days' and became a choreographer 'whose ballets bear the essential stamp of originality and dramatic truth'.[196]

In October, one unsatisfactory ballet assignment came Helpmann's way – he was asked by the Grand Ballet du Marquis de Cuevas in Paris to finish off a staging of *The Sleeping Beauty* that had been begun by Bronislava Nijinska. He was responsible only for Act III. It is remembered chiefly for its outré designs for costumes and headdresses by de Cuevas's young nephew, Raymondo de Larrain.

Throughout all the later tangled and tragic affairs of Vivien Leigh and Laurence Olivier, Benthall and Helpmann did much to support Leigh, remembering always the friendship they had with her from the Old Vic days in 1937. In 1961 Helpmann devoted himself almost entirely to her interests – she had just been divorced from Olivier. Beginning in June, she undertook a long tour of Australia and New Zealand with an Old Vic Drama company. This was extended in the first half of 1962 to the Far East and South America. Helpmann accompanied her for part of the time, and directed the plays – *Twelfth Night*, *Duel of Angels* and *The Lady of the Camellias* – in which she starred.

In Mexico City in March 1962 he joined the company briefly to act in a recital of 'Great Scenes from Shakespeare'. That month he also appeared as The Old Man in an excellent BBC-TV production by Stuart Burge of Strindberg's *The Ghost Sonata*, and worked, on location in Spain, on the film *55 Days at Peking*, acting Prince Tuan. At last asked by de Valois to do another ballet for the Royal Ballet (she would be retiring from the artistic directorship in 1963), he began planning *Elektra*, a theme that had engrossed him for some time. He probably realised that this would be the last commission he would have from the company with which he had once been totally identified.

Elektra, premiered on 26 March 1963, was a short work whose complete artistic unity proved once again Helpmann's ability to work with designers and composers. With his associates Arthur Boyd and Malcolm Arnold, he provided clues to the mood and style of the ballet he had in mind. Boyd, a member of a widely talented Australian family, was one of the most strongly individual and imaginative of Australian painters, and his concept for *Elektra* was powerfully theatrical. In an interview in the *Daily Express*, Helpmann said Boyd had been selected 'because his colours and the way he uses them seemed right for what I had in mind. But all I have told him is that I want a door and some stairs, and the rest is up to him'. About Malcolm Arnold, he said that he only

> told him roughly what I wanted – for instance, that it should start with a tremendous noise to focus immediate attention, then almost silence to emphasise the threat as the Eumenides enter. Then, after about half a minute, something like a scream of terror to mark the entrance of Elektra. All I have is the central idea of concentrating the Elektra theme of fear, hate and sex.[197]

What emerged was certainly sensational, and people reacted violently one way or the other. Helpmann's choreography was ahead of its time in its acrobatic physicality, now common currency in classical ballet but then associated with 'adagio dancers' in nightclubs and cabaret, and its steps and poses picked up with insight Boyd's remarkable vision of human anatomy, with its splayed legs and disturbing contortions. Richard Buckle understood it. In the *Sunday Times* he described the audience ovation, and wrote of the action:

> It opens with drums and brass in a burst of boiling rage. Scarlet floorcloth and a flight of scarlet steps set off Arthur Boyd's huge images of love and death drawn in black and white. [Nadia] Nerina, made up witchlike with streaming vermilion hair, gloating over her avenging axe, is Elektra. [David] Blair, naked and redheaded, is Orestes. There are eight male purple Erinyes or Spirits of Vengeance who fling Elektra through the air in a variety of breathtaking dives ... *Elektra* is tremendously effective. It may [not] be vulgar, but it isn't genteel. Helpmann has not lost his blazing

sense of theatre; and his new work, though less profound, is the nearest thing to Martha Graham's *Phaedra* on this side of the drink ... Malcolm Arnold's railway music is clearly composed as film music would be or, in fact, as Graham's score are, as an atmospheric accompaniment to the drama ... The sets of Arthur Boyd ... must be seen – they are a shot in the arm. And the ballet is the more welcome for revealing to us the volcanic passions hitherto concealed beneath Nadia Nerina's pretty placid countenance.[198]

Buckle's praise could not save *Elektra* when critics such as Oleg Kerensky, Noel Goodwin, Peter Williams and Clive Barnes (who claimed that he only managed to stagger to the gent's lavatory before he was violently sick) totally condemned it. Some members of the audience were sufficiently disgusted with this kind of critical venom to write letters to magazines. *Dance and Dancers* proved their editorial fairness by printing one from Pauline Selby (they carefully included her title of 'Miss' to suggest that she was a blinkered fan), who said that 'Mr Barnes's frivolous, irrelevant and indeed distasteful tirade' might be 'due to the fact that he is unutterably confused'.[199]

Several other dance events happened for Helpmann in 1963. One was an excellent Margaret Dale BBC-TV production of *Checkmate*, in which he resumed his original role of the Red King (this time termed White, as the film was not shown in colour). Another was a tour that he directed of a divertissement programme for a small group of Royal Ballet dancers led by Fonteyn and Nureyev. This began in early August at the Herodus Atticus Theatre in Athens and worked its way round the Mediterranean by way of the Riviera to Israel. It continued to Japan (Tokyo, Osaka, Nagoya and Kyoto) and ended in Honolulu on 22 September. In October he repeated his roles for a film of *The Soldier's Tale* made at Syon House, which failed to capture the strength and impetus of the Edinburgh Festival production.

An unexpected assignment was an enormously ambitious Royal Ballet staging of *Swan Lake* at Covent Garden, which had important choreographic additions by Ashton and was produced by Helpmann. It was not a success – both Helpmann's contribution and Ashton's extensive new choreography were highly controversial and had a very mixed reception from London critics. It opened with a prologue (as some later versions have done) showing Odette's transformation into a swan; it cut out Benno and the huntsmen and enlarged the role of von Rothbart. The would-be fiancées in Act III were given separate identities and families, and it expanded the last act with Ashton's praised new elegiac arrangement for the swans. Mary

Clarke, in *The Dancing Times* was positively in favour, declaring that 'the most important achievement in this new version ... is the way in which the story has been given its real importance'. All through, 'inconsistencies have been ironed out and where necessary new details of production added to make all clear'. She felt that 'the magnification of the Rothbart character lifts the whole ballet on to a much more dramatic plane'. What she did not like was the choreographic re-arrangement of the national dances, and Carl Toms's designs.[200]

22

In the early 1960s, if the London ballet world was closing towards Helpmann, a gate was opening in Australia. In 1960 the Borovansky Ballet in Melbourne, left leaderless with the death of Edouard Borovansky in December 1959, gained a new artistic director in Peggy van Praagh. Van Praagh, a product of Ballet Rambert and Antony Tudor's London Ballet, had been a member of Sadler's Wells Ballet and, later, assistant director of Sadler's Wells Theatre Ballet. In taking over the Borovansky Ballet, she had been warmly encouraged by de Valois, Helpmann and Fonteyn. That job lasted only a year, but in 1962 a new company, the Australian Ballet, was launched with van Praagh as founding artistic director. By 1963 it was steadily gaining ground, a company full of lively young Australian talent helped along by international stars such as Erik Bruhn, Rudolf Nureyev and Sonia Arova.

Van Praagh, naturally, was looking for choreographers. The March 1962 Royal Ballet premiere of Helpmann's *Elektra*, with its all-Australian team of creators, prompted her to approach him with the suggestion that he might stage a new work for her company. He told her of his idea for a ballet featuring Australia's remarkable bush denizen, the lyrebird. During his theatre tour in Australia with Katharine Hepburn, Helpmann had happily introduced her – an avid sightseer – to Australia's famous flora and fauna, and she had particularly enjoyed their early morning rendezvous in the Dandenong Mountains near Melbourne, where they were able to see the lyrebird's amazing courtship dance. Now Helpmann planned to use this as an ingredient for another all-Australian ballet.

This time the designs were by Sidney Nolan and the score by Malcolm Williamson. The story was simple. It opened with the lyrebird's dance; then a typical group of young Aussies arrived to picnic in the bush, the boys kicking a football about, drinking beer, and showing off to the girls. A male outsider approached one of the girls, and became involved in a fight over her with the boys. He was left badly knocked about, but the girl returned. After an increasingly passionate duet, the boy (rather unbelievably honourable) tore himself away. To the deserted girl, the returning lyrebird symbolised both love and fulfilment.

To get some verisimilitude into the ballgame, Helpmann asked a champion football player to coach the dancers, and an ex-boxer was enlisted to help them with the fights. Nolan's forest scene and his wonderful costume for the lyrebird with its astonishing tail were echoed by Helpmann in avian movements that testified to close observation, and were brilliantly interpreted by Barry Kitcher. The roles of the girl and the outsider were danced with immense dramatic feeling by Kathleen Gorham and Garth Welch.

The premiere of *The Display* at the Adelaide Festival on 14 March 1964 was a triumph and a talking-point. For ballet in Australia, it had immense importance. As the critic in the *Sydney Morning Herald* wrote, it was 'that long-awaited event, a wholly Australian ballet with respect to its inspiration, its composition, and to the talented company of dancers which performed it'.[201] Harold Tidemann in the *Adelaide Advertiser* called it 'a significant ballet of imagination and colour which might well be a milestone in Australian ballet and theatre generally'.[202]

Frank Harris in the *Sydney Mirror* wrote, 'Here was something of the land itself – an Australian theme brilliantly choreographed by Robert Helpmann, with a score by Malcolm Williamson worthy of a concert performance and Sidney Nolan's beautifully luminous bush decor ... the whole thing was breathlessly arresting. We were confronted with an Australian ballet which had that blessed quality of unity'.[203] There were, of course, reservations from other writers. Although Geoffrey Hutton in the *Melbourne Age* felt that it was an exciting event and 'a brilliant piece of stagecraft', he felt that 'as a comment on life, it does not go far beyond Grand Guignol ... It is not a pretty ballet; it is intended to shock, and it succeeds'.[204]

This particular visit to Australia, which began in February, launched another light-hearted piece of news (something Helpmann was always inventive in feeding to the eager Australian press!). He was now in the habit of breaking his journeys in Honolulu, where he could pursue, on Waikiki beach, a teenage Australian passion for surfing. This time he also made what the Australian newspapers called 'a surfie stomp record', singing two songs, and it was naturally immediately put out on a TV show (*Sydney Sun-Herald*, 1 February). The two sides were contrasted – on one side was the fast-beat *Surfer Doll* and on the other a pretty little ballad, *I Still Could Care*.

A further association with the Royal Ballet at Covent Garden came in April 1964, when a programme to mark Shakespeare's quatercentenary was planned. This was a triple bill made up of the premieres of Ashton's *The Dream* and Kenneth MacMillan's *Images of Love*, and a revival of Helpmann's *Hamlet*, in which Nureyev danced the title role. There was the now usual carping from a section of the critics, but this time around there was an extremely positive assessment from Alexander Bland (the pseudonym of a team of the art critic Nigel Gosling and his wife, the former Rambert leading dancer Maude Lloyd) in the *Observer:*

> It *[Hamlet]* turned out to be not only much the best ballet of the three but a remarkable ballet by any standards. It starts with the advantage of Tchaikovsky's dramatic score, whose near-hysteria has been seized on by Helpmann and his surrealist designer, Leslie Hurry, with glorious confidence. This is that theatrical rarity, a complicated idea very simply worked out. The ingenious exits and entrances, the way in which the whole story is not only recounted but commented on (in Freudian terms from innumerable angles), all within 18 minutes, reveal a miracle of construction. It is a nightmare flashback in the mind of the dying prince. Father and uncle fuse mistily together; the stage fills and empties; the fiancée's shroud is lifted to reveal the mother's corpse; skull and royal orb identify; forbidden kisses foreclose; swords flash and poison burns. As darkness shuts down, the royal corpse is lifted high. It is a part which has been waiting for Nureyev and he takes it over with a deathly authority.[205]

Richard Buckle, writing in *The Sunday Times,* used the nutshell technique: 'Nureyev as Hamlet was tremendous, dead right. And Helpmann's clever, spasmodic work on Tchaikovsky's score is as compulsive now as then.'[206] In the *New Statesman,* Annabel Farjeon was also succinct: 'This work stands out as the only one [of the evening] which has been conceived as though by a single imagination. It remains lurid and exciting.'[207]

At this point, the Melbourne *Age* published a detailed profile of Helpmann by John Hetherington. He was one of the people who could relate the young Bobby Helpman of the J.C. Williamson days and the fifty-five-year-old who was currently making headlines:

> His features have lost their boyishness and hardened into narrow aquilinity; in profile, the sun-tanned face, with its rather prominent eyes and crowned by strong-growing dark hair, is like the image of a Red Indian engraved on a coin. His lithe and muscular figure is only a fraction heavier than it ever was ... The thing about him which you remember long after you leave him is his tough-minded candour, his innocence of humbug.

After making the point that 'few living Australians have a better title to talk about success' than Helpmann, he quotes him as saying,

> Success is an illusion, it makes no lasting difference. I used to think if I could go to London and be the premier dancer of a ballet company I would be happy forever. I believed if I could play Hamlet in London or direct an opera at Covent Garden, then I could want no more. I've done those things, but nothing is changed. Success means you can afford to go to a better restaurant or have three suits instead of one, but it makes no difference inside you. You never lie back in bed and say 'Ha, I'm a success!' It isn't a permanent state of being, only a passing glow.[208]

Back in England in April, Helpmann was reunited with Vivien Leigh in a gala opening of the new Yvonne Arnaud Theatre in Guildford. They played the first Oberon–Titania scene from the *Dream*; Leigh recited the 'Quality of mercy' speech from the *Merchant*, and Helpmann (presumably with a borrowed dog) contributed Launce's soliloquy from *The Two Gentlemen of Verona*.

In August he directed and choreographed *Camelot* at Drury Lane Theatre. Considerable rewriting and revision had been done from the show that had been running in New York, and the new production, starring Laurence Harvey and Elizabeth Larner, was designed by a young Australian discovery of Helpmann's, John Truscott. It was enthusiastically welcomed by Harold Hobson in *The Sunday Times* as 'a musical that dazzles the senses and purifies the heart'. He wrote that Helpmann 'had directed the piece with great regard for the dialogue, the staging and the pageantry', but severely criticised the farcical treatment of King Pellinore. Most of the other critics simply howled with dismay over everything.[209]

In September Helpmann was back in Sydney with a new staging of *The Soldier's Tale*, in which he again played The Devil. He received a CBE (Commander of the Order of the British Empire) at Buckingham Palace in November and, more interestingly, accomplished a brilliant tour de force as the Narrator in *A Wedding Bouquet* with the Royal Ballet at Covent Garden. Looking very much like the Bridegroom (the role he had created in 1937), he sat at a small, white-draped table, with champagne in a bucket, and declaimed the Gertrude Stein text in its original version (Constant Lambert had often curtailed or added to it), reflecting every stage of the Berners score and the Stein words with immaculate understanding. Knowing the choreography from its inception, he related perfectly to the dancers and, because one of his special vocal gifts as an actor was his ability to vary the significance of a phrase even in its final inflection, he produced memorable versions of such delicately poignant lines as 'Bitterness ... bitterness ... bitterness is entertained by all.' He even earned an accolade from Clive Barnes in *The Spectator:*

> At the first performance of this sumptuously staged revival it seemed that only the narrator, Robert Helpmann, had the right spirit. Croaking balefully over his champagne, registering disasters with a malicious indifference, shadowing into sadness, Helpmann, like no one else, was the embodiment of Ashton, Berners and, of course, Gertrude Stein.[210]

At the end of November, Helpmann went to Italy to mount *The Sleeping Beauty* at the Rome Opera, which had a disastrous first night. He was saddled with extraordinary and unsuitable designs: the sleeping Aurora was found in a tomblike structure by a lakeside; the costumes were excessively fussy and coloured largely in purple, yellow and sea green. The leading roles were excellently taken by Carla Fracci and Attilio Labis, but the resident corps de ballet was barely adequate either in numbers or technical ability to cope with such a work.

23

The success in Australia of *The Display* had two results. In January 1965 Helpmann began to rehearse a second ballet, *Yugen*, for the Australian Ballet, and on 4 March he was offered and accepted the position of co-artistic director of the company with van Praagh. The understanding was that he would spend two or three months (unspecified) each year in Australia, but inevitably his connection was considerably closer than that implied. He told the *Sydney Morning Herald* that he was convinced of the 'tremendous potential' of the Australian Ballet. Of his own function, and that of van Praagh, he said, 'I am only co-artistic director. Peggy van Praagh will be with them throughout the year. She is the one who does all the hard work, the ground work, the basic work. She has ploughed the furrow. The ballet is ready now to sow the seed.'[211]

Helpmann saw his usefulness in international terms. Australia, even in 1965, was remarkably remote from the rest of the Western world and needed to maintain all possible contacts with important Western artistic developments. Because of its geographical context, it also had to strengthen cultural understanding with its Far Eastern and South East Asian neighbours. As a global traveller, with a great number of influential friends and associates in the performing arts in many countries, he was unusually qualified to be a liaison between his native country and the rest of the world. As a theatre artist whose standards were highly professional, he could also do much to ensure that the Australian Ballet would measure up well in relation to top companies elsewhere.

Yugen, premiered on 18 February 1965, was in complete contrast to *The Display*. The title, a Zen Buddhist term about the graceful and refined expression of beauty, was untranslatable. Helpmann greatly admired Japanese art and theatre, and in 1962 had been in Tokyo with Vivien Leigh and the Old Vic Drama company. The following year he had been associated with a Fonteyn–Nureyev tour to Tokyo, Osaka, Nagoya and Kyoto. He had met Japanese theatre directors and composers, seen an impressive production of *King Lear,* and directed a Japanese drama company in *The Tempest*. In 1964 he worked out a scenario from the Noh play *Hagoromo,* which is about the Moon Goddess who visits the earth every night to swim in a lake, leaving her wings temporarily at the water's edge. They are found by a fisherman who, thinking they are shells, takes them to his village. The goddess follows him there to win them back, so that she can return to the sky. The play itself is acclaimed in Japan as being a supreme example of lyric theatre, combining dance, song, poetry and spectacle. In *Yugen,* while firmly denying that he was trying to create a Japanese ballet, Helpmann aimed at reflecting in Western terms the tranquillity and radiance of moonlight on lake water.

The music was a commissioned score from a Japanese composer and conductor, Yuzo Toyama, and the designs were by Desmond Heeley. In the choreography, Helpmann used *pointe* work and lifts to great advantage, but grafted in elements of Japanese dance movement, fan manipulation and martial arts. The ballet was well received in Australia, where its essential fluency and simplicity, its intensely lyrical atmosphere and visual beauty, were greatly enjoyed. Once again, the leads were danced by Gorham and Welch. One of the critics most impressed by the work was Julian Russell, reviewer for the *Sydney Sun,* who wrote:

> As a spectacle, the ballet is exquisite choreographically and refreshingly original. It has the economy of ... a series of Japanese prints, each one beautiful in itself and all in harmony. Despite the simplicity of its story, the ballet is full of incident, in turn graceful, vigorous and always imaginative.[212]

Naturally, there were dissentient views, some of them distinctly bitter, and later in 1965, when the Australian Ballet appeared in London in connection with the Commonwealth Festival of the Arts (part of a substantial overseas tour), both *Yugen* and *The Display* were savaged by most of the critics as trite, pretentious and naive. Oleg Kerensky, surprisingly, came out in favour, describing *The Display* in the *Daily Mail* as

> a powerful dramatic work about a picnic party which bursts into violence ... there was exciting athletic dancing for the boys and a magnificent emotional role for the heroine, admirably performed by Kathleen Gorham. She also appeared as the Moon Goddess in *Yugen,* an absolutely charming Japanese folk tale using many of the spectacular effects of Noh drama.[213]

In an unpublished article about Helpmann's career and personality, written in October 1965, A.V. Coton, the critic for the *Daily Telegraph,* contributed an interesting opinion about Helpmann's value to the Australian Ballet:

I became aware – again – of the immense diversity of his skill, for in my view the most notable aspect of these works was the manner in which ... he had made ballets precisely fitted to the Australian cultural need. He has drawn themes from home life and that of a half-familiar neighbouring culture. He has carefully exploited the available performing talent. He has exactly tuned in to a national subconscious desire to achieve cooperation with native composers and designers; and as theatrical works both ballets seem perfectly geared to the taste of and feeling for ballet in Australia now. This has been a more cunning achievement than appears at a cursory glance, for it suggests that Helpmann has firmly taken the measure of exactly how much is possible in Australian ballet under his co-directorship with Peggy van Praagh.[214]

Earlier in 1965, Helpmann had tried to help Vivien Leigh to resume her acting career after a five-year break by directing a play she wanted to put on in England. *La Contessa* was by Paul Osborne, based on Maurice Druon's story about the Italian Marquesa Casati. It sank with little trace, never reaching London. Where Helpmann was concerned, his links with the Royal Ballet were sufficiently re-forged to mean that *Cinderella* was revived by the Royal Ballet at Covent Garden at the end of the year, with Ashton and Helpmann (Ashton had now been knighted) in place as the Stepsisters. They were photographed for the *Daily Mail* 'limbering up the middle-aged muscles' at ages fifty-nine and fifty-six, respectively. The performance was something everyone could enjoy writing about. Clement Crisp reported in *The Spectator:*

Fonteyn is in superlative form, phrasing so beautifully and musically that you could cry for sheer joy, and Ashton and Helpmann are back in their original devastating and devastated drag as the flower of the Ugly Sisterhood. Helpmann is the bossy one as usual; afflicted this season with a nasty facial hair problem and oeillades worthy of a bolting horse, he flaunts and prances, snatching the biggest of everything from men to oranges. Ashton is the other poor dear, desperately shy and put upon, paddling about the stage like the oldest of the ugly ducklings, and so appealing and marvellously funny that he almost becomes the heroine of the ballet and you long for the shoe to fit him.[215]

In January 1966 Helpmann was named Australian of the Year, a prestigious award for which nearly forty people had been considered. In March the Australian Ballet revived *Elektra,* which went down well.

Gorham once more was superbly cast, and it was sad that it was her last season before retirement. Beth Dean, writing in the *Sydney Morning Herald,* approved of the ballet:

> Lust is its own devouring in Robert Helpmann's choreographic translation of the Greek philosophy of inevitable justice in *Elektra.* The idea is expressed in a reasoned pressure of movement in a setting by Arthur Boyd of erotic black and white pen and ink curlings above a vermilion flooring. It is displayed against the distraught tensions of Malcolm Arnold's music. Some viewers will be shocked by the erotic emphasis of the work but there is no denying its theatrical impact. It is a powerful statement and a development for the Australian Ballet who, in this work, take one step closer to maturity.[216]

Writing for London readers in *Ballet Today,* Diana Mann was brave enough to declare that she liked it: 'Helpmann's dance drama *Elektra* was given a dramatic and energetic performance, and despite well-remembered pannings by London critics several years ago I fully enjoyed the ballet, a mixture of Malcolm Arnold's clanging music, Arthur Boyd's stark body-infested surrealist decor and Helpmann's erotic athletic choreography.'[217]

Helpmann was now closely concerned with promoting and arranging overseas tours for the Australian Ballet, and this had a two-way benefit – the dancers could see and evaluate what was going on in international ballet, and the rest of the world could discover the quality of a company they knew little about. The next major undertaking began in February 1967. On their way to appear in May at 'Expo 67' in Montreal, they danced in New Zealand, Hawaii and Vancouver. The company members were conscious of themselves as ambassadors for Australian culture and also, in some places, as pioneers of classical ballet. After Montreal they appeared in Jamaica and Trinidad, in Brazil, Argentina, Colombia and Mexico. In Montreal, each participating country provided a special day, and Helpmann was invited to direct the Australia one. He organised an entertainment that included wood-chopping, tennis and sheepdog displays as well as Australian pop groups and singers.

He himself was dodging about the world, dancing in the Royal Ballet *Cinderella* in London and New York before reaching Canada. The Ashton–Helpmann duo of Stepsisters continued to be a feature of Royal Ballet programmes for some years, and they were performing at Covent Garden at the turn of 1967/68, when Helpmann was knighted in the New Year Honours. Alexander Bland in *The Observer* commented with a play on the

English 'pantomime dame' tradition, 'Twas the knight after Christmas, and all thro' the House the Covent Garden audience warmed last Tuesday to the sight of Sir Robert's Ugly Sister joining Sir Fred's to make the first pair of dames of the British Empire.'[218] Peter Williams, in *Dance and Dancers*, felt that the two men were better than ever:

> Last year I remember thinking that perhaps they were overdoing it a bit; this year they were more muted and therefore more convincing. It may seem that much of the horseplay is impromptu, following the centuries old traditions of the *Commedia dell'Arte*, but the basic form is wholly consistent, although with certain moments left to individual interpretation, rather like a cadenza in a concerto ... every time you see these two it is like seeing them for the first time ... for my money these sacred monsters – one so timid, the other so overbearing – are the best clowns that the Christmas season has to offer.[219]

For the record, it is interesting to remember that these monstrous characterisations were caricatures of the two men's personalities. Sir Fred, although intensely insecure, was in no way truly timid; Sir Robert, although histrionic and extrovert, was in no way insensitively overbearing.

24

Sir Robert had, naturally, been pleased to receive his knighthood – and also to receive personally written congratulations from two of his particular admirers, Queen Elizabeth the Queen Mother and HRH the Princess Margaret. To my own letter he merely replied, 'I'm so glad I got it while Ma was still here to enjoy it' – and enjoy it greatly she did. He was soon getting amusement from filming as the wicked Child Catcher in *Chitty Chitty Bang Bang*.

However, he was back in Australia in February 1968 to go with the ballet company on a major Asian tour. Starting in Singapore, they took in Malaysia, Thailand, Cambodia, the Philippines, Korea, Indonesia, Hong Kong, Taiwan and four cities in Japan, and their success was an important factor in improving cultural relations between Australia and its neighbours. (Only those who have spent time there ever fully appreciate how vital this area of communication is for Australia.)

Helpmann was also a consultant on the 1968 Adelaide Festival of Arts, and was already planning events as director-designate for the next Festival in 1970. In Tokyo in March he started work on his next ballet, another all-Australian production: *Sun Music,* to a score by Peter Sculthorpe, with designs by Kenneth Rowell. Sculthorpe's 'Sun Music I' had been launched by the Sydney Symphony Orchestra at the Commonwealth Festival in 1965, and was widely praised. 'Sun Music III and IV' were published in 1967 but II was as yet unpublished during the creation of the ballet. The music – adventurous and experimental in its techniques – consisted of five movements, illustrating the various powers of the sun. When the ballet was staged in Sydney in August 1968, *Sun Music* was as controversial as *Elektra,* but impressively vigorous and theatrical. It was enthusiastically received by F.R. Blanks, writing in the *Sydney Morning Herald*:

A flamboyant and often brooding obsession with sun worship fuses *Sun Music* into something more than mere ballet – it is a turbulent *tour de force* of total theatre ... [it] must inevitably count as one of the finest, certainly the most purely virtuosic, creations to have come from Helpmann. The first two [sections] have a distinctly Australian flavour by way of ochre colours, aboriginal-inspired tattoos and the desolating sense of the sun and nature as enemy. Sculthorpe's scientifically sonorous music, played by the orchestra at first and for the second scene amplified on tape, is perfectly in tune with the spirit. Throughout, the music suggests that it has all this time been searching for a choreographer to give it meaning, and in Helpmann has ended the search in perfection.[220]

Harold Tidemann, writing in the Adelaide *Advertiser,* called it 'a major breakthrough for the Australian arts':

[Helpmann's] flair for moulding choreography, music and décor was never more apparent than in *Sun Music,* a masterpiece of classically inspired dance drama. It might be termed a symphonic ballet in five movements with the theme the effect of the sun on mere mortals ... the action ranged from dramatic desert sequences to some lyrical lovemaking, passion and violence, leading up to a devastating finale of destruction.[221]

Geoffrey Hutton wrote in the Melbourne *Age*:

Sun Music is a massive, sensational and allusive ballet which drenches the ears and eyes with sound and colour and movement ... The work stems from Sculthorpe's avant-garde music which explores a whole range of sound effects in the brass and percussion, set against skittering upper partials on the strings, and taped human voices shouting from the depths. Rowell's decor accepts the challenge, splashing colour over the stage and flooding it with sudden shadows, drawing on Asian and Mexican motifs and switching to abstractionism. As a piece of stage mechanics it has architectural volume. It also has a sense of surprise, of sheer shock, and here the three collaborators are completely in unison. Helpmann has choreographed five turbulent scenes in a style of semi-abstract expressionism ... His range of movement, as always, is wide, linking classical steps with acrobatics, massing his dancers in surging groups or pyramids, using gymnastic tricks and every movement which the trained athlete can accomplish.[222]

As with other choreographers, Helpmann had his special list of so-called 'muses'. Initially, of course, it had been Fonteyn for *Comus* and *Hamlet;* Celia Franca was cast as Gertrude in *Hamlet* and the Prostitute in *Miracle in the Gorbals,* while Pauline Clayden had created the Suicide in *Miracle.* June Brae had been a vital contributor to *Adam Zero,* Nadia Nerina to *Elektra.* In Australia, he had worked closely with Kathleen Gorham on *The*

Display and *Yugen,* and cast her in the revival of *Elektra.* Now he pulled Josephine Jason out of the corps de ballet to lead the large cast in *Sun Music.* Both Gorham and Jason were dramatic dancers who felt deeply privileged to have the chances they were offered. Gorham, on her retirement, said in an interview in *Walkabout*:

> There have been various influences on my career but ... I have loved most of all working with Helpmann. Until I did three ballets of his here I'd never met him. I was too shy to go up to him earlier ... and show my gratitude as a dancer for his artistry ... [Later] I told him, 'You are a creative performer and I am an interpretative performer, and I am concerned whether I have interpreted this creation correctly.'[223]

Neither Helpmann nor anyone else had any doubts about the brilliance of her interpretations.

Helpmann celebrated his sixtieth birthday in 1969 in Mount Gambier, and the Australian Ballet managed to put on one performance at the small King's Theatre there to supplement various civic entertainments in honour of him. In July the company revived *Coppélia* in Sydney, and he played Coppelius to great acclaim. Most of the year was absorbed in work connected with the Adelaide Festival of 1970, but he was in London in November to narrate *A Wedding Bouquet* and dance in *Cinderella* with the Royal Ballet. He supervised a revival of *Le Coq d'or,* and at the Friends of Covent Garden Christmas Party donned a tutu and danced on *pointe* in a send-up of the Kingdom of Shades entrée in *La Bayadère.*

Directing the Adelaide Festival was a major task and he tackled it with immense energy. Like the Edinburgh Festival, it represented all the arts, and the 1970 line-up was unusually prestigious. Australian commentators recognised that this was due to Helpmann's international reputation. Included were the Royal Shakespeare Company with Judi Dench and Donald Sinden, Benjamin Britten and Peter Pears with the English Opera Group, the Warsaw Philharmonic Orchestra, and art exhibitions from Pompeii and Mexico. Where ballet and dance were concerned, the main events involved the Australian Ballet, the Royal Thai Ballet, the Balinese Dance Company and the Georgian State Dance Company. Nureyev was guest artist with the Australian Ballet. He appeared in a revival of Helpmann's *Hamlet*, which, although new to the company's repertoire, was greatly admired, and staged his version of Petipa's *Don Quixote*, dancing Basilio. Nureyev and Helpmann got on extremely well. They understood and appreciated each other, but had not worked together until that season.

Nureyev's *Don Quixote* was a revision of the staging he had already done for the Vienna State Opera, but the Australians achieved a triumph from its very first night in Adelaide, bringing to it immense vigour and pace. Lucette Aldous's Kitri was unforgettable in its technical brilliance and splendid musicality, and the rest of the company had excellent opportunities. Where mime roles were concerned, there were ideal performances from Ray Powell as Sancho Panza and Colin Peasley as Gamache, while Helpmann was dominant in the title role. It was a very different assignment from his impressive creation in de Valois's ballet in 1950. In the Petipa version, however, he was equally at home, adapting perfectly to the mood of light-hearted romantic comedy of the action and the lively Minkus score. He managed the difficult task of making the role an essential feature of the ballet rather than a mere cipher, and smoothly united the delightful comedy of the duel with Gamache with a fine lyricism in the Dryad scene, reminiscent of the Vision scene of *The Sleeping Beauty*. Fortunately, the production was presented in both London and New York, and is preserved on film. The excitements and successes of the Festival were marred for him, however. His beloved mother died in a private hospital in Adelaide on 15 April.

After Maytie Helpman's death, Sheila Helpmann, who had been her loving companion in her later years, picked up on the threads of her own career. She acted on stage, in films and television, and elegantly compèred top fashion shows. In October 1971, she had a leading role in *Mixed Doubles* at the Independent Theatre in Sydney. This was a multi-authored 'entertainment on marriage' picked up from a 1969 staging at the Comedy Theatre, London – an anthology of eight short plays directed by Robert Levis. They were described in the programme as 'an amusing if acid picture of the progress of marriage life from honeymoon to cemetery'. In four of them Sheila was partnered by Max Osbiston: they were *Score* by Lyndon Brook, *Night* by Harold Pinter, *Countdown* by Alan Ayckbourn and *Resting Place* by David Campton. In an interview with Ursula Connor in the *Sydney Morning Herald*, she referred to her return to the stage:

> I never go on stage completely calm. It's not facing an audience that worries me – a Helpmann always loves an audience! It's whether I could do it justice. I find myself thinking, What if I can't learn a part any more?[224]

A versatile performer, in 1974 she was the New York society hostess in J.C. Williamson's centenary musical production, *Irene*, and two years later did a five-week stint for the popular Australian television soap opera *Number 96*. Cast as the mother of the character Dudley Butterfield, in her own words she was

a silly, vague, maddening creature. I don't know why her son doesn't thump her, but he loves her. I usually play either slick, sophisticated women or slightly sinister ladies ... but it's been a lot of fun, and I've grown quite fond of the silly old dear.[225]

Sinister ladies surfaced again in 1977 with the film *The Getting of Wisdom*, directed by Bruce Beresford, in which she played the terrifying headmistress Mrs Gurney. A much-loved sister to her two brothers, Sheila regularly spent time with Robert when he was in London and with Max in Stratford, Ontario. She was the last of the three to die – in Sydney on 19 July 1994.

Max remained with the theatre company in Stratford, Ontario, until his death on 5 April 1987. Additional acting engagements took him regularly to other Canadian cities, and he also worked with Canadian television. Amicably divorced from Barbara Chilcott, he had a later relationship with the actress Kate Reid, whom he met when they both played in a television version of *Mother Courage* in 1965. In 1969 he joined the Theatre Management Administration of the Avon Theatre in Stratford. An excellent supporting actor, he played key cameo roles in most of the Stratford productions. A handsome bronze plaque (with portrait) commemorates him at the theatre.

In July 1970, Helpmann was with the Royal Ballet in New York as the Narrator in *A Wedding Bouquet*, and in July he was in London for a special engagement, as the on-stage narrator-compère of 'A Tribute to Sir Frederick Ashton', which marked Ashton's (reluctant) retirement from the directorship of the Royal Ballet. Still the best-ever Gala, this was a remarkable anthology programme, staged by Michael Somes, John Hart and Leslie Edwards, with a biographical commentary written by William Chappell; and this unique occasion owed a very great deal to Helpmann's charm and expertise in pulling it all together. The critics liked it very much. John Percival summed it up in *The Times* as

simply the most splendiferous lecture-demonstration that can ever have been given. Robert Helpmann was the uniquely-qualified expositor of Sir Fred's life and career. Starting at the champagne-decked table from

A Wedding Bouquet and making his second half entry in the balloon from *Les Sirènes*, Helpmann was in charge throughout.[226]

Another overseas tour at the turn of the year 1970/71 took the Australian Ballet coast-to-coast in the United States and Canada. The tour opened in Los Angeles on 26 December and ended in Boston on 3 March. *Don Quixote* was included, with Nureyev as guest artist and Helpmann occasionally appearing as Quixote. His own choreography was generally disliked; American critics found *The Display* and *Sun Music* impossible to enjoy.

In December 1971 Helpmann directed a new, but not particularly successful, production of *Peter Pan* at the London Coliseum, and returned as guest artist to the Royal Ballet in a role he had not danced since 1947: the Red King in *Checkmate*. In this revival in honour of Sir Arthur Bliss's eightieth birthday, Helpmann elicited a well-merited set of eulogies from the major London critics. Clement Crisp was impressed by the staging, saying in the *Financial Times* that the ballet was 'a remarkable commentary upon the war-menaced years of the thirties, when it was created'. He went on:

> The performance was dominated by Monica Mason's balefully evil portrayal of the Black Queen, and by the return of Sir Robert Helpmann to the role of the Red King, a part which he created ... For the first time in my experience, the Red King achieved his proper stature. Helpmann brings out both the doddering weakness and the essential dignity of the figure, and the ballet gained enormously from his presence.[227]

John Percival wrote in *The Times*:

> The real star performance is Robert Helpmann's as the stumbling old Red King. To my generation he was a legend in this role, which he created but quite soon relinquished. The legend was not exaggerated. He not only brings out with unmatched vividness the role's obvious qualities, the weariness through which flashes of an almost extinct authority still momentarily blaze, but gives them a credible context. The sly cunning with which he tries to make up for his lost strength takes on an almost heroic quality in this unsentimentally clear portrait of an old man fighting desperately for his life.[228]

Helpmann had tried before to get Ashton to make the trip to Australia to appear with him in a staging of *Cinderella*, and Ashton finally agreed to this in 1972. Interviewing Ashton in London for the *Sydney Morning Herald*, Lynne Bell commented,

> Fred – or Freddie – and Bobby [Helpmann] have been friends for 38 years. When Sir Frederick wrote *Cinderella* back in 1948 he did so with Helpmann and himself in mind for the Ugly Sisters. He says vaguely that, yes, perhaps it reflects something of their characters ... 'I have to watch him,' says Sir Frederick with a laugh. 'He steals all the scenes if I don't.[229]

Helpmannn also wanted to persuade Ashton to create a new ballet for the company. He said in an interview in the *Sydney Morning Herald*:

> It's a great thing for him to come out, because although we do several of his ballets they are ballets done somewhere else in the world. It is very important we do ballets especially created for us, but it is very hard to get choreographers to do that until they come out and work with the company ... I hope once Sir Frederick works with the company he will be mad about it, and do an original ballet with us.[230]

He never did. The performances of the Stepsisters were immensely popular in Australia and Ashton was duly honoured and feted. Julian Russell pointed out in the *Sydney Sun* that 'they were marvellously matched, offering beautifully timed comedy interspersed with graceful, agile interludes'.[231] Brian Hoad in *The Bulletin* mentioned what a 'stuffed and starched' audience it was, but continued:

> Helpmann and Ashton: two knights of the realm dolled up as a couple of ugly sisters swishing, skipping and tottering around the stage finally proved irresistible, and unfroze the most dignified of the dignitaries. Helpmann, the fabulous mimic, the quintessential pantomime dame, sweetly nasty, heartily bitchy, mocking at the foibles of the sexual condition with pungent randiness as, adjusting overtight corset and flapping feathered fan, he makes yet another somewhat desperate pass at yet another passing cavalier ... Ashton as the shy, silly but happy creature who before the evening is out has pulled off a minor miracle and generated the kind of magic which has the power to touch the human heart.[232]

Ashton oversaw a staging *of La Fille mal gardée*, but no persuasions could prevail on him to stay long enough to give the Australians a new ballet. The nearest he came to it was to discuss the possibility of creating one to the Offenbach music for *Le Papillon*, which Richard Bonynge had recently recorded, but the score as a whole held no attraction for him. He did, however, join Helpmann in South Africa in August, where they danced in *Cinderella* for PACT Ballet.

25

In November 1972 Helpmann worked as co-director with Nureyev on an ambitious film of the Australian Ballet's *Don Quixote* – it was very much a cooperative creation. They took over a couple of disused hangars in Melbourne's old Essendon Airport as a film studio. Barry Kay, who had designed the stage version, applied himself to a different concept for the cinema; Geoffrey Unsworth, admired for *Cabaret* and *2001: A Space Odyssey*, was director of photography; and the music was specially recorded by the Elizabethan Theatre Trust's Melbourne orchestra, conducted by John Lanchbery. There were countless problems, including a formidable heatwave. As a ninety-four percent Australian venture, its production was widely covered by the Australian press. Completed in December, it had a socially brilliant launching in July 1973 at the Concert Hall of the new Sydney Opera House.

The London Coliseum saw the stage version of *Don Quixote* the following November, when the company was in brilliant form after having travelled by way of dates in India, Russia, Poland, Czechoslovakia and Romania. On the whole, the British critics responded with pleasure and Helpmann came in for some kind words. Clement Crisp was impressed, as he made clear in the *Financial Times*:

> Amid the whirlwind of steps and stamping there is a figure of nobility and peculiarly touching dignity – Sir Robert Helpmann as the Don himself. Levashov with the Bolshoi was moving in the role, but Helpmann, playing with the greatest subtlety and economy, turns the butt of the piece into a character having a mad White Knight like distinction. Here, for an instant, Cervantes' dreamer comes alive and, grateful as I am for the chance to see the company in full cry, I was more excited by Helpmann's performance than by anything else in the evening.[233]

When it came to *Sun Music*, of course, choreographically Helpmann was generally panned. Oleg Kerensky, however, wrote with fairness in the *International Herald Tribune*:

> Sir Robert Helpmann's *Sun Music*, a 45-minute Australian equivalent of *The Rite of Spring*, has received a bad press and some booing. But it is

undeniably theatrical and contains some extremely beautiful scenic and lighting effects. The opening scene, with the dancers growing in the sun like plants and the finale, with them shrivelling up in the heat, are both extremely effective. But there is a sequence in the middle, consisting of athletic exercises on huge rubber beach balls, danced to recorded aboriginal grunts, which inevitably provokes some unsympathetic laughter.[234]

Back in Australia in December, Helpmann and van Praagh staged a successful new production of *The Sleeping Beauty*, enchantingly designed by Kenneth Rowell, to mark the Australian Ballet's first appearance at the Sydney Opera House. In March 1974, at another Adelaide Festival, Rowell also designed what proved to be Helpmann's last ballet, the plotless *Perisynthyon*. Initially, there was to be commissioned music. First of all, Richard Meale was asked for a score, then Malcolm Williamson, but Helpmann was not happy with either and he reverted, very much at the last minute, to a score he greatly admired and had earlier thought of using for a ballet, Sibelius's *Symphony No. 1 in E minor*. He had only rarely before choreographed to existing music. This late change was unfortunate, as it meant that the ballet was put on with insufficient preparation, and first impressions were indelible. The critics were much divided. Quite a few brought out their daggers, dismissing the work as disastrously muddled, disappointing and gimmicky. Others saw more in it, despite its weaknesses. William Shoubridge, calling it 'a curious patchwork quilt of a ballet', wrote in the Adelaide *Advertiser*:

Its opening scene must rank as one of the most stunning in all ballet. Suspended high above the darkened stage, Perisynthyon (John Meehan) swirled and dipped like some midnight moth, then joined the *corps de ballet* in scenes that gradually progressed through some *tour de force* dancing to a thrilling climax. Helpmann has managed ... to weld together pure classic steps and modern movement into a tightly knit whole that had choreographic as well as dramatic continuity.

He accused the corps of looking 'sloppy and poorly drilled' and said 'Helpmann, unlike Maurice Béjart, seems unable to handle large group movement and gives the corps little else than a stilted series of changes from pose to pose. But he truly excels when he intensifies the drama with smaller groups, bringing out the essence of what he has to say in spectacular solos and pas *de deux*.' [235]

Jill Sykes, writing in the *Sydney Morning Herald*, also found the opening scene 'absolutely stunning':

> As John Meehan twirls in suspended animation, pivoting from a rope looped around his ankle, it seemed that Sir Robert had reached out for a new dimension in dance, freeing it from gravity and the ground ... I was disappointed the ideas were not developed; mere mortal elevation in the classical dance sense could become something of an anticlimax. Grouping a series of dance impressions in the terms of the movements of Sibelius' Symphony No. 1, Sir Robert has created a ballet without any significant theme but with an unworldly, sometimes menacing atmosphere.[236]

My own estimate at the time was that the score was used with understanding and sympathy, and that the action was dramatically effective and fluent. The ensembles I also felt to be insufficiently inventive, but the ebb and flow of solos, duets and trios was consistently interesting and the use of ramps, upper levels and hidden trampolines admirable. Helpmann was using the kind of acrobatic and gymnastic techniques that would be very much in vogue in dance theatre a dozen years later.

When *Perisynthyon* was shown a month later in Sydney, Sykes reported on 15 April that it was 'looking much more sure of itself ... the production seems tighter and it's enjoyable entertainment'. This did not save its life. John Cargher, writing from Adelaide in *The Australian*, made the point that it was seriously under-rehearsed and that 'the ensemble was so ragged at times as to make the choreographer's intention null and void'. However, there was much that he liked about it. Speaking of possible 'major surgery', he said 'the good outweighs the bad by a considerable margin. *Perisynthyon* has the potential to become a major hit without too much reworking'.[237] Helpmann did not, however, make any effort to revise or rework *Perisynthyon*. In his personal life (about which he talked little) there was great sadness in September 1974, when Michael Benthall died at the age of fifty-five. They had been partners for many years, enjoying the closest artistic association in various branches of the theatre. This had changed during the 1960s, with Helpmann's work increasingly centred on Australia, with peripheral travelling to the United States and the Far East, and with Benthall's intensified family responsibilities after his father's death, followed by his sad descent into alcoholism. Although they still shared a London home, their paths became considerably diverged. A great deal of separation, however, never meant that affection was destroyed on either side, and Helpmann was with Benthall constantly in London during his last illness.

At the end of 1974 Peggy van Praagh retired, and Helpmann continued as sole artistic director of the Australian Ballet. He began planning a ballet version of *The Merry Widow*, which would be the first three-act production created especially for the company. He did not intend to choreograph this himself but to set it all out as producer. He had, of course, appeared as a leading dancer in the operetta in his days with J C. Williamson, and he had also choreographed it for Cyril Ritchard and Madge Elliott in London in 1943. He was rightly convinced that it would be an immensely popular show with the general public, and therefore would make money for the company. Money to make it, however, was needed. An Industries Assistance Commission inquiry was being held for the performing arts, which came out with a blunt statement to the effect that the Australian Ballet was bankrupt and that the Government was not committed to subsidising it forever. Peter Bahen, the ballet's administrator, challenged this, commenting that 'it might be proved that we are technically bankrupt, but then we always have [been] and always would be considered in this light'. The Commission climbed down far enough to say that they were 'just making the point that your show was not commercially viable'. Helpmann then maintained, in the *Sydney Morning Herald*, that they could not cut down on expenses because 'basic classical techniques could be maintained only through the presentation of the expensive three-act spectaculars like *Swan Lake* and *The Sleeping Beauty*, and a great deal of public interest lay in the pure spectacle and magnificence of these productions'.[238] It was becoming increasingly apparent that there was little sympathy from the finance side of Australian government for such an expensive branch of the arts. This was undoubtedly one of the factors contributing to the Australian Ballet Board's decision to terminate Helpmann's contract as artistic director. An additional point to remember is that he had been making it increasingly plain that he felt the Board was becoming dominated by moneymen who had no experience or understanding of artistic matters. This hardly made him popular with the people in question.

Before the production of *The Merry Widow*, Helpmann was asked to appear in an hour-long ballet created especially for television by Gillian Lynne. She was commissioned by the Australian Broadcasting Commission and the Australian Ballet, and spent three preliminary weeks in Melbourne in March 1975, getting to know the company. She wrote the scenario for *The Fool on the Hill* in collaboration with her co-director, Bob Hird, and created the choreography when she went back in August. Filming took place toward the end of September. The story was about a Walter Mitty type of young man and his dreams, and the music was an arrangement of songs from the Beatles' album *Sergeant Pepper's Lonely Hearts Club Band.* Tim Goodchild was brought over as designer. Lynne who, as a young dancer, had been chosen by Helpmann for a special role in *Adam Zero,* returned the compliment by casting him as Sergeant Pepper. Helpmann was delighted. He had a continuing interest in all kinds of jazz, pop and rock music.

The problems between Helpmann and the Board of Directors of the Australian Ballet were publicised in October 1975. A bland and formal press handout dated 20 October announced that he would 'conclude his term as Director of the Australian Ballet at the end of June 1976'. Polite tribute was paid to how he had 'imparted much of his diverse theatrical knowledge and experience to the dancers of the Australian Ballet over the past eleven years'. Helpmann, however, refused to play the Board's game. A few days earlier he had phoned Jill Sykes of the *Sydney Morning Herald:* 'The Board's announcement gives the impression that it was my decision to leave the Australian Ballet, which is quite incorrect', he said. 'I want the public and the dancers to know that I didn't decide to leave them. I would have stayed with them until I dropped dead.'[239]

The last months of his directorship were very much occupied with *The Merry Widow,* which had its premiere in Melbourne on 13 November. Helpmann features on programmes in a limited capacity as producer, but it was very much his own special project. He had written the scenario; he had, against some odds, negotiated with the reluctant estates of the composer (Lehar) and the librettist; he had commissioned Lanchbery to arrange the music, Ronald Hynd, who had a special affinity with the period and style, to do the choreography, and Desmond Heeley to design the spectacular sets and costumes. He had collaborated with Hynd on casting; and when Marilyn Rowe, who was to be the first to dance the title role, developed continued trouble with an ankle joint, which had already kept her off the stage for a year, he insisted that she be sent to Denmark to a renowned specialist in dancers' injuries, Professor Thomassen, who ensured that with an operation and exercises she returned to full form.

At this point, he was surrounded by people he knew well and completely trusted. Hynd had turned to freelance choreography after a fine career as *premier danseur* with the Royal Ballet, and his wife, Annette Page, who worked on the production, had danced the Suicide in *Miracle in the Gorbals* when it was revived in 1958. Heeley had designed *Yugen.* Lanchbery had

worked on the film *of Don Quixote*. Additionally, the previous April,
Helpmann had appointed a new personal assistant, Elizabeth Anderton, a
former principal dancer with the Royal Ballet touring company, who had
spoken very warmly about him to the *Sydney Sun-Herald*, calling him 'a
marvellous person to work with. We have the same sense of humour. He is
the easiest person to get along with – except when he loses his temper,
which isn't very often!'[240]

From the first night, it was obvious that the Australian Ballet had a
smash hit on their hands with *The Merry Widow*. Of course, it was the kind
of show that led some people to hold up their hands in horror over its
popular appeal, although most simply enjoyed it and the public was willing
to pay to see it. Reviewing it in the *Sydney Morning Herald*, Jill Sykes wrote
that

> it has all the escapist ingredients that have lured people to the theatre
> for centuries. Desmond Heeley's costumes and sets are absolutely
> stunning; the action is steeped in romanticism, relaxingly predictable,
> and ends happily ever after; and Lehar's tuneful music, skilfully arranged
> by John Lanchbery, is not only familiar but beloved.

However, she carped about the choreography for the ensembles:

> Only in the soloists' roles [Hynd] has created dance movements that are
> something out of the ordinary, that stay in the mind for their freshness,
> tenderness and warmth ... *The Merry Widow* is a living monument to Sir
> Robert Helpmann's faith in glamour and romance. It was his idea and
> he staged it, putting a lifetime's knowledge into it.[241]

The four leading roles were splendidly danced by Rowe, Meehan, Aldous
and Kelvin Coe, and Paul Saliba contributed a captivating comedy
performance as the maître d' of Chez Maxim. John Cargher wrote in *The
Australian*:

> One hopes that the company's dismissed artistic director, Robert
> Helpmann, will be given credit for having brought about this remarkable
> first full-length Australian ballet. Since Helpmann co-created the
> adaptation and supervised the whole thing, the credit given to him need
> not be based on sentiment. It would be hard to imagine how Lehar's
> masterpiece could have been turned into ballet to greater effect.

He was much more enthusiastic than Sykes had been about Hynd's choreography:

Time and again he astonishes by suddenly changing direction when a conventional *enchaînement* is apparently reaching its logical climax. There is not a dull moment. There is humour, blessedly without slapstick comedy, there is romance without false tears, and there is technical virtuosity without ever losing sight of the story line.[242]

In *The Age*, Leonard Radic called it

Sir Robert Helpmann's swansong with the company. And what a splendid swansong it is. The people who run the company can rationalise their dismissal of Sir Robert how they will. The fact remains that with this balletic rewrite of the Lehar operetta, Helpmann has given the company its one indisputable triumph.[243]

Neil Jillett wrote in the *Melbourne Herald*,

A rave is the only appropriate response to the world premiere of the first full-length work commissioned by the Australian Ballet ... it is a masterpiece of wit and swooning romanticism. [It] enchants the eye and ear and lifts the spirit.

Jillett put his finger on a problem (in the Vilia sequence) about which Helpmann and Hynd were only too aware:

The copyright holders' misguided insistence that some singing should accompany the dancing leads to the production's one serious weakness. The ooh-ah vocalising drags the ballet's mood from Edwardian Paris into 1940s Hollywood.[244]

The company were soon on tour again. They took *The Merry Widow* to Washington DC, New York and London, with Fonteyn as an enchanting guest artist. While in the States, Helpmann was called in by American Ballet Theatre to supervise its production of *The Sleeping Beauty*, which had been staged by Mary Skeaping in the spring, for its season opening in December in Washington DC. He also contributed a guest artist appearance as Carabosse. In 1977 Sadler's Wells Royal Ballet, then directed by Peter Wright, engaged him to guest with them as the Red King in *Checkmate* and

Coppelius in *Coppélia* and the programmes were brought to Sadler's Wells. It was an excellent idea, as many people who had seen little of him on stage were able for the first time to gauge his standing in two major roles. Writing in the *Financial Times*, Clement Crisp brilliantly summed up these performances:

> A consummate droll, Helpmann has ever had immense fun in showing us Dr Coppelius in the worst possible light: senile, slightly malicious, and doddering on the point of lunacy. He is riotously and wonderfully in control in the part once again: the tripping walk, the petulance, the feeling at moments that the role is being taken by a malevolent sheep are all framed in a joyous comic performance. And there are, too, the passages when Helpmann the actor, who impressed us in *The White Devil* and as Hamlet, and the dancer whose dignity as a prince in the classic repertoire was carried with a wonderful ease, is seen. When Swanilda as Coppélia comes to life, Helpmann's seriousness is truly Hoffmannesque; his pathos at the end of Act 2 is simple and affecting ... British ballet owes Helpmann a vast debt – his present performances in *Coppélia* and *Checkmate* increase it still further.[245]

26

Later in 1977 Helpmann was in Australia acting, in what he described as his fourteenth film, *The Mango Tree*, based on Ronald McKie's novel and directed by Kevin Dobson. His role was of a drunken derelict called The Professor, whom he described to the *Sydney Daily Telegraph* as 'an intellectual who, despite being a drunk, has a great influence on the star of the film, a teenage boy ... at the end of World War I in northern Queensland'.[246]

In 1978 he directed a substantial antipodean tour of 'Stars of World Ballet' in association with Michael Edgley. Programmes of varied classical and modern duets (as well as Flemming Flindt in his own ballet *The Lesson*) represented not only Fonteyn but also a fine group of international stars from the Bolshoi Ballet, American Ballet Theatre, Stuttgart Ballet and Royal Ballet. Fonteyn danced with Ivan Nagy a Romeo and Juliet *pas de deux* choreographed by George Skibine. Jill Sykes, in the *Sydney Morning Herald*, spoke of the show as 'offering new delights with every performance ... The programme changed constantly, bringing in different *pas de deux* and new partnerships between the dancers.' Fonteyn, with Wayne Eagling, gave 'a passionate performance' in Ashton's *pas de deux Hamlet with Ophelia*, which had been created in 1977 for Fonteyn and Nureyev as *Hamlet Prelude*.[247]

Also in 1978, Helpmann's biography by Elizabeth Salter was published by Angus & Robertson, and he gave an interview to Marie Knuckey that was published in the *Sydney Morning Herald*. She said he was 'absolutely unprovokable':

> Could this be the quicksilver Sir Robert I had seen in action before? Who when he talked to an audience never just talked, but gave a three-dimensional performance; dramatising his words like an actor, moving like a dancer? Whose witty comments made any interview a delight, even or especially when those comments had the cutting edge of a diamond?..He looked at me with a wicked glint in his eye and said firmly, very firmly: 'I am not irritateable today'.

Points about beliefs and opinions, however, emerged. He believed in luck. 'I think timing and luck are how things happen. If I'd arrived in England six months earlier or six months later, things might have been very different.' He felt that the 'only way you learn is to be taught by experts', and suggested that young actors should work with experienced directors, and young directors should work with experienced actors. 'I don't think the blind should be leading the blind all the time.' When he went to the theatre, 'I expect to be entertained. I don't expect to be lectured. I want to be excited.' He disliked 'amateurism, stupidity, snobbism. I dislike incompetent people. I dislike people who are not willing to learn.' On the other hand, he liked 'people who give friendship'. Friendship was very important. 'I *know* a lot of people, but I don't have that many friends.'[248]

In 1971 the Australian Broadcasting Commission had set up a long series of interviews with Helpmann about his life and career. In the course of them he talked of many famous people with whom he had worked, always with amusing anecdotes and great warmth of appreciation for their qualities. The interviewer picked him up on this: 'You have almost always spoken of them with affection. Surely there are some people you heartily dislike?' Helpmann thought about this and replied, 'No. There's really nobody I heartily dislike. I have a kind of built-in red light about that, and so I have always avoided them. I was always seeking out something they had that I could learn from them.' He summed up a little, speaking of de Valois's constant advice and her extraordinary vision, of the fact that she was a great producer and one of the greatest administrators in ballet. He spoke with great feeling about Baylis, and of her acute instinct for choosing the people who could serve the purposes of her theatres. He said of Lambert that he was underrated as a composer because of his devotion to ballet, and of the fact that he could talk about 'eight different subjects at the same time and all intelligently'. He spoke of Sophie Fedorovitch's quiet modesty and her marvellous ability for 'eliminating everything except the absolute essentials ... she was perfect for Ashton's splendid economy of movement and they worked wonderfully together'. He spoke of Ashton's great sense of the theatre and of how he always picked up 'the least trace of falseness in anyone's performance', of how 'he allows you to do your own characterisation, and then moulds it'. He had already talked about the Sitwells, Lord Berners, Stein and Toklas, Arthur Bliss and the Lunts. He spoke of Katharine Hepburn's discipline and thoroughness, and her integrity: 'I never met a human being so entirely honest. She never believed in lying in any shape or form.' About theatre people in general he said, 'You almost always read the bad things about them, with great headlines ... but all through my life I have found people in the theatre helpful, hard-working, charming, and disciplined'.[249]

In July 1978 Helpmann was appointed artistic director of Sydney's oldest fully professional, non-commercial theatre, the Old Tote Theatre Company.

For some time this long-standing company had been in trouble, both financially and in failing to establish a current firm identity. Helpmann was to take up his appointment in January 1979, and was energetically planning a first season. This came to nothing, however, as the company lost its federal financing and, in spite of considerable outrage on the part of press and public, had to go into liquidation. August 1978 saw a production by him of *Dracula* at Her Majesty's Theatre, Sydney. This was a dramatisation by Hamilton Deane and John L. Balderston and, at Helpmann's request, starred the Australian film actor John Waters. Romola Costantino (*Sydney Morning Herald*) enjoyed it, praising the 'delicate, fanciful, art-nouveau designs in black, white and grey' by Edward Gorey. As to the production, she wrote: 'Helpmann raises this household-word ghoul to loftier levels than those of a customary music-hall villain ... no director, surely, could have set the whole cast gliding and gesturing more elegantly ... in short, *Dracula* is delicious'.[250]

The next few years were not wasted. On 23 May 1979, he was at Covent Garden for 'A Tribute to Margot Fonteyn' for her sixtieth birthday; he had himself reached seventy the previous month. It was a splendid and nostalgic evening. It featured a clever solo, *Salut d'amour*, devised by Ashton – Clement Crisp (*Financial Times*) reported that it was 'made of hints, phrases, from some of the ballets in which he has celebrated her beauty, talent, musicality, classic decorum, her grace of spirit and body'. He also recorded the closing item:

> '*Façade* – with the bonus of Sir Robert Helpmann back in the black velvet, hair-oil and curlicues of the Dago. To see Fonteyn and Helpmann up to their old and splendid tricks, all except the turning of the debutante head over heels, whose omission made for a grand new joke – was to see time rolled back 30 years, and not believe that the years had passed. Dame Margot was as zany and faintly amazed by it all as ever; Sir Robert even more luxuriant in rings and rolling eyes. Would that today's performers had as much comic verve and resource.[251]

In 1980 Maina Gielgud put on an attractive 'master class' production called *Steps, Notes and Squeaks* at the Old Vic, and Helpmann, along with de Valois and Svetlana Beriosova, was one of the coaches. In March 1981, in the USA, he directed Lilli Palmer in a two-character show (the second character, a maid, never spoke) about Sarah Bernhardt, *Sarah in America*; this was written by Ruth Wolff to celebrate Bernhardt's nine tours of America between 1880 and 1918. In June he staged a revival of the ballet

Hamlet for Anthony Dowell at Covent Garden; this was later taken to New York. John Percival interviewed him for *The Times*, and was told that when he arrived he 'took it for granted that everyone knew what it was about. Then I heard two boys talking in the corridor. One asked, 'What actually happened to Ophelia?' and the other replied 'She drowned – didn't she go out in a boat?'. So I called them all together and explained what happens in the play.'[252]

In June that year, Helpmann directed and choreographed Handel's *Alcina* for the Australian Opera in Sydney. Interviewed by Richard Coleman for the *Sydney Morning Herald*, he said, 'the music is exquisite, the decor charming, the story perfectly idiotic, and Joan Carden, who will sing the title role, absolutely wonderful'. He spoke of changes he intended to make to stress Alcina's identity as a wicked enchantress and to clarify the story. These included staging it as 'an opera within an opera' and using 'all the stage effects that all those wonderful old theatres had – the sea, rocks turning into a palace, the transformations'.[253]

In America in 1982 he appeared with Diana Rigg in an ill-fated musical, *Colette.* This had multiple backers who poured $1.5 million into a show that had little chance of working. It opened in Seattle (5th Avenue Theater) on 9 February but was immediately seen to be a total turkey. Wayne Johnson wrote in the *Seattle Sunday Times* that

> it failed to achieve any real measure of affecting life ... It had some good moments, created primarily by two superb English actors, Diana Rigg and Sir Robert Helpmann. But those moments remain isolated; they never coalesce to become a piece with audience-involving momentum.[254]

The director, Dennis Rosa, was sacked and a new one appointed. A new scenic designer was brought in, and a very much revised version was tried out on 21 March at Denver; but it lost its backers (to general relief!) and survived no longer. Back in Seattle, on 28 February a *Sunday Times* reporter, Carole Beers, had interviewed Helpmann about the show. He was quoted as saying the show was 'too busy, too expensive, tries to do too much. It's the New York syndrome of changing directors in midstream, All you should do is follow one man's vision and stick to it. Too many people spoil the thing.' He said that his was 'the best-written part in the play – especially the final, moving scene with Colette'. His involvement had come from the fact that Roger Stevens (one of the producers) saw his production of *Sarah in America* and wanted him to take the role of Jacques in *Colette* – partly because he not only knew the Paris context of the 1930s and 1940s, but had actually met Colette in 1948 when he and Fonteyn were dancing in Paris.

Margaret Rawlings, an English actress friend of mine, came backstage and asked if I wanted to meet Colette. I wanted nothing more than to meet this legendary writer and actress. This was when Colette was in her late 70s, four years before she died. We went to one of her salons in her apartments in the Palais Royal. There she was, surrounded by her cats, her husband Maurice and her daughter. She was propped up on a pillow and couldn't move around much because of severe arthritis. Her hands were crippled. But she surprised me. She was so alive, so animated, so flirty, even in her 70s. She would kind of look at you sideways and she would laugh a great deal. She was utterly fascinating. She was one of those people who become a legend in their time. But she actually lived up to the legend. Not many do.[255]

27

Helpmann acted for the last time in Britain in May 1982, as what Kurt Gänzl calls 'the wickedly scabrous Cardinal Pirelli' in a revival of Sandy Wilson's *Valmouth* at the Chichester Festival, a performance that Gänzl praised as 'finely understated'.[256] Patrick Garland in *The Listener* described Helpmann in rehearsal – 'white hair falling elegantly across the shoulders of his mink coat, in a fastidious blue-print of Cardinal Pirelli's tango, extolling the virtues of the cathedral of Clemenza'.[257] The production itself (by John Dexter) did not conceal the fact that, as John Barber wrote in the *Daily Telegraph*, 'what once was described as fantasticated smut now seems harmless today and even, I confess, occasionally tepid'.[258] Irving Wardle in *The Times* found little to like in this 'party for peacocks', but decided that the 'collectors' item' was 'the return of Robert Helpmann ... [his] hooded smirks and baleful *oeillades*, his capacity to express elegant corruption down to his beringed fingertips, lodge one imperishable image'.[259] For me, the production misfired almost entirely, and I was not surprised that it did not transfer to London.

For Helpmann, 1983 began with a staging of Gounod's opera *Roméo et Juliette* in Sydney, for Glenys Fowles and Anson Austin, and during that season Joan Sutherland took over the title role in *Alcina*.

In October, also in Australia, he was acclaimed for an acting tour de force as Lord Alfred Douglas in Justin Fleming's play about Oscar Wilde, *The Cobra*. This was set in London in 1942, with Douglas re-living scenes of his life with Wilde. In advance, Helpmann told Sonia Humphrey of the *Weekly Australian*, 'I play Douglas as an old man; the three other characters are the young Alfred, Wilde and the Marquess of Queensberry. It's the longest part I've ever done – he never stops talking!'[260] Janise Beaumont in the *Sydney Sun-Herald* reported him as saying that the play 'is about relationships generally and about how we can destroy each other. The tragedy of human beings is the incapability of two people loving equally at the same time – the imbalance of it.' He himself had 'had two very long relationships in my life, so I know. Yes, the balance did come finally, but one had to wait for it. Loving at the same pitch is rarely possible, but I've known a few good marriages, although one has to think ...'

In this unusually frank interview, he also spoke of the motivation of actors: 'For me, the motivation is more escape from reality than ego. I've never indulged in drugs, but I imagine that being in a successful play has the same effect as a high. While doing it, I'm escaping from unpleasantness.' Although he had smoked since he was nine, he had just given up without too much difficulty. 'I can be strong when the issue is to do with myself.' He spoke of 'not having suffered many shattering experiences' but of being able to deal with those that did come along, partly thanks to the discipline he learnt as a dancer. Looking back to early days, he said 'We were called bright young things, but I don't think we were anything to write home about. I was into everything, you know.' He suggested that the fact of there being fewer options available then was one of the main differences between his youth and teenagers of today. 'Also, we weren't vicious. There was no viciousness.'[261]

The Cobra was premiered in the Opera House Drama Theatre in Sydney on 7 October 1983, directed by Richard Wherrett. H.G. Kippax in the *Sydney Morning Herald* welcomed Helpmann's return to acting:

> As a dancer at his peak he seemed compounded of sinew and mercury with something sulphurous for seasoning. The qualities remain unimpaired, and here masterfully complement Mr Fleming's literate text ... The physical control in his acting is absolute. So is his vocal command. How expressively he speaks, stroking sour comedy from man's spleen, stabbing in attack, elegiac in the last fantasy as he reaches out to an imagined, suppliant Wilde to bless him with forgiveness.[262]

John Moses in *The Australian* wrote of Fleming's 'new and brilliant play', and also had praise for Helpmann, saying that his casting had been a masterstroke:

> What a complete man of the stage he is! His performance is that of a consummate theatre craftsman; feline, waspish, graceful and petulant by turn, the voice perhaps a little lacking in its former resonance but not in nuance, nor in elegance. This is acting in the grand manner. It should not, on any account, be missed.[263]

In November Helpmann joined up with great friends, Googie Withers and John McCallum, who were what they described as 'breaking new ground by playing in poker machine clubs' in the Ted Willis play *Stardust*, in which, according to McCallum, he was 'very droll and amusing and of course so utterly different from anybody else'.[264]

At the turn of 1983/84, Helpmann was also involved in some unimportant feature and television films. There was *Puzzle*, a thriller about murder and missing gold bars directed by Gordon Hessler; and *Patrick*, about a comatose patient with strange powers, directed by Richard Franklin, in which Helpmann was a callous doctor. In April 1984 Helpmann was in Mount Gambier when the South Australian Premier formally renamed the enlarged local theatre as The Sir Robert Helpmann Theatre. Helpmann's reply, reported in the local *Evening Express*, was typical: 'There always comes a time when one is completely at a loss for words, which is strange for me, because friends say I talk too much!' It certainly meant a great deal to him, given not only that he had been born in Mount Gambier but that his roots there went back to his great-grandfather.[265]

In January 1985 there was a good deal of publicity in the Australian papers about the appearance of Helpmann and Sheila in an episode of the popular Seven Network television series *A Country Practice*. They had never acted together since they were children. In a *Woman's Day* article by Julie Kusko, Sheila was quoted as saying:

I've always wanted to work with Robert and it never seemed to happen. At one stage there was talk about J.B. Priestley writing a play for the three of us [including her actor brother Max] but it never worked out.

She recalled how 'when we were kids I was a bit in awe of him because he was always ordering us around. Everybody had to dress up and were told exactly what we had to do. He was directing even then.' But when they met as adults after years of separation, they 'got on very well. He's so easy-going really, a tolerant person and not moody. He's got a very even temperament; things don't upset him.'[266]

After that, Helpmann was in the United States directing, in collaboration with Christopher Brown, his partner since 1970, a revival of the operetta *The Merry Widow* for San Diego Opera Ballet at the Civic Theater. An earlier production there had been directed by Tito Capobianco, and Donald Dierks compared the two in his review in the *San Diego Union-Tribune*:

Robert Helpmann clearly likes fun and good jokes as well as the next fellow, but his directing style is more evenhanded and reserved than was that of Tito Capobianco ... It was also clear that Helpmann was a dancer and choreographer before he was a stage director. He was able to move the large cast and chorus around on stage with balletic grace and dramatic purpose, and he created some handsome stage pictures along the way ... what gave Helpmann's work its quality was his comic reserve. He helped the cast to be amusing, but he made clowns of no one.[267]

In June, back at the Sydney Opera House, he (and Christopher Brown) directed Joan Sutherland in Bellini's *I Puritani* for the Australian Opera. His last stage appearances were as the Red King in *Checkmate* with the Australian Ballet in May 1986. Jill Sykes wrote in the *Sydney Morning Herald*: 'It gives Robert Helpmann a chance to remind us what an extraordinary man of the theatre he still is.' After discussing the contemporary cast, she ended, 'There was, of course, a scene-stealer in their midst. With rolling eyes, a few grand gestures, and a moving moment in which he shows the defiance of his distant youth, Helpmann's tottering Red King compels the attention in a way that none of his highly charged young colleagues could equal.'[268]

That year, on September 28, he died of emphysema in a Sydney hospital.

Australia realised what it had lost. It began by giving him the unprecedented tribute of a state funeral, held on 2 October at St Andrew's Cathedral, Sydney, with a packed congregation, a set of celebrated pallbearers, and a large crowd outside in the street. Some weeks after the funeral, his sister Sheila and Christopher Brown carried his ashes to Waikiki to scatter them on the waves.

On 7 October, the Senate of the Parliament of the Commonwealth of Australia at Canberra expressed 'its deep regret' and 'placed on record its appreciation of his long and meritorious service to Australian ballet.'. All senators present stood in silence. This was also unusual. It was pointed out that 'it is only in exceptional circumstances that motions of condolence are moved for distinguished Australians who have not sat in the Parliament'. Helpmann's career was then set out at length, and various senators added tributes. One of them, Senator Stanley James Collard, summed up by saying:

He always regarded himself as an Australian, although much of his life was spent away from these shores ... His love of the theatre and his ability to use it as a medium of communication and expression knew no bounds. He put this country on the map in the cultural arena. He was always looking for new challenges and was never content to rely on past successes ... He was one of our great ambassadors.

In the House of Representatives, the Prime Minister, Bob Hawke, said that 'no one should underestimate Sir Robert Helpmann's role in the development of the growing maturity of Australia's art and culture ... He demonstrated to the world the diversity of this nation's talents and capabilities'. The Leader of the Opposition, John Howard, declared that 'he will be remembered as an artist of international stature'. The Minister for Arts, Heritage and Environment, Barry Cohen, spoke of 'the awesome breadth of his artistic talent', and another Representative, David Miles Connolly, commented on how 'he used his infinite imagination in so many fields throughout his life'.[269]

The Australian Ballet followed on 15 October with a memorial service at the State Theatre in the Victorian Arts Centre in Melbourne, which apparently managed to be 'theatrical, entertaining and amusing, but at the same time serious and dignified'.[270] A small-scale but crowded Service of Thanksgiving – on 25 November at St. Paul's Church, Covent Garden, known as the Actors' Church – was the only tribute paid in London, which had seen so much of his life and work, and the Royal Ballet merely dedicated a performance to him in its usual perfunctory way. Plenty of mixed obituaries turned up both in Australia and in Britain, but Helpmann might well have settled for what de Valois wrote in the *Daily Telegraph*, very much off the cuff after the news of his death was broken to her:

> To work with Robert Helpmann was always an inspiration. There was at work an alerted intelligence with an acute sense of perception. Bobby had a sense of humour that surmounted everything. Sometimes it was expressed by word of mouth, sometimes by an outburst of 'mime'; at other times by just a look – and the latter could prove to be the most potent of all, for his timing on such occasions was as faultless as it was fatal ...

She continued:

> A few months ago, in his native Australia, Bobby paid farewell to his much-loved world of the theatre. It took the form of a gesture to the ballet. He gave a performance of his famous role, The Red King in *Checkmate*. Australia greeted his performance with an ovation that from all accounts was, as ever, well merited. Thus, down through the years of a life that had spread itself through many parts of the world, he returned in the end to his first love – the world of the ballet. I am left with the honour of receiving that touching gift from him; his final appearance in a role that will always remain the property of Robert Helpmann.[271]

He would also have been touched by what Michael Somes wrote:

> It would be impossible and presumptuous of me to try and assess the enormous contribution he made to the development and success of British ballet. Perhaps only those of us (from all branches of the theatre) who were fortunate enough and privileged enough to work and learn from him, can know how much we owe to his influence and example ... Bobby was not only a great artist but a kind and generous human being, who could, and was willing to, share his talent for the benefit of others. Above all, on and off the stage, we owe him hours of laughter.[272]

Another long-term associate, Joy Newton, a leading dancer and ballet mistress of Sadler's Wells Ballet, confirmed Somes's assessment, saying that he 'was always such fun – a kind man, irresistible mischief but no malice'.[273]

I said that I would return to the unpublished article written by A.V. Coton in October 1965. Coton first met Helpmann when he was 'as nervous a young critic as Helpmann was a dancer', when Tyrone Guthrie introduced them during his production of the Old Vic's *A Midsummer Night's Dream* in 1937. In the article, Coton makes some particularly relevant remarks:

> Helpmann's willingness – and ability – to tackle any sort of interesting notion was clear from his earliest days in English ballet ... English ballet [then] used a much wider range of subjects than we find today; or possibly we remember more sharply the diversities of theme, music, decor and choreographic styles that our ballet displayed during those excitingly experimental times ... Not a ballet I can recall from all that achievement in which at some time Helpmann did not dance, never hesitating to pull his weight as a minor soloist or in the corps de ballet when not performing a leading role ... Character is destiny, and Robert Helpmann is a very positive example of one who has recognised this hard fact early in life ... Helpmann, I believe, has never taken on anything that he thought impossible, simply because he has had absolute faith in his own intelligence, imagination and craftsmanship. This does not mean that every role, every act of creation, has borne the stamp of excellence; it does mean that he has never failed to make something theatrically interesting out of what he has done.

Continuing, Coton makes a very pertinent and valuable comment:

Everything Helpmann had done, either in performance or in direction, has emphasised the qualities of precise movement and precise gesture. He recognises that everything that any sort of performer does is based on, controlled by, and given total theatrical weight by his quality of movement. Perhaps this is the exact thing I have for long tried to define as the most valuable asset in Helpmann's equipment – his almost encyclopedic knowledge of what can happen in a theatre centres on this absolute sense of the value of movement.[274]

I have only briefly touched on one important facet of Helpmann's personality, the one that both de Valois and Somes mentioned, the one that cannot be proved to those who never experienced it: his brilliance as a raconteur, a spontaneous offstage performer, an expert duelling interviewee, an entertaining companion. Time and again, people were disarmed and enchanted by his wit and his irrepressible sense of fun. He was one of a select group of such talents whose gifts cannot be reflected in the written word. Peter Virgin, the biographer of Sydney Smith (one of the scintillating speakers of the early nineteenth century), used words about Smith that could well apply to Robert Helpmann:

Most of his jokes were told in less than half a minute. Often he would pick up and elaborate upon comments other people had made. There was nothing contrived about his wit; it was spontaneous, varied and dazzling ... His best remarks are succinct ... He could of course be mischievous ... uproariously funny at one moment, solemn the next.[275]

Where Helpmann is concerned, one testimony about this, from Annabel Farjeon, may be a fitting end to this book:

Bobby Helpmann was one of the very, very few whose wit in private and public life could make his presence in a room or on the stage a hair-raising delight. The spontaneity of his droll humour, the acuteness of his sallies, that could both devastate and enchant with their elegance and ribaldry, have given me the supreme pleasure of laughter that makes one rock and weep.[276]

Notes

1 Mary Helpman, *The Helpman Family Story: 1796–1964* (Adelaide: Rigby, 1967).

2 BBC Radio Home Service, 'The Robert Helpmann Story', 17 October 1960. From notes made by the author.

3 Keith S. Thomson, *HMS Beagle: The Ship that Changed the Course of History* (Phoenix, 1995).

4 as (1).

5 Harcourt Algeranoff, *My Years With Pavlova* (Heinemann, 1957).

6 as (2).

7 Quoted in Elizabeth Salter, *Helpmann* (Angus & Robertson, 1978).

8 Quoted in Evan Senior, 'The Vera van Rij Ballet Recital', *TownTopics* (Adelaide), 9 September1932.

9 Esmond Knight, *Seeking the Bubble* (Hutchinson, 1943).

10 Ninette de Valois, *Come Dance With Me* (Hamish Hamilton, 1957).

11 Gordon Anthony, *Studies of Robert Helpmann* (photographs). Foreword by Ninette de Valois (Home & van Thal, 1946).

12 as (11).

13 Leslie Edwards, *In Good Company* (Dance Books, 2003).

14 The Sitter Out, *The Dancing Times*, November 1933.

15 Jasper Howlett, *Talking of Ballet* (Philip Allen & Co., 1936).

16 H.B. Sibthorp, unpublished notes, *The Vic-Wells Ballet*, in the Theatre Museum, London.

17 R.B.M., *The Era*, 11 April 1934.

18 The Sitter Out, *The Dancing Times*, July 1934.

19 as (16).

20 P.W. Manchester, *Vic-Wells: A Ballet Progress* (Gollancz, 1942).

21 Harold Turner in *The Vic-Wells Association Magazine*, March 1936.

22 Ernest Newman, *The Sunday Times*, 26 January 1936.

23 Robert Hewison, *Footlights – A Hundred Years of Cambridge Comedy* (Methuen, 1983).

24 Mary Clarke, *The Sadler's Wells Ballet* (A. & C. Black, 1955).

25 Robert Helpmann, interview by Ellis Blane, Australian Broadcasting Commission, 1971. From notes made by the author.

26 as (16).

27 *Time and Tide*, 17 October 1936.

28 Margot Fonteyn, *Autobiography* (W.H. Allen & Co., 1975).

29 Arnold L. Haskell, *Balletomane at Large* (Heinemann, 1972).

30 ed. William Chappell, *Well, Dearie! The Letters of Edward Burra* (Gordon Fraser, 1985).

31 Julie Kavanagh, *Secret Muses: The Life of Frederick Ashton* (Faber & Faber, 1996).

32 Annabel Farjeon, 'Choreographers: Dancing for de Valois and Ashton', *Dance Chronicle*, Vol. 17, No. 2,1994.

33 as (20).

34 as (1).

35 Janet Rowson Davis, 'Ballet on British Television', *Dance Chronicle*, Vols 13, No. 2,1990; 15, Nos 1 and 2,1992; 16, No. 2, 1993; 19, No. 1, 1996.

36/37 Patricia Don Young, *Dramatic School* (Peter Davies, 1954).

38 Horace Horsnell, *Observer*, 1 January 1938.

39 James Agate, *The Sunday Times*, 1 January 1938.

40 Horace Horsnell, *Observer*, 10 April 1938.

41 as (20).

42 as (13)

43 Philip Page, *The Daily Mail*, 19 March 1939.

44 The Sitter Out, *The Dancing Times*, May 1939.

45 Richard Buckle, 'Commentary', *Ballet*, September–October 1939.

46 as (20).

47 as (32).

48 as (28).

49 as (1).

50 as (25).

51 Horace Horsnell, *Observer*, 2 February 1940.

52 as (11).

53 *The Bystander*, June 1940.

54 *Observer*, 26 May 1940.

55 as (7).

56 as (10).

57 *The Times*, 28 January 1941.

58 Horace Horsnell, *Observer*, 3 February 1941.

59 *Evening Standard*, 28 January 1941.

60 C.F.D., *Yorkshire Post*, 4 March 1941.

61 C.F.D., *Yorkshire Post*, 6 March 1941.

62 as (20).

63 as (11).

64 Horace Horsnell, *Observer*, 18 January 1942.

65 Dyneley Hussey, *The Spectator*, 23 January 1942.

66 Herbert Farjeon, *Tatler*, 28 January 1942.

67 The Sitter Out, *The Dancing Times*, February 1942.

68 Arthur Franks, *Twentieth Century Ballet* (Burke, 1954).

69 C.W Beaumont, *Leslie Hurry* (Faber & Faber, 1946).

70 Raymond Ingram, *Leslie Hurry: an Exhibition of Theatrical Designs & Illustrations* (London, 1990).

71 *Leslie Hurry, Paintings & Drawings*. Introduction & a poem by Jack Lindsay (Grey Walls Press, 1950).

72 Elspeth Grant, *Daily Sketch*, 20 May 1942.

73 Horace Horsnell, *Observer*, 24 May 1942.

74 Dyneley Hussey, *The Spectator*, 29 May 1942.

75 Herbert Farjeon, *Tatler*, 10 June 1942.

76 A.V. Coton, *Dance Chronicle* (UK, privately printed), May–June 1942.

77 *The Dancing Times*, September 1942: Helpmann, 'The Function of Ballet', speech to the Royal Academy of Dancing, 17 July 1942.

78 *The Dancing Times*, July 1944: Lieut. David James, RNVR, 'A Balletomane in a German Prison'.

79 Helpmann, radio talk, BBC Forces Programme, 18 June 1942, from notes made by the author.

80 Horace Horsnell, *Observer*, 29 November 1942.

81 Elspeth Grant, *Daily Sketch*, 29 November 1942.

82 James Redfern, *The Spectator*, 27 November 1942.

83 The Sitter Out, *The Dancing Times*, January 1943.

84 Edwin Evans, *Time & Tide*, 30 January 1943.

85 *The Times*, 26 January 1943.

86 Edwin Evans, *Time & Tide*, 14 April 1943.

87 *The Times*, 26 May 1943.

88 Arnold L. Haskell, *The National Ballet* (A & C Black, 1947).

89 William Chappell, 'Development of the Ballet', *New Writing & Daylight*, Summer 1943.

90 Leo Kersley, Obituary of Robert Helpmann, *Equity News*, December 1986.

91 *The Times*, 23 December 1943.

92 W.A. Darlington, *The Daily Telegraph*, 12 February 1944.

93 *The Times*, 12 February 1944.

94 Desmond McCarthy, *New Statesman*, 19 February 1944.

95 Horace Horsnell, *Tatler*, 2 March 1944.

96 James Redfern, *The Spectator*, 28 February 1944.

97 *John o'London's Weekly*, 25 February 1944.

98 *News Chronicle*, 19 February 1944.

99 H.R. Jeans, *Manchester Daily Mail*, 31 August 1944.

100 *News of the World*, 9 September 1944.

101 *The Leader*, 21 September 1944.

102 The Sitter Out, *The Dancing Times*, December 1944.

103 Robert Helpmann, 'A Choreographer Speaks', *New Theatre*, March–April 1947.

104 Arnold L. Haskell, *Miracle in the Gorbals* (Albyn Press, 1946).

105 Herbert Farjeon, *Sunday Graphic*, 29 October 1944.

106 *The Times*, 27 October 1944.

107 Edwin Evans, *Time & Tide*, 11 November 1944.

108 W. McNaught, *Manchester Guardian*, 28 October 1944.

109 The Sitter Out, *The Dancing Times*, December 1944.

110 Arthur Franks, *Twentieth Century Ballet* (Burke, 1954).

111 *The Times*, 6 February 1945.

112 *La Dernière Heure* (Brussels), 16 February 1945.
('In the first [*Rake*], Mme Ninette de Valois shows extraordinary gifts of observation, the character of each individual being depicted with impressive truth. In *Hamlet*, which is faithful to the way the tragedy unfolds, Robert Helpmann's fresh ideas, such as the fluid identification in Hamlet's mind between Ophelia and the Queen, demonstrate clearly that this is an expressive art that can depict the most subtle psychological nuances. For all that, it would not be right to conclude that this is a just a matter of dramatic miming. The dance never loses its pre-eminence.')

113 *La Libre Belgique* (Brussels), 26 February 1945. ('a miniature drama whose powerful evocation using purely choreographic means is gripping and poignant')

114 Ninette de Valois, speech to Vic-Wells Association, Morley College, 16 June 1945 (notes made by the author).

115 Compere, 'My Friends the Stars', *Evening News*, 2 June 1945.

116 Helpmann, 'Dance & Drama', *Bandwagon*, July 1945.

117 Mary Clarke, 'London Letter', *Dance (The American Dancer)*, October 1945.

118 as (7).

119 as (103).

120 *The Times*, 11 April 1946.

121 Philip Hope-Wallace, *Time & Tide*, 20 November 1946.

122 The Sitter Out, *The Dancing Times*, May 1946.

123 Janet Leeper, *Our Time*, May 1946.

124 Merlyn Severn, *Double Exposure* (Faber & Faber, 1956).

125 as (103).

126 James Agate, *The Sunday Times*, 25 May 1947.

127 Peter Ustinov, *New Theatre*, May 1947.

128 Clifford Bax, *Theatre Newsletter*, 22 May 1947.

129 Monk Gibbons, *The Red Shoes Ballet* (Saturn Press, 1948).

130 as (129).

131 as (129).

132 as (129).

133 Helpmann, interview in *Autumn Parade 1947*.

134 Harold Hobson, *The Sunday Times*, 18 April 1948.

135 Ivor Brown, *Observer*, 18 April 1948.

136 Alan Dent, *News Chronicle*, 16 April 1948.

137 Philip Hope-Wallace, *Time & Tide*, 24 April 1948.

138 *New Statesman*, 1 May 1948.

139 Alan Dent, *News Chronicle*, 1 May 1948.

140 *The Times*, 26 April 1948.

141 Harold Hobson, *The Sunday Times*, 30 May 1948.

142 Fred Majdalany, *Daily Mail*, 23 July 1948.

143 C.A. Lejeune, *Observer*, 25 July 1948.

144 Dilys Powell, *The Sunday Times*, 25 July 1948.

145 David Vaughan, *Frederick Ashton and his Ballets* (A. & C. Black, 1977).

146 J.H.M., *Manchester Guardian*, 18 December 1948.

147 *The Times*, 24 December 1948.

148 *New Statesman*, 1 January 1949.

149 *The Listener*, 14 April 1949. Helpmann, 'The Ballet Dancer', text of a BBC Forces Educational Programme broadcast 19 June 1948, repeated 1 April 1949 on BBC Radio Home Service.

150 John Martin, *New York Times*, 13 October 1949.

151 John Martin, *New York Times*, 19 October 1949.

152 Walter Terry, *New York Herald Tribune*, 19 October 1949.

153 John Martin, *New York Times*, 26 October 1949.

154 Walter Terry, *New York Herald Tribune*, 26 October 1949.

155 Robert Sylvestor, *New York Daily News*, 26 October 1949.

156 Elisabeth Schwarzkopf, interview, *The Stage*, 3 March 1950.

157 *The Times*, 21 February 1950.

158 Kurt Gânzl, *The British Musical Theatre* (Macmillan 1986).

159 Walter Terry, *New York Herald Tribune*, 29 September 1950.

160 John Martin, *New York Times*, 29 September 1950.

161 Sol Hurok, *Sol Hurok Presents ... The World of Ballet* (Hale, 1955).

162 *Daily Mail*, 21 February 1951.

163 Monk Gibbon, *The Tales of Hoffmann* (Saturn Press, 1951).

164 George A. Romero, interview, *Daily Telegraph*, 31 December 2005.

165 George Rylands, 'Festival Shakespeare in the West End', in Allardyce Nicoll (ed.), *Shakespeare Survey Volume 6: The Histories* (Cambridge University Press, 1953).

166 Brooks Atkinson, *New York Times*, 26 April 1953.

167 W.A. Darlington, *Daily Telegraph*, 11 March 1953.

168 *The Times*, 8 January 1954.

169 Eric Blom, *Observer*, 10 January 1954.

170 *The Stage*, 9 July 1953.

171 Ivor Brown, *Observer*, 18 April 1954.

172 Harold Hobson, *Observer*, 18 April 1954.

173 Helpmann, 'Formula for Midsummer Magic', *Theatre Arts Monthly*, September 1954.

174 *Weekly Scotsman*, 9 September 1954.

175 Felix Aprahamian, *The Sunday Times*, 12 September 1954.

176 Maurice Wiltshire, *Daily Mail*, 2 March 1955.

177 Stephen Williams, *Evening News*, 2 March 1955.

178 T.C. Worsley, *New Statesman*, 11 March 1955.

179 Helpmann, interview with Marjorie Plunkett, *Australian Women's Weekly*, 9 March 1955.

180 *Sydney Morning Herald*, 17 May 1955.

181 *Sydney Morning Herald*, 25 May 1955.

182 Annabel Farjeon, *New Statesman*, 12 May 1956.

183 *The Vic-Wells Association Magazine*, June 1956.

184 *The Times*, 6 March 1957.

185 Anthony Cookman, *The Tatler & Bystander*, 20 March 1957.

186 Elizabeth Franks, *News Chronicle*, 26 November 1957.

187 R.E.L, *The Stage*, 28 November 1957.

188 Andrew Porter, *Financial Times*, 6, 22, 28 March 1958.

189 C.W. Beaumont, *The Sunday Times*, 27 April 1958.

190 Andrew Porter, *Financial Times*, 22 April 1958.

191 Helpmann, 'Surrender to Make Believe', radio talk, Australian Broadcasting Corporation Weekly, 6 August 1958.

192 T.C. Worsley, *Financial Times*, 12 December 1959.

193 Eric Johns, *The Stage*, 7 January 1960.

194 Brooks Atkinson, *New York Times*, 20 April 1960.

195 Vivien Leigh, interview with BBC radio, October 1960.

196 *Dance Gazette (R.A.D.)*, No 115, September 1960.

197 Helpmann, interview with Jeremy Hornsby, *Daily Express*, 4 January 1963.

198 Richard Buckle, *The Sunday Times*, 31 March 1963.

199 Pauline Selby, letter in *Dance & Dancers*, June 1963.

200 Mary Clarke, *The Dancing Times*, January 1964.

201 *Sydney Morning Herald*, 16 March 1964.

202 Harold Tidemann, *Adelaide Advertiser*, 16 March 1964.

203 Frank Harris, *Sydney Mirror*, 31 August 1964.

204 Geoffrey Hutton, *Melbourne Age*, 24 October 1964.

205 Alexander Bland, *Observer*, 5 April 1964.

206 Richard Buckle, *The Sunday Times*, 5 April 1964.

207 Annabel Farjeon, *New Statesman*, April 10 1964.

208 John Hetherington, *Melbourne Age*, 25 April 1964.

209 Harold Hobson, *The Sunday Times*, 23 August 1964.

210 Clive Barnes, *The Spectator*, 11 December 1964.

211 *Sydney Morning Herald*, 11 December 1964.

212 Julian Russell, *Sydney Sun*, 19 February 1965.

213 Oleg Kerensky, *Daily Mail*, 2 October 1965.

214 A.V. Coton, unpublished article, October 1965 (author's collection).

215 Clement Crisp, *The Spectator*, 31 December 1965.

216 Beth Dean, *Sydney Morning Herald*, 18 March 1966.

217 Diana Mann, *Ballet Today*, July/August 1966.

218 Alexander Bland, *Observer*, 7 January 1968.

219 Peter Williams, 'The Royal Ballet at the Royal Opera House, Covent Garden', *Dance & Dancers*, February 1968.

220 F.R. Blanks, *Sydney Morning Herald*, 3 August 1968.

221 Harold Tidemann, *Adelaide Advertiser*, 3 August 1968.

222 Geoffrey Hutton, *Melbourne Age*, 25 October 1968.

223 Kathleen Gorham, interview by Stan Marks, *Walkabout*, December 1967.

224 Sheila Helpmann, interview with Ursula Connor, *Sydney Morning Herald*, 14 October 1971.

225 Sheila Helpmann, interview in Sydney *Time* (TV journal), 21–27 February 1976.

226 John Percival, *The Times*, 15 July 1970.

227 Clement Crisp, *Financial Times*, 17 December 1971.

228 John Percival, *The Times*, 17 December 1971.

229 Frederick Ashton, interview by Lynne Bell, *Sydney Morning Herald*, 16 February 1972.

230 Helpmann, interview in *Sydney Morning Herald*, 7 February 1972.

231 Julian Russell, *Sydney Sun*, 21 March 1972.

232 Brian Hoad, *The Bulletin*, 25 March 1972.

233 Clement Crisp, *Financial Times*, 3 October 1973.

234 Oleg Kerensky, *International Herald Tribune*, 12 October 1973.

235 William Shoubridge, *Adelaide Advertiser*, 22 March 1973.

236 Jill Sykes, *Sydney Morning Herald*, 25 March 1973.

237 John Cargher, *The Australian*, 29 March 1974.

238 Jill Sykes, *Sydney Morning Herald*, 18 June 1975.

239 Jill Sykes, *Sydney Morning Herald*, 18 October 1975.

240 Elizabeth Anderton, interview by Paula Goodyer, *Sydney Sun-Herald*, 27 April 1975.

241 Jill Sykes, *Sydney Morning Herald*, 29 November 1975.

242 John Cargher, *The Australian*, 17 November 1975.

243 Leonard Radic, *Melbourne Age*, 14 November 1975.

244 Neil Jillett, *Melbourne Herald*, 14 November 1975.

245 Clement Crisp, *Financial Times*, 3 May 1977.

246 *Sydney Daily Telegraph*, 28 June 1977.

247 Jill Sykes, *Sydney Morning Herald*, 8 July 1977.

248 Helpmann, interview by Marie Knuckey, *Sydney Morning Herald*, 17 July 1977.

249 as (25).

250 Romola Costantino, *Sydney Morning Herald*, 21 August 1978.

251 Clement Crisp, *Financial Times*, 24 May 1979.

252 John Percival, *The Times*, 4 April 1981.

253 Richard Coleman, *Sydney Morning Herald*, 2 May 1981.

254 Wayne Johnson, *Seattle Sunday Times*, 11 February 1982.

255 Carole Beers, *Seattle Sunday Times*, 28 February 1982.

256 as (158).

257 Patrick Garland, *The Listener*, 22 April 1982.

258 John Barber, *The Daily Telegraph*, 20 May 1982.

259 Irving Wardle, *The Times*, 20 May 1983.

260 Helpmann, interview with Sonia Humphrey, *Weekly Australian*, 2 February 1983.

261 Helpmann, interview with Janise Beaumont, *Sydney Sun-Herald*, 9 October 1983.

262 H.G. Kippax, *Sydney Morning Herald*, 7 October 1983.

263 John Moses, *The Australian*, 8 October 1983.

264 Letter from John McCallum to the author, 2 April 1998.

265 *Mount Gambier Evening Express*, 14 April 1984.

266 Sheila Helpmann, interviewed in *Woman's Day*, 14 January 1985.

267 Donald Dierks, *San Diego Union-Tribune*, 4 February 1985.

268 Jill Sykes, *Sydney Morning Herald*, 9 May 1986.

269 *A Tribute to the Memory of Sir Robert Helpmann, C.B.E.* (The Parliament of the Commonwealth of Australia, Canberra). Extracts from the Journals and Parliamentary Debates of the Senate, No. 130, dated 7 October 1986; extracts from the Votes and Proceedings of the House of Representatives, No. 122, dated 7 October 1986. Printed by the Authority of the Commonwealth Government Printer.

270 *The Australian Ballet News*, November 1986.

271 Ninette de Valois, 'Helpmann: a rare sense of the theatre', *The Daily Telegraph*, 29 September 1986.

272 Michael Somes, obituary in *UPROHR* (newsletter of the Royal Opera House, Covent Garden), Christmas 1986.

273 Joy Newton, conversation with the author, September 1995.

274 as (214).

275 Peter Virgin, *Sydney Smith* (Harper Collins, 1994).

276 Annabel Farjeon, letter, *The Dancing Times*, January 1987.

APPENDICES

Abbreviations used in Appendices

AB – Australian Ballet
arr – arranged
bk – book
c – costumes
cdb – corps de ballet
chor – choreography
cr – created role
des – designs
dir – directed/director
divt – divertissement
HM – Her/His Majesty's
JCW – J.C. Williamson Ltd
ldg – leading
m – music
mat – matinee
OH – Opera House
OV – Old Vic
pdd, pd3, pd6 – *pas de deux, pas de trois, pas de six*
RB – Royal Ballet
ROHCG – Royal Opera House, Covent Garden
sc – scenery
SWB – Sadler's Wells Ballet
SWRB – Sadler's Wells Royal Ballet
SWT – Sadler's Wells Theatre
SWTB – Sadler's Wells Theatre Ballet
Th – Theatre
trad – traditional
VWB – Vic-Wells Ballet

APPENDIX 1– Works choreographed and roles danced

Acis and Galatea (ballet), chor Letty Littlewood, m Handel. Cr *Acis*. Open Air Th, Regent's Park, London, 4 June 1934.

Adam Zero (ballet), chor RH, m Bliss (commissioned), des Roger Furse, bk Michael Benthall. Cr *Adam Zero/The Principal Dancer*. SWB, ROHCG, 10 April 1946 (revised 16 December 1947). Ldg roles: RH, June Brae, David Paltenghi, Gillian Lynne, Alexis Rassine.

Agreement of the Peoples, An (pageant celebrating British–Soviet Alliance), movement arr RH. Empress Hall, London, 20 June 1942.

Apache Dance (in divt as pupil of Nora Stewart), *Pdd.* charity concert, Adelaide. c.1922.

Apparitions (ballet), chor Ashton, m Liszt, des Cecil Beaton. Cr *The Poet*. VWB, SWT, 11 February 1936.

Arabella (opera), chor not known, m R. Strauss. Cr *Ldg Dancer*. CG Opera, ROHCG, 17 May 1934.

Arlecchino (theatrical capriccio), chor Andrée Howard, masque Wilfred Franks, m and words Busoni. Cr *Arlecchino* (acted and danced). BBC-TV, 12 February 1939.

As You Like It (play by Shakespeare), chor Letty Littlewood, m not known. Cr *Pdd*. Open Air Th, Regent's Park, London, 31 July 1934.

Baiser de la fée, Le (ballet), chor Ashton, m Stravinsky, des Sophie Fedorovitch. Cr *A Villager*. VWB, SWT, 26 November 1935.

Barabau (ballet), chor de Valois, m Rieti, des Edward Burra. *Barabau*. VWB, SWT, 22 August 1940 (revival in revised version).

Battle of the Flowers, The (chor Vera van Rij?) *Pdd.* Vera van Rij Dance Recital, Australia Hotel, Adelaide, 5 September 1932.

Birds, The (ballet), chor RH, m Respighi, des Chiang Yee. SWB, New Th, London, 24 November 1942. Ldg roles: Moyra Fraser, Beryl Grey, Alexis Rassine, Gordon Hamilton.

Blue Danube Waltz (divt), chor Alicia Markova, m J. Strauss. Cr *Pdd*. VWB, ROHCG, 13 February 1934 (Vic-Wells Dance).

Business à la Russe (ballet), chor RH., m/des unknown, bk Gabriel Toyne. Cr *The Young Man*. Rawlings/Toyne Drama Company, Criterion Th, Sydney, April 1932.

Carnaval (ballet), chor Fokine, m Schumann, des Elizabeth & Marsh Williams. *Valse Noble*, VWB, SWT, 24 October 1933 (1st night VWB revival); *Florestan*, VWB, OV, 6 November 1933; *Harlequin*, VWB, SWT, 9 October 1934; des after Bakst; *Pierrot*, VWB OV, 7 January 1935; *Eusebius*, VWB, SWT, 10 January 1936, BBC-TV, 11 October 1937.

Casse-Noisette (The Nutcracker) (ballet), chor Lev Ivanov, m Tchaikovsky, des Hedley Briggs. *An Incroyable/Danse Chinoise*, VWB, SWT, 30 January 1934 (1st night VWB revival); BBC-TV, 28 March 1934 *Danse Chinoise*, (transmission also included Helpmann in *Coda to the Sugar Plum Fairy*); *The President/The Nutcracker Prince*, VWB, SWT, 30 October 1934; *Danse Espagnole pdd*, VWB, SWT, 2 October 1936 (new des Mstislav Doboujinsky) BBC-TV, 11 March 1937.

Cenerentola, La (opera), chor de Valois, m Rossini. Cr *Pdd*. CG Opera, ROHCG, 14 June 1934.

Checkmate (ballet), chor de Valois, m Bliss, des E. McKnight Kauffer. Cr *The Red King,* VWB, Th des Champs-Elysées (as *Echec et mat)*, Paris, 15 June 1937; BBC-TV, 8 May 1938; BBC1 TV prod Margaret Dale, 31 July 1963 (*The White King*); RB revival ROHCG; 14 December 1971, SWRB, Pavilion, Bournemouth, 21 April 1977; AB, Sydney OH, 6 May 1986 (final stage appearance 24 May 1986).

Chopin 'Obertas' (divt), chor Vera van Rij, m Chopin. Cr *Pdd.* Vera van Rij Dance Recital, Australia Hotel, Adelaide, 5 September 1932.

Chopin Prelude in A Flat Major (divt), chor Ashton, m Chopin. Cr *Pdd.* Liverpool Ballet Club (guest artist), Crane Th, Liverpool, 21 April 1939.

Chopin Waltz (divt). Not identified; possibly the one from *Les Sylphides.* Chor not known, m Chopin. *Pdd.* Gala, Cambridge Th, London, 9 June1938.

Cinderella (ballet), chor Ashton, m Prokofiev, des Jean-Denis Maclès. Cr *A Stepsister.* SWB, ROHCG, 23 December 1948; BBC-TV 29 December 1969; AB, Elizabethan Th, Sydney, 17 March 1972; PACT Ballet, Johannesburg (guest artist), September 1972.

Comus (ballet), chor RH, m Purcell, des Oliver Messel. Cr *Comus.* SWB, New Th, London, 14 January 1942. Ldg roles: RH, Margot Fonteyn, Margaret Dale, John Hart, John Field, Moyra Fraser. With speeches. Speeches were omitted for a short period from 28 August 1943.

Coppélia (ballet), chor Petipa/Cecchetti, m Delibes, des Edwin Callaghan. *A Village Dancer,* VWB, SWT, 21 March 1933 (1st night VWB revival, two-act version, and Helpmann's 1st appearance with VWB); *Ldg Village Dancer,* VWB, SWT, 15 October 1935; *Franz,* VWB, SWT, 6 December 1935, SWB, SWT, 15 April 1940 (1st night SWB revival, three-act version inc ldg czardas, des William Chappell); *Dr Coppelius,* SWB, New Th, London, 30 September mat 1941; BBC-TV prod Margaret Dale, 27 October 1957; RB Touring Company, Empire Th, Sydney, 1 November 1958; AB, HM Th, Sydney, 25 July 1969; ABC (Australian Broadcasting Commission) TV, 1969; SWRB, Pavilion, Bournemouth, (guest artist), 20 April 1977.

Création du monde, La (ballet), chor de Valois, m Milhaud, des Edward Wolfe. *A God.* VWB, OV, 30 October 1933.

Danse, La/Valse, La (ballet), chor RH with Wendy Toye, m Ravel, des unknown. Royal Academy of Dancing Production Club, Rudolf Steiner Hall, London, 19 March 1939; Ballet de la Jeunesse Anglaise, Cambridge Th, London, 9 May 1939. RAD programme, Westminster Th, 18 July 1939. Ldg roles: Sadie Jacobs (Sara Luzita), Travis Kemp.

Dante Sonata (ballet), chor Ashton, m Liszt, des Sophie Fedorovitch. Cr *Ldg Child of Darkness.* VWB, SWT, 23 January 1940.

Display, The (ballet), chor RH, m Malcolm Williamson (commissioned), des Sidney Nolan. AB, HM Th, Adelaide, 14 March 1964; Australian TV, Channel 7's Sing Sing Sing, 18 September 1964; TC N9-TV, Australia, 4 July 1965. Ldg roles: Kathleen Gorham, Garth Welch, Bryan Lawrence, Barry Kitcher.

Don Juan (ballet), chor Ashton, m R. Strauss, des Edward Burra. Cr *Don Juan.* SWB, ROHCG, 25 November 1948.

Don Quixote (ballet), chor Petipa/Laurent Novikov, m Minkus. cdb. Pavlova Ballet, HM Th, Melbourne, 5 April 1926.

Don Quixote (ballet), chor de Valois. m Roberto Gerhard, des Edward Burra. Cr *Don Quixote*. SWB, ROHCG, 20 February 1950.

Don Quixote (ballet), chor Petipa/Rudolf Nureyev, m Minkus. des Barry Kay. *Don Quixote*. AB, HM Th, Adelaide, 28 March 1970; Nouveau Ballet (guest artist), Marseilles OH, 15 November 1971; TCN9-TV, Australia, 1 August 1970; Filmed, premiere Sydney OH concert hall, 19 July 1973.

Douanes (ballet), chor de Valois, m Geoffrey Toye, des Hedley Briggs. *A Gendarme*, VWB, SWT, 3 October 1933; *Cook's Man*, VWB, SWT, 29 October 1935 (1st night revised version, des Sophie Fedorovitch).

During the Ball (ballet), chor Nini Theilade, m R. Strauss, des unknown. Cr *The Charming Man*. Open Air Th, Regent's Park, London, 4 June 1934.

Elektra (ballet), chor RH, m Malcolm Arnold (commissioned), des Arthur Boyd. RB, ROHCG, 26 March 1963, ldg roles: Nadia Nerina, David Blair, Monica Mason, Derek Rencher; AB, HM Th, Adelaide, 15 March 1966, ldg roles: Kathleen Gorham, Bryan Lawrence, Janet Karin, Warren de Maria.

Emperor's New Clothes, The (ballet). See *Roi nu, Le*.

Façade (ballet), chor Ashton, m Walton, des John Armstrong. *Scotch Rhapsody*/cr *Country Dance, The Squire*. VWB, SWT, 8 October 1935 (1st night VWB revival); *The Squire*, BBC-TV, 8 December 1936; *Yodelling Song/A Mountaineer* and *Tango/ The Dago*, VWB, Arts Th, Cambridge, 3 June 1939; cr *Foxtrot*, VWB, SWT (revised version, new Armstrong designs), 23 July 1940; *Nocturne Peruvienne /Tango*, New Th, London, 4 August 1941; *Nocturne Peruvienne/Tango*, RB Touring Company, Empire Th, Sydney, 27 October 1958, AB, Princess Th, Melbourne, 8 September 1972; *Tango* Gala Matinee, Drury Lane Th, London, 6 December 1962, Stars of World Ballet, Regent Th, Sydney, 2 July 1979, RB A Tribute to Margot Fonteyn, ROHCG, 23 May 1979. Spoke poems to music of *Façade*, Festival Chamber Group, Union Hall, Adelaide, 13 March 1964 (no choreography).

Fairy Queen, The (masque), chor Ashton, m Purcell, des Michael Ayrton. *Spirits of the Air Pdd* danced as divt in a gala programme, Ny Norsk Ballet (guest artist), Det Nye Teater, Oslo, 30 January 1950. (See also Appendix 2)

Fantasticks, The (play), chor de Valois, m unknown. Cr *A Person of the Ballet (Pd6)*. Lyric Th, Hammersmith, 21 June 1933; Open Air Theatre, Regent's Park, 19 July 1933.

Faust (opera), chor de Valois, m Gounod, des unknown. *Pdd*. VW Opera, SWT, 5 October 1934.

Fête Polonaise (ballet), chor de Valois, m Glinka, des Owen P Smyth. *Mazurka*, VWB, SWT, 10 October 1933; *Adage and Variation*, VWB, SWT, 2 October 1934 (des Edmund Dulac).

Fine and Dandy (revue), chor RH 'Winterhalter Waltz', m Tchaikovsky, c William Chappell. Saville Th, London, 30 April 1942.

Fledermaus, Die (opera), chor ?de Valois, m J. Strauss. *Pdd*, VW Opera, SWT, 31 January 1935; chor Ashton, cr *Pdd*, VW Opera, SWT, 28 October 1936.

Fonteyn Groups (often with Nureyev): dir RH; Athens Festival and 'Sunshine Tour', 9 August 1963 continuing to Nice, Cannes, Tel Aviv, Haifa, Jerusalem, Tokyo, Osaka, Nagoya, Kyoto, finishing Honolulu (RH with them at Athens and then on from Tel Aviv); Royal Academy of Dancing Gala, Th Royal Drury Lane, London, 5 December 1963; Stars of World Ballet tour, Regent Th, Sydney, 27 June 1978 and 2 July 1979.

Fool on the Hill, The (ballet), chor Gillian Lynne, m The Beatles, des Tim Goodchild. Cr *Sergeant Pepper*. AB, made for ABC-TV, 21 May 1976.

Footlights Revues: These, called May Week Revues, were presented by the Footlights Dramatic Club at the Arts Th, Cambridge, annually from 1936 to 1939. Helpmann choreographed dances and ensembles: *Turn Over a New Leaf,* dir George Rylands, 8 June 1936, included a cabaret scene featuring a samba danced by Tito and Harmodio de Arias; *Full Swing,* dir Donald Beves, 8 June 1937, included a spoof version of *Les Sylphides* danced by men students; *Pure and Simple,* dir George Rylands, 8 June 1938; *The All-Male Revue,* dir Donald Beves, 6 June 1939.

Frasquita (operetta), dances and ensembles invented and arr Minnie Everett, m Lehar, des unknown. Cr *Specialty Dancer/El Tango* (Act I), JCW, Grand OH, Wellington, New Zealand, 27 December 1926. JCW, HM Th (later Th Royal), Sydney, 16 April 1927.

Fun and Games (revue), chor RH 'The Old Shoemaker', m Manning Sherwin, des unknown, bk Richard Hearne. Saville Th, London, 21 August 1941. Revived in *The Shephard Show* (revue), Princes Th, London, 26 September 1946; *Music for You,* BBC-TV, 21 October 1953.

Giselle (ballet), chor Coralli/Perrot, m Adam, des Barbara Allen. *Hilarion*, VWB, OV 1 January 1934 (1st night VWB revival); *Albrecht*, VWB, SWT, mat 6 October 1934; Liverpool Ballet Club (guest artist), Crane Th, Liverpool, 15 December 1938 (des from 1935 W. Chappell).

Gods Go a-Begging, The (ballet), chor de Valois, m Handel, des Hugh Stevenson. Cr *Ldg Nobleman*. VWB, SWT, 10 January 1936; BBC-TV, 8 June 1938.

Golden City (musical), co-dir with Benthall/chor RH, a music-hall divt, a 'coons' carnival, a saloon fight, a Zulu war dance, m John Tore, des Audrey Cruddas. Adelphi Th, London, 15 June 1950.

Good News (vaudeville cabaret). *Specialty Dancer*. Palais Royal, Adelaide, summer season 1928.

Hamlet (ballet), chor RH, m Tchaikovsky (Fantasy Overture), des Leslie Hurry. Cr *Hamlet*, SWB, New Th, London, 19 May 1942, Ldg roles: RH, Fonteyn, Celia Franca, David Paltenghi; RB Touring Company, Empire Th, Sydney, 4 November 1958; AB, HM Th, Adelaide, 24 March 1970, Ldg roles: Rudolf Nureyev, Josephine Jason, Carolyn Rappel.

Haunted Ballroom, The (ballet), chor de Valois, m Geoffrey Toye, des Motley. Cr *The Master of Treginnis*. VWB, SWT, 3 April 1934.

Hommage aux belles viennoises (ballet), chor de Valois, m Schubert, des Owen P. Smyth. Pdd. Liverpool Ballet Club (guest artist), Crane Th, Liverpool, 13 May 1938.

Hussar, The (solo divt), chor Ceslaw Konarski *(The Polish Hussar)*, m trad. Fonteyn–Helpmann Concert Group, Assembly Hall, Tunbridge Wells, 2 June 1950.

Ile des sirènes, L' (ballet), chor Alfred Rodrigues, m Debussy, des Loudon Sainthill. Cr *The Mariner*. Fonteyn–Helpmann Concert Group, Assembly Hall, Tunbridge Wells, 2 June 1950.

Jar, The (ballet), chor de Valois, m Casella, des William Chappell. Cr *Don Lollo Zirafa*. VWB, SWT, 9 October 1934.

Job (masque for dancing), chor de Valois, m Vaughan Williams, des Gwen Raverat. *A Son /War, Pestilence and Famine*, VWB, SWT, 18 April 1933; *Satan*, VWB, SWT, 26 September 1933 (1st ldg role with VWB); excerpts, BBC-TV, 11 November1936.

Judgment of Paris, The (ballet), chor Ashton, m Lennox Berkeley, des William Chappell. Cr *Paris*. VWB, SWT, 10 May 1938.

Katinka (operetta), ballets and ensembles arr Hazel Meldrum, m Friml. Cr *Russian Dance* (Act I), *Cabaret Pdd* (Act III). JCW, Th Royal, Melbourne, 17 May 1930; ballets and dances arr Ada Barber, same roles, JCW, Th Royal, Adelaide, 3 October 1930.

Katja the Dancer (musical), chor Minnie Everett/Minnie Hooper, m J. Gilbert. Cr *Dancer*. Th Royal, Melbourne, 1928.

Lac des cygnes, Le (Swan Lake) (ballet), chor Petipa/Ivanov, m Tchaikovsky, des Hugh Stevenson. *Prince Siegfried*. VWB, SWT, 20 November 1934 (1st night VWB revival, 4-act version); Act II only, BBC-TV, 13 December 1937. See also *Swan Lake*.

Little Serenade, A (ballet), chor M. Martin-Harvey, m Mozart. Cr *The Student*. Open Air Th, Regent's Park, London, 9 July 1934.

Lord of Burleigh, The (ballet), chor Ashton, m Mendelssohn, des George Sheringham. *The Lord of Burleigh*. VWB, SWT, 6 November 1933.

Love's Labour's Lost (play by Shakespeare), arr dances RH. OV Drama Company, OV, 11 October 1949.

Masques, Les (ballet), chor Ashton, m Poulenc, des Sophie Fedorovitch. *A Personage*. Ballet Rambert, Mercury Th, London, 13 November 1938.

Merry Widow, The (operetta), ballets and ensembles arr Minnie Everett, m Lehar. Cr Ldg dancer, *Butterflies* (Act III). JCW, Th Royal, Melbourne, 26 April 1930.

Merry Widow, The (operetta), (1) chor RH, m Lehar, des William Chappell. HM Th, London, 4 March 1943. (2) co-dir RH with Christopher Brown, chor RH with John Hart, m Lehar, des Carl Toms. San Diego Opera, Civic Theater, San Diego, 3 February 1985. (see also Appendix 2)

Merry Widow, The (ballet), scenario/production RH, chor Ronald Hynd, m Lehar, des Desmond Heeley. AB, Palais Th, Melbourne, 13 November 1975, Ldg roles: Marilyn Rowe, John Meehan, Lucette Aldous, Kelvin Coe; National Ballet of Canada, O'Keefe Centre, Toronto, 8 November 1986, Ldg roles: Karen Kain, John Meehan, Yoko Ichino, Kevin Pugh; CBC-TV, 27 December 1987.

Midsummer Night's Dream, A (play by Shakespeare), chor and m unknown. *child extra*, Allan Wilkie Shakespeare Company, Adelaide, 1917.

Midsummer Night's Dream, A (play by Shakespeare), chor RH (except Nocturne, chor Ashton), m Mendelssohn, des Robin and Christopher Ironside. Cr *Nocturne Pdd* (as Oberon), also danced in ensembles. OV Drama Company, Empire Th, Edinburgh, 31 August 1954. (see also Appendix 2)

Miracle in the Gorbals (ballet), chor RH, m Bliss (commissioned), des Edward Burra. Cr *The Stranger*. SWB, Princes Th, London, 26 October 1944. Ldg roles: RH, Pauline Clayden, Celia Franca, David Paltenghi.

Music for Ballet (ballet), chor de Valois, m Bliss. Cr *Pdd.* SWB Gala, Cambridge Th, London, 4 May 1936.

Neapolitana (ballet), chor Letty Littlewood, m Mendelssohn. Cr *Luigi.* Open Air Th, Regent's Park, London, 9 July 1934.

New Moon, The (operetta), chor Minnie Everett/Minnie Hooper, m Romberg. Cr Dancer JCW, HM Th, Sydney, 4 January 1930.

Nocturne (ballet), chor Ashton, m Delius, des Sophie Fedorovitch. Cr *A Young Man.* VWB, SWT, 10 November 1936; BBC-TV, 8 June 1938.

Nursery Suite (ballet), chor de Valois, m Elgar, des William Chappell. *Georgie-Porgie.* VWB, OV, 26 December 1933.

Nutcracker, The. See *Casse-Noisette.*

Olympians, The (opera), chor Pauline Grant, m Bliss. Cr *Mercury.* CG Opera, ROHCG, 29 September 1949.

Orpheus (opera), chor de Valois, m Gluck. Cr *A Fury.* VW Opera, SWT, 29 November 1933.

Orpheus and Eurydice (ballet), chor de Valois, m Gluck, des Sophie Fedorovitch. Cr *Orpheus.* SWB, New Th, London, 28 May 1941.

Pagliacci, I (opera, Prologue only, sung by Percy Heming). chor unknown, m Leoncavallo. Cr *Pierrot, Pdd.* Gala mat, London Coliseum, 27 March 1939; BBC-TV, 9 April 1939.

Partie Carré (ballet), chor Marjorie Stewart, m H. Mayer. Cr *A Bather.* Open Air Th, Regent's Park, London, 30 July 1934.

Party 1860 (ballet), chor trad, m trad. Cr *The Host.* Open Air Th, Regent's Park, London, 4 June 1934.

Pas de deux (divt). chor Ashton., m unknown. Cr *Tango Exhibition Dance Pdd .* Silver Rose Ball (charity), London, 18 December 1935. (Repeated Vic-Wells Coronation Ball, R. Albert Hall, 15 March 1937)

Patineurs, Les (ballet), chor Ashton, m Meyerbeer, des William Chappell. Cr *Pdd.* VWB, SWT, 16 February 1937; BBC-TV, 3 May 1937; *Variation and pd3* VWB, SWT, 3 April 1940.

Peer Gynt (play by Ibsen), movement and groupings arr RH, m Grieg, des Reece Pemberton. OV Drama Company, New Th, London, 31 August 1944.

Perisynthyon (ballet), chor RH, m Sibelius (*Symphony No. 1 in E minor*), des Kenneth Rowell. AB, HM Th, Adelaide, 21 March 1974. Ldg roles: John Meehan, Gail Ferguson, Francis Croese.

Perpetuum Mobile (divt), chor Ashton, m J. Strauss. Cr *Pdd.* VWB (Gala Variety Show), SWT, 11 January 1937.

Petrushka (ballet), chor Fokine, m Stravinsky, des Alexandre Benois. *Petrushka.* RB, ROHCG, 21 April 1958.

Pomona (ballet), chor Ashton, m Lambert, des John Banting. *Vertumnus.* VWB, SWT, 17 October 1933; Arts Th, Cambridge (revival), 28 September 1937.

Precipice (play with music by Frances Gregory), dir Gabriel Toyne. *Duval, a member of the Hohlakov Ballet* (acted and danced in ballet, *La Mort*). Savoy Th, London, 5 June 1934.

Promenade (ballet), chor de Valois, m Haydn, des Hugh Stevenson. *The Lepidopterist.* SWB, Th Marigny, Paris, possibly 21 February 1945.

Prometheus (ballet), chor de Valois, m Beethoven, des John Banting. Cr *Prometheus.* VWB, SWT, 13 October 1936; *The Friend* VWB, SWT, 10 November 1936.

Prospect Before Us, The (ballet), chor de Valois, m Boyce, des Roger Furse. Cr *Mr O'Reilly.* SWB, SWT, 4 July 1940; SWTB (guest artist), SWT, 13 February 1951.

Psyche (ballet), chor Nini Theilade, m Franck. Cr *Eros.* Open Air Th, Regent's Park, London, 30 July 1934.

Queen High (musical), dances and ensembles arr Elsie Stevenson, m L. Gensler. Cr *Dancer.* JCW, Th Royal, Melbourne, 24 December 1927.

Quest, The (ballet), chor Ashton, m Walton, des John Piper. Cr *St George.* SWB, New Th, London, 6 April 1943.

Rake's Progress, The (ballet), chor de Valois, m Gavin Gordon, des Rex Whistler. *The Rake.* VWB, SWT, 27 September 1935; RB Touring Company, Empire Th, Sydney, 27 October 1958; BBC-TV, 8 April 1939.

Red Shoes, The (film), chor RH, *The Red Shoes Ballet* (Massine's role choreographed by himself) and short section of *Hearts of Fire* ballet, m Easdale (commissioned), des Hein Heckroth. Cr *Ldg dancer.* 22 July 1948. Ldg roles: RH, Shearer, Massine. Also acted role of Ivan Boleslawsky.

Rendezvous, Les (ballet), chor Ashton, m Auber, des William Chappell. Cr *Pd3/Pd6*, VWB, SWT, 5 December 1933; *Variation and Andante*, VWB, OV, 31 December 1934.

Roi nu, Le (The Emperor's New Clothes) (ballet), chor de Valois, m Françaix, des Hedley Briggs. Cr *The Emperor.* VWB, SWT, 7 April 1938.

Rondino (solo) chor RH, for Leonie Leahy, Elizabethan Th, Sydney, 29 September 1964.

Rose Marie (operetta), chor Minnie Everett/Minnie Hooper, m Friml/Stothart. Cr *Dancer.* JCW, Australia, 1930.

Russian Dance (divt). chor trad, m trad. *Solo.* Vera van Rij Dance Recital, Australia Hotel, Adelaide, 5 September 1932.

Schwanda [the Bagpiper] (opera), chor Margareta Wallmann, m Weinberger. Cr *Ldg dancer in Court Scene polka* and *Furiant in Act III.* CG Opera, ROHCG, 11 May 1934.

Seascape (ENSA show), chor RH, m 'What Shall We Do with a Drunken Sailor?' (song) (men's hornpipe *Pd6*). Royal Albert Hall, London, 12 September 1943.

Siesta (divt), chor Ashton, m Walton. Cr *Pdd.* VWB, SWT, 24 January 1936.

Sinbad the Sailor (pantomime), chor based on Fred Leslie, The Spider's Web in Act II, m Alma Palmer. *The Spider.* The Rose Ballet in Act II: *Solo Dancer*, JCW, HMTh, Melbourne, 23 December 1931.

Sirènes, Les (ballet), chor Ashton, m Berners, des Cecil Beaton. Cr *Adelino Canberra.* SWB, ROHCG, 12 November 1946.

Sleeping Beauty, The (ballet), chor Petipa, m Tchaikovsky, RH dir Act III only (earlier acts dir Nijinska), des Raymondo de Lorraino. De Cuevas Ballet, Th des Champs-Elysées, Paris, 25 October 1960; dir. Rome Opera Ballet, Rome OH, November 1965; AB, dir in collaboration with Peggy van Praagh, des Kenneth Rowell, Sydney OH, 9 December 1973; AB, dir Sydney OH, 26 March 1976; American Ballet Theatre, Kennedy Center OH, Washington DC, 16 December 1976; dir prod staged by Skeaping after Petipa/Sergeyev, des Oliver Messel, danced *Carabosse* (guest artist).

Sleeping Princess (Beauty), The (ballet), chor Petipa, m Tchaikovsky. *Pdd* (unidentified) at 15th Annual Fancy Dress Dance, ROHCG, 5 March 1935; *Aurora Pdd*, VWB Costume Dance, ROHCG, 24 February 1936; *Bluebird Pdd*, Charity gala, London, 1936; Ballet in entirety, *Prince Charming*, VWB, SWT, 2 February 1939; *Fourth Suitor/Prince Charming*, VWB, SWT, 9 January 1940; *Carabosse/P Charming*, SWB, New Th, London, 6 October 1941; *Prince Florimund* (formerly *Prince Charming*) /*Carabosse*, SWB, ROHCG, 20 February 1946; *Prince Florimund/Carabosse*, La Scala, Milan (guest artist in production by Margherita Wallmann), 24 April 1950; Acts I and III, BBC-TV, 25 March 1939, and Act III, 22 May 1939.

Snow Maiden, The (opera), chor de Valois, m Rimsky-Korsakov. *A Tumbler*. VW Opera, SWT, 5 October 1933.

*Soldier's Tale, The (*L'Histoire du Soldat*)* (theatre piece), dir G. Rennert, chor RH, m Stravinsky. Cr *The Devil* (acting and dancing). Glyndebourne Opera Company, King's Th, Edinburgh, 6 September 1954, Ldg roles: RH, Shearer; filmed by Ipsilon Films, dir. Lord Birkett, press show 12 October 1964, Ldg roles: RH, Svetlana Beriosova; Australian Elizabethan Th Trust gala, dir RH Elizabethan Th, Sydney, 29 September 1964, Ldg roles: RH, Kathleen Gorham. (see also Appendix 2)

Song of Norway (operetta), dir/chor RH, 'The Concerto Ballet', m Grieg, des for ballet Sophie Fedorovitch. Palace Th, London, 7 March 1946.

Spectre de la rose, Le (ballet), chor Fokine, m Weber. *The Spirit of the Rose*, VWB, OV, 15 January 1934; Open Air Th, Regent's Park, London, 4 June 1934.

Stars of World Ballet, dir RH, see Fonteyn Groups.

Steps of the Ballet/Birth of a Ballet (film, see Appendix 2).

Steps, Notes and Squeaks (Maina Gielgud), rehearsal excerpts, OV Th, 3 June 1980.

Stop Press (revue), chor Charles Weidman for 'Lonely Heart Column' and 'Revolt in Cuba', Albertina Rasch for 'The Beggar's Dream', m various. *Ldg Dancer* in 'Lonely Heart Column', 'The Beggar's Dream', 'Revolt in Cuba', 'Echo of Former Romance'. Adelphi Th, London, 21 February 1935.

Sun Music (ballet), chor RH, m Peter Sculthorpe, des Kenneth Rowell. AB, HM Th, Sydney, 2 August 1968. Ldg roles: Josephine Jason, Karl Welander, Kelvin Coe.

Swan Lake (ballet), dir RH (additional chor by Ashton), m Tchaikovsky, des Carl Toms. RB, ROHCG, 12 December 1963. See also *Lac des cygnes, Le*.

Sylphides, Les (ballet), chor Fokine, m Chopin. *Ldg Dancer, solo and pdd*. VWB, OV, 19 March 1934.

Sylvia (divt, as pupil of Nora Stewart), chor trad, m Delibes. *Pizzicato solo (en travestie)*. Charity concert, Exhibition Hall, Adelaide, 1920.

Tales of Hoffmann, The (opera film), chor Ashton, m Offenbach. *Dapertutto solo* (also mimed roles of *Dr Coppelius, Dapertutto, Lindorf, Dr Miracle*). Shown at Metropolitan OH, New York, 1 April 1951. London premiere, Carlton Th, 18 April 1951.

Tchaikovsky Pas de Deux (divt). Not identified, possibly *Casse-Noisette* or *Aurora pdd*. Phyllis Bedells Farewell Matinee, London Hippodrome, 8 November 1935.

Terrible Triplets, The (revue number in Sid Field Show), chor RH for Laurence Olivier, Vivien Leigh and Danny Kaye. London Palladium, 26 June 1951.

This Year of Grace (revue), dances arr Kathinka Starace, bk/m Noel Coward. *A Male Passenger* in 'A London Tube Station'; *A Young Gentleman* in 'Teach me to dance like Grandma'; *Baroness Kurdle* in 'The Lido Beach (Italy)'; *Waiter* in 'Love, Life and Laughter'; *A Dancer* in 'Dance, Little Lady'; *The Patient* in 'The Ministering Angel' (written by Ronald Jeans). JCW, Th Royal, Melbourne, 30 March 1929. Also *Another Boy* in sketch based on 'Young Woodley' (Theatre Guide section), JCW, Th Royal, Sydney, 25 May 1929.

Tip Toes (musical), ballets and ensembles arr Minnie Hooper, m Gershwin. *A Dancer*. JCW, Newcastle, NSW, 4 May 1927. HM Th, Sydney, 7 June 1927.

Tribute to Ashton (see Appendix 2).

Tsar Saltan (opera), chor de Valois, m Rimsky-Korsakov. Cr *A Dancer in Guidon's Court/A Clown in the Island of Bujan*. V W Opera, SWT, 11 October 1933.

Two Gentlemen of Verona, The (play by Shakespeare), arr dances RH, m Cedric Thorpe Davis, des Tanya Moiseiwitsch. OV Drama Company, OV, 22 January 1957. (see also Appendix 2)

Ugly Duckling, The (musical, perf as pupil), chor and m not known. *The Ugly Duckling*. Th Royal, Adelaide, 5 Oct 1922.

Walpurgis Night (ballet), chor Ivan Clustine. m Gounod.. *A Dancer*. Pavlova Ballet, HM Th, Melbourne, March–April 1926.

Wanderer, The (ballet), chor Ashton, m Schubert, des Graham Sutherland. Cr *The Wanderer*. SWB, New Th, London, 27 January 1941.

Wedding Bouquet, A (ballet), chor Ashton, m & des Berners. Cr *The Bridegroom*. VWB, SWT, 27 April 1937; BBC-TV, 25 April 1938; *The Narrator*, RB, ROHCG, 25 November 1964.

Wild Rose (musical adapted from Jerome Kern's *Sally*), chor RH 'Flor Fina Ballet', m Victor Herbert, des Frederick Dawson. Princes Th, London, 6 August 1942.

Winter's Tale, The (play by Shakespeare), dance arr RH. Shakespeare Memorial Th, Stratford-upon-Avon, 5 June 1948.

Wise and Foolish Virgins, The (The Foolish Virgins) (ballet), chor de Valois, m Kurt Atterberg, des William Chappell. *A Musician*, VWB, SWT, 10 October 1933; *The Bridegroom*, VWB, SWT, 28 November 1933.

Wise Virgins, The (ballet), chor Ashton, m J.S. Bach, des Rex Whistler. *The Father*, SWB, OH Manchester, 20 November 1940; *The Bridegroom*, SWB, New Th, London, 26 July 1941.

Yugen (ballet), chor RH, m Yuzo Toyama (commissioned), des Desmond Heeley. bk adapted from play *Hagoromo*. AB, HM Th, Adelaide, 18 February 1965. TCN9-TV, Australia, 4 July 1965. Ldg roles: Kathleen Gorham, Garth Welch.

Projects: *Corroboree* (m John Antill, des William Constable), SWB, 1947/48. *The Picture of Dorian Gray* (m Clifton Parker [commissioned], des Sophie Fedorovitch), SWB, 1943. *Inez de Castro*, SWB, 1946.

APPENDIX 2 – Roles as an actor on stage, film or TV; and work as a stage director apart from choreography

After the Ball (operetta by Noel Coward), dir/chor RH, des Doris Zinkeisen. Royal Court Th Liverpool, 1 March 1954, Globe Th, London, 10 June 1954.

Aladdin (pantomime), m Cole Porter, dir/chor RH, des Loudon Sainthill. London Coliseum, 17 December 1959.

Alcina (opera by Handel), dir/chor RH, des John Truscott. Australian Opera, Sydney, 26 June 1981.

Alice's Adventures in Wonderland (film), dir William Sterling. *The Mad Hatter.* Premiere, 5 December 1972.

Antony and Cleopatra (play by Shakespeare), dir Michael Benthall. *Octavius Caesar.* Olivier Company, Manchester Opera House, 1 May 1951; St James's Th, London, 11 May 1951; Ziegfeld Th, New York, 20 December 1951; dir RH, m Gordon Jacob, des Loudon Sainthill, OV Drama Company, OV, 5 March 1957. Pompey scenes cut.

Arlecchino (theatrical capriccio by Busoni). *Arlecchino.* See Appendix 1.

As You Like It (play by Shakespeare), dir RH, m Gordon Jacob, des Domenico Gnoli. OV Drama Company, OV, 1 March 1955.

Barretts of Wimpole Street, The (play by Rudolf Besier), dir Gabriel Toyne. *Septimus.* Criterion Th, Sydney, 23 April 1932.

Big Money, The (film), dir John Paddy Carstairs. *The Bogus Clergyman.* Premiere, 30 May 1958 (made in 1956).

Box for One (play by Peter Brook), dir Tony Richardson. *The Caller.* BBC-TV, 18 February 1953; dir William Sterling, ABV2 Melbourne TV, 17 August 1958.

BBC broadcast & television talks included: *The Choreographer at Work,* 28 March 1948; *The Production of Hamlet,* 31 March 1948; *The Musician's World (The Ballet Dancer),* 19 June 1948; Poetry Reading, own selection, BBC radio, 27 February 1949; *Desert Island Discs* (Roy Plomley), 19 June 1953; *The Robert Helpmann Story,* BBC Home Service, 17 October 1960; *An Evening with Robert Helpmann,* BBC TV 26 May 1963; *The Story of Ninette de Valois* (told in six parts by RH), prod Peggy Bacon: 9 February 1964, 16 February, 23 February, 1 March, 8 March, 15 March; *Helpmann,* BBC1 TV Omnibus, 30 September 1973; *Desert Island Discs,* BBC radio, 23 December 1978; Parkinson interviews, ABN 2 Sydney TV, 25 April 1979 and 28 July 1980.

Caesar and Cleopatra (play by Shaw), dir Michael Benthall. *Apollodorus.* Olivier Company, Manchester OH, 24 April 1951; St James's Th, London, 10 May 1951; Ziegfeld Th, New York, 19 December 1951.

Caligula (play by Jean-Paul Sartre), dir Noel Iliff. *Caligula.* BBC radio, 5 April 1949.

Camelot (musical by Lerner–Loewe), dir RH, des John Truscott. Th Royal, Drury Lane, 19 August 1964.

Caravan (film, Gainsborough Films), dir Arthur Crabtree. *Wycroft.* Premiere 12 April 1946.

Catch as Catch Can (play by Jean Anouilh), dir David Benedictus. *Fouché.* BBC TV, 30 September 1964.

Chitty Chitty Bang Bang (film), dir Ken Hughes. *The Child Catcher.* Premiere, 16 December 1968.

Cobra, The (play by Justin Fleming), dir Richard Wherrett. *Lord Alfred Douglas.* Sydney Th Company, Sydney OH, 5 October 1983.

Colette (musical play, book/lyrics Tom Jones, m Harvey Schmidt), dir Dennis Rosa, co-prod Harry Rigby. *Jaques.* 5th Ave Th, Seattle, USA, 10 February 1982. 2nd prod with a new director and designs, Denver 21 March.

Comedy of Errors, The (play by Shakespeare, cut version in double bill), dir Walter Hudd. *Dr Pinch.* OV Drama Company, OV, 23 April 1957.

Contessa, La (play by Paul Osborne from *Film of Memory* by Maurice Druon). dir RH, sc Desmond Heeley, c Beatrice Dawson. Th Royal, Newcastle, 6 April 1965.

Contrabandits (episode 'In for a Penny'), TV Series. *Don Steele.* ABC-TV, 6 September 1968.

Coq d'or, Le (opera by Rimsky-Korsakov), dir/chor RH. Royal Opera Company, ROHCG, 7 January 1954.

Country Practice, A (episode, 'Save the Last Dance for Me'), TV series. *Sir Adrian Dormin,* Australian TV, c 14 January 1985.

Dracula (play by Hamilton Deane & John L Balderston after Bram Stoker), dir RH, des Edward Gorey, HM Th, Sydney 18 August 1978.

Duel of Angels (play by Jean Giraudoux, trans Christopher Fry), dir RH, des Roger Furse. Helen Hayes Th, New York, 19 April 1960; OV Drama Company, HM Th, Melbourne, 12 July 1961, des Felix Kelly.

Fairy Queen, The (masque by Purcell based on *A Midsummer Night's Dream*), dir Frederick Ashton & Malcolm Baker Smith. *Oberon.* CG Opera, ROHCG, 12 December 1946, see also Appendix 1.

55 Days at Peking (film), dir Nicholas Ray. *Prince Tuan.* Premiere, London, 6 May 1963.

Finian's Rainbow (musical), dir/chor RH. Grand Th, Blackpool, 29 March 1961.

Gaslight (play by Patrick Hamilton), dir Cleland Finn. *Jack Manningham.* BBC-Radio, 8 December 1948.

Ghost Sonata, The (play by Strindberg), dir Stuart Burge. *The Old Man.* BBC-TV, 16 March 1962.

Golden City – see Appendix I.

Hamlet (play by Shakespeare), dir Tyrone Guthrie & Michael Benthall. *Hamlet.* OV Drama Company, New Th, London, 11 February 1944; dir Michael Benthall, Shakespeare Memorial Th, Stratford-upon-Avon, 24 April 1948.

He Who Gets Slapped (play by Leonid Andreyev adapted by Judith Guthrie), dir Tyrone Guthrie. *'Prince'.* Duchess Th, London, 17 June 1937.

Heathen! (musical by Eaton Magoon, Jnr), dir credited RH (but he had nothing to do with the NY staging). Rose Th, New York, 18 May 1972.

Henry V (film of play by Shakespeare, Two Cities Film), dir Laurence Olivier *The Bishop of Ely.* Premiere 23 November 1944.

I Hate Men (play written and dir by Peter Godfrey), *The Young Man/Waiter.* Gate Th, London. 28 February 1933.

Insect Play, The (play by the Brothers Capek), dir ?Nancy Price. *Felix the Butterfly, Mr Cricket, Chief of the Yellow Ants.* Playhouse Th, London, 27 April 1938.

Iron Petticoat, The (film, Remus), dir Ralph Thomas. *Ivan Kropotkin.* Premiere 9 August 1956.

King John (play by Shakespeare), dir Michael Benthall. *King John.* Shakespeare Memorial Th, Stratford-upon-Avon. 15 April 1948.

Lady of the Camellias, The (play), dir RH, des Carl Toms. OV Drama Company, HM Th, Melbourne, 8 August 1961.

Madame Butterfly (opera by Puccini), dir RH. Royal Opera Company, ROHCG, 17 January 1950.

Maker of Dreams, The (play by Oliphant Down), dir Lanham Titchener. *Pierrot.* BBC TV, 13 April 1938.

Mango Tree, The (film, Australia), prod Michael Pate. *The Professor.* Premiere 16 December 1977.

Marriage-go-round, The (play by Leslie Stevens), dir RH, m Leslie Bridgewater, des Hutchinson Scott. Royal Lyceum Th, Edinburgh, 22 September 1959; Piccadilly Th, London, 29 October 1959.

Measure for Measure (play by Shakespeare), dir Michael Benthall. *Angelo.* OV Drama Company, Tivoli Th, Sydney, 31 May 1955.

Merchant of Venice, The (play by Shakespeare), dir Michael Benthall. *Shylock.* Shakespeare Memorial Th, Stratford-upon-Avon, 19 April 1948; dir Benthall, OV Drama Company, Tivoli Th, Sydney, 14 May 1955; dir Benthall, OV Drama Company, OV, 11 December 1956; Baalbek, 25 July 1957; dir RH, OV Drama Company, Far East tour (Japan), c March 1962 – probably only excerpts in a recital of *Great Scenes from Shakespeare.*

Merry Widow, The (operetta by Lehar) see Appendix 1.

Message from Mars, A (play by Richard Ganthony), prod Beatrice Holloway and Robert Gregg. *A newsboy.* Criterion Th Sydney, c 1926.

Midsummer Night's Dream, A (play by Shakespeare), dir Tyrone Guthrie. *Oberon,* OV Drama Co, OV, London, 26 December 1937; repeated 26 December 1938; BBC radio, dir Val Gielgud, 23 April 1944; excerpts broadcast in Hamburg (Forces Radio), dir and acted *Oberon* and *Bottom,* between 19 and 24 November, 1945; dir Michael Benthall, *Oberon,* OV Drama Company, Empire Th, Edinburgh, 31 August 1954; Metropolitan OH, New York, 21 September 1954; recording, Columbia ALP 1262/4 1954, reissued Music for Pleasure, Listen for Pleasure, No. 7062. See also Appendix 1.

Millionairess, The (play by Shaw), dir Michael Benthall. *The Egyptian Doctor.* Royal Court Th, Liverpool, 5 May 1952; New Th, London, 27 June 1952; Shubert Th, New York, 17 October 1952.

Murder in the Cathedral (play by T.S. Eliot), dir RH, des Alan Barlow. OV Drama Company, OV, 31 March 1953. Columbia Gramophone Records 33CX 1056 and 33CX 1057.

Nekrassov (play by Jean-Paul Sartre), dir George Devine. *Georges de Valera.* Royal Lyceum Th, Edinburgh, 19 August 1957 (Festival); Royal Court Th, London, 17 September 1957; excerpt on BBC-TV, 16 September 1957.

Nude with Violin (play by Noel Coward), dir Coward and John Gielgud. *Sebastien.* Globe Th, London, 25 November 1957; Comedy Th, Melbourne, dir RH, 21 June 1958; ITV, dir Lionel Harris, 21 July 1959.

Old Lady Shows Her Medals, The (play by J.M. Barrie), Theater Guild on the Air Production, NBC broadcast. *Private Dowey.* 3 February 1952.

One of our Aircraft is Missing (film), dir Powell–Pressburger. *De Jong.* Premiere 24 April 1942.

Patrick (film, Australia), dir Richard Franklyn. *Dr Roget.* Premiere 18 September 1978.

Peter and the Wolf (Prokofiev). *Narrator.* Royal Philharmonic Orchestra, Gaumont State Th, Kilburn, London, 6 March 1949; London Symphony Orchestra, Empress Hall, 17 April 1949; London Philharmonic Orchestra, ROHCG, 12 February 1950; Royal Festival Hall, 7 November 1953; on Fonteyn–Helpmann Concert Ballet tour, starting Assembly Hall, Tunbridge Wells, 2 June 1950; Pro Arte Orchestra, Royal Festival Hall, 1 November 1963; Australian Youth Orchestra, Adelaide Town Hall, 12 March 1964.

Peter Pan (play by J.M. Barrie, m Grant Foster), dir RH, des Anthony Holland. London Coliseum, 27 December 1971.

Precipice – see Appendix I.

Puritani, I (opera by Bellini), dir RH (with Christopher Brown). Australian Opera, Sydney OH, 24 June 1985.

Puzzle (film), dir Gordon Hessler, Australian TV. *Buckminster Shepherd.* c December 1978.

Quiller Memorandum, The (film, Rank), dir Michael Anderson. *Weng.* Premiere 10 November 1966.

Red Shoes, The (fim) – see Appendix I.

Richard III (play by Shakespeare),.. dir Douglas Seale. *Richard III.* OV Drama Company, OV, 29 May 1957.

Romeo & Juliet (play by Shakespeare), dir RH, m Brian Easdale, des Loudon Sainthill. OV Drama Company, OV, 12 June 1956.

Romeo et Juliette (opera by Gounod), dir RH, des Kenneth Rowell. Australian Opera, Concert Hall, Sydney, January 29 1983 (without nuptial procession & ballet).

Sarah in America (play by Ruth Wolff), dir RH. Kennedy Center, Washington DC, 2 March 1981.

Soldier's Tale, The (L'Histoire du soldat) (Stravinsky), dir Gunther Rennert, chor RH. *The Devil.* Glyndebourne Opera Company, King's Th, Edinburgh, 6 September 1954; film (Ipsilon Films), dir Lord Birkett, chor RH, London press show, 12 October 1964; dir RH, Gala, Elizabethan Theatre, Sydney, 29 September 1964.

Song of Norway – see Appendix I.

Stardust (play by Ted Willis), *The Manservant*, Civic Theatre, Newcastle, NSW 15 November 1984.

Steps of the Ballet (Birth of a Ballet) (film, Crown Film Unit), dir Muir Matheson. *Narrator.* 30 September 1948. (pre-release)

Swinging the Gate (revue), dir Norman Marshall. *Impersonations,* and on occasion *two other items.* Ambassadors Th, London, 22 May 1940.

Tales of Hoffmann, The (film) – see Appendix I.

Taming of the Shrew, The (play by Shakespeare), dir Tyrone Guthrie. *Gremio/ Nicholas/A Tailor.* OV Drama Company, OV, London, 28 March 1939; dir Michael Benthall, *Petruchio,* OV Drama Company, Tivoli Th, Sydney, 24 May 1955.

Tempest, The (play by Shakespeare), dir RH, m Malcolm Arnold, des Leslie Hurry. OV Drama Company, OV, London, 13 April 1954, dir RH, Japanese National Theatre Company, Nessei Th, early December 1967.

Titus Andronicus (play by Shakespeare in cut version, in double bill), dir Walter Hudd. *Saturninus.* OV Drama Company, OV, 23 April 1957.

Tribute to Sir Frederick Ashton, dir Michael Somes, John Hart. *Compere.* RB, ROHCG, 24 July 1970.

Twelfth Night (play by Shakespeare), dir RH, des Loudon Sainthill. OV Drama Company, HM Th, Melbourne, 25 July 1961.

Two Gentlemen of Verona, The (play by Shakespeare), dir Michael Langham. *Launce.* OV Drama Company, OV, 22 January 1957. See also Appendix 1.

Valmouth (play with music by Sandy Wilson), dir John Dexter. *Cardinal Pirelli.* Chichester Festival Th, 19 May 1982.

Wedding Bouquet, A (ballet). See Appendix 1.

Wedding Ring, The (farce by Kieran Tunney & Simon Wardell), dir RH. Manchester OH, 4 August 1952.

White Devil, The (play by John Webster), dir Michael Benthall. *Flamineo.* Th Royal, Brighton, 17 February 1947; Duchess Th, London, 6 March 1947; excerpts on BBC radio, 30 April 1947.

APPENDIX 3 – *Chronology*

1917
A Midsummer Night's Dream – child extra. Allan Wilkie Shakespeare Company, Adelaide.

1920
Sylvia pizzicato solo – pupil performance. Charity concert, Exhibition Hall, Adelaide.

1922
5 Oct *The Ugly Duckling* (musical) – pupil performance. *The Ugly Duckling.* Th Royal, Adelaide.
Apache Dance (pdd) – pupil performance. Louise Larson Studio, Adelaide.
A Message from Mars (play) – a newsboy. Criterion Th, Sydney.

1926
5 –14 Apr *Don Quixote* (ballet) and *Walpurgis Night* (ballet) – cdb. Pavlova Ballet, HM Th, Melbourne.
On tour with Pavlova Ballet: 17 Apr – 20 May HM Th, Sydney; 26 May–early July New Zealand; 12–20 July HM Th, Brisbane; 22 July Charity Matinee, Sydney; 23 July Charity Matinee, Melbourne; 24 July–4 Aug Th Royal, Adelaide.
27 Dec *Frasquita* (operetta), Speciality Dancer/El Tango. JCW, Grand OH, Wellington, New Zealand.

1927
16 Apr *Frasquita* (as above), HM Th (then Th Royal), Sydney, then on tour.
7 May *Tip Toes* (musical), a dancer. JCW, HM Th, Sydney. Opened 4 May in Newcastle, NSW. then on tour.
24 Dec *Queen High* (musical), a dancer. JCW, Th Royal, Melbourne.

1928
summer season *Good News* (vaudeville cabaret), speciality dancer. Palais Royal, Adelaide.
date unknown *Katja the Dancer* (musical), a dancer. JCW, Th Royal, Melbourne.

1929
30 Mar–Aug *This Year of Grace* (revue), various roles. JCW, Th Royal, Melbourne.

1930
4 Jan *The New Moon* (operetta), Ldg dancer. JCW, HM Th, Sydney.
26 Apr *The Merry Widow* (operetta), Ldg dancer. 'Butterflies'. JCW, Th Royal, Melbourne.
17 May *Katinka* (operetta), Russian Dance, Cabaret, pdd. JCW, Th Royal, Melbourne.

1931
23 Dec *Sinbad the Sailor* (pantomime), The Rose Ballet, and dance scena The Spider's Web, The Spider. JCW, HM Th, Melbourne.

1932

23 Apr *The Barretts of Wimpole Street* (play). Septimus. Toyne/Rawlings Company, Criterion Th, Sydney. Also *Business à la Russe* (ballet), chor RH, cr The Young Man.
5 Sep *Chopin 'Obertas'*, pdd; also Russian Dance, solo Vera van Rij Dance Recital, Australia Hotel, Adelaide, and *Battle of the Flowers*.
Dec Sailed to Europe.

1933

28 Feb *I Hate Men* (play), Young Man/Waiter. Gate Th, London.
21 Mar *Coppélia* (ballet 2 acts), A Village Dancer, VWB (1st appearance with company), SWT.
18 Apr *Job* (ballet), A Son/War, Pestilence and Famine. VWB, SWT.
21 June *The Fantasticks* (play), cr A Person of the Ballet, pd6. Lyric Th, Hammersmith and Open Air Th, Regents Park 19 July.
26 Sep *Job* (ballet), Satan. VWB, SWT.
3 Oct *Douanes* (ballet), A Gendarme. VWB, SWT.
5 Oct *The Snow Maiden* (opera), A Tumbler. VW Opera, SWT.
10 Oct *Fête Polonaise* (ballet), mazurka; *The Wise and Foolish Virgins* (ballet), A Musician. VWB, SWT.
11 Oct *Tsar Saltan* (opera), cr A Dancer in Guidon's Court/A Clown in Island of Bujan. VW Opera, SWT.
17 Oct *Pomona* (ballet), Vertumnus. VWB, SWT.
24 Oct *Carnaval* (ballet), valse noble. VWB, SWT.
30 Oct *La Création du monde* (ballet), A God. VWB, OV.
6 Nov *The Lord of Burleigh* (ballet), The Lord of Burleigh; *Carnaval* (ballet), Florestan. VWB, OV.
28 Nov *The [Wise and] Foolish Virgins* (ballet), The Bridegroom. VWB, SWT.
29 Nov *Orpheus* (opera), cr A Fury. VW Opera, SWT.
5 Dec *Les Rendezvous* (ballet), cr pd3, pd6. VWB, SWT.
26 Dec *Nursery Suite* (ballet), Georgie-Porgie. VWB, OV.

1934

1 Jan *Giselle* (ballet), Hilarion. VWB (1st company perf), SWT.
15 Jan *Le Spectre de la rose* (ballet), The Spirit of the Rose. VWB, OV.
30 Jan *Casse-Noisette* (ballet), An Incroyable/Danse Chinoise. VWB (1st company perf), SWT.
13 Feb Vic-Wells Dance, *Blue Danube Waltz*, pdd. ROHCG.
19 Mar *Les Sylphides* (ballet), Ldg dancer. VWB, OV.
28 Mar BBC TV divt: Danse Chinoise/Coda to the Sugar Plum Fairy.
3 Apr *The Haunted Ballroom* (ballet), cr The Master of Treginnis. VWB, SWT.
11 May *Schwanda* (opera), Ldg dancer in court scene polka, Furiant in Act III. CG Opera, ROHCG.
17 May *Arabella* (opera), Ldg dancer. CG Opera, ROHCG.
4 June Ballet group, Open Air Th, Regent's Park, London: *During the Ball* (ballet), cr The Charming Young Man; *Acis and Galatea* (ballet), cr Acis; *Party 1860* (ballet), cr The Host.
5 June *Precipice* (play), Duval (acted/danced). Savoy Th, London. No perfs on Mondays, when Helpmann was dancing at Regent's Park.
14 June *La Cenerentola* (opera), cr pdd. CG Opera, ROHCG.

9 July Ballet group, Open Air Th, Regent's Park, London: *A Little Serenade* (ballet), cr The Student; *Neapolitana* (ballet), cr Luigi.

30 July Ballet group, Open Air Th, Regent's Park, London: *Psyche*(ballet), cr Eros; *Partie Carré* (ballet), cr A Bather.

31 July *As You Like It* (play), pdd. Open Air Th, Regent's Park, London.

2 Oct *Fête Polonaise* (ballet), adage and variation. VWB, SWT.

5 Oct *Faust* (opera), pdd. VW Opera, SWT.

6 Oct *Giselle* (ballet), Albrecht. VWB, SWT.

9 Oct *The Jar* (ballet), cr Don Lollo Zirafa; *Carnaval* (ballet), Harlequin. VWB, SWT.

30 Oct *Casse-Noisette* (ballet), The President/The Nutcracker Prince. VWB, SWT.

20 Nov *Le Lac des cygnes* (ballet), Prince Siegfried. VWB (1st company perf, 4-act version), SWT.

31 Dec *Les Rendevous* (ballet), Variation and Andante, VWB, OV.

1935

7 Jan *Carnaval* (ballet), Pierrot. VWB, OV.

31 Jan *Die Fledermaus* (opera), pdd. VW Opera, SWT.

21 Feb *Stop Press* (revue), Ldg dancer ('Lonely Heart Column', 'The Beggar's Dream', 'Revolt in Cuba', 'Echoes of a Former Romance'). Adelphi Th, London.

27 Sep *The Rake's Progress* (ballet), The Rake. VWB, SWT.

8 Oct *Façade* (ballet), Scotch Rhapsody/ cr Country Dance, The Squire. VWB, SWT.

15 Oct *Coppélia* (ballet), Ldg village dancer. VWB, SWT.

29 Oct *Douanes* (ballet), Cook's Man. VWB (revised version), SWT.

8 Nov *Tchaikovsky Pas de Deux* (divt). Not identified; probably *Aurora* or *Casse-Noisette*. Phyllis Bedells Farewell Matinee, London Hippodrome.

26 Nov *Le Baiser de la fée* (ballet), cr A Villager. VWB, SWT.

6 Dec *Coppélia* (ballet 2 acts), Franz. VWB, SWT.

18 Dec Silver Rose Ball (charity), Tango Exhibition Dance pdd, chor Ashton.

1936

10 Jan *Carnaval* (ballet), Eusebius; *The Gods Go a-Begging* (ballet), cr Ldg nobleman. VWB, SWT.

24 Jan *Siesta* (ballet), cr pdd. VWB, SWT.

11 Feb *Apparitions* (ballet pdd), cr The Poet. VWB, SWT.

24 Feb *Aurora Pas de Deux* (divt), pdd. Vic-Wells Costume Dance, ROHCG.

4 May *Music for Ballet* (ballet), cr pdd. Gala, Cambridge Th, London.

8 June *Turn over a New Leaf* (revue), RH arr. Samba cabaret. Cambridge University Footlights Dramatic Club, Arts Th, Cambridge.

2 Oct *Casse-Noisette Act III* (ballet), Danse Espagnole pdd. VWB, SWT.

13 Oct *Prometheus* (ballet), cr Prometheus. VWB, SWT.

28 Oct *Die Fledermaus* (opera; new version chor Ashton), cr pdd. VW Opera, SWT.

10 Nov *Prometheus* (ballet), The Friend; *Nocturne* (ballet), cr The Young Man. VWB, SWT.

11 Nov BBC TV excerpts from *Job* (ballet) Satan. VWB.

8 Dec BBC TV: *Façade* (ballet), Country Dance/The Squire VWB.

1937

11 Jan *Perpetuum Mobile* (divt), cr pdd. Gala variety, SWT.

16 Feb *Les Patineurs* (ballet), cr pdd. VWB, SWT.

11 Mar BBC TV: *Casse-Noisette Act III* (ballet), Danse Espagnole. VWB.
27 Apr *A Wedding Bouquet* (ballet), cr The Bridegroom. VWB, SWT.
3 May BBC TV: *Les Patineurs* (ballet), pdd. VWB.
8 June *Full Swing* (revue), RH arr dances and ensembles. Cambridge University Footlights Dramatic Club, Arts Th, Cambridge.
15 June *Checkmate* (ballet), cr The Red King. VWB, Th des Champs-Elysées, Paris.
11 Oct BBC TV: *Carnaval* (ballet), Eusebius. VWB.
13 Dec BBC TV: *Le Lac des cygnes Act II* (ballet), Prince Siegfried. VWB.
26 Dec–5 Feb 1938 *A Midsummer Night's Dream* (play), Oberon. OV Drama Company, OV.

1938
7 Apr *Le Roi nu (The Emperor's New Clothes)* (ballet), cr The Emperor. VWB, SWT.
13 Apr BBC TV: *The Maker of Dreams* (play), Pierrot.
25 Apri BBC TV: *A Wedding Bouquet* (ballet), The Bridegroom. VWB.
27 Apr *The Insect Play* (play), Felix the Butterfly, Mr Cricket, Chief of theYellow Ants.
8 May BBC TV: *Checkmate* (ballet), The Red King. VWB.
10 May *The Judgment of Paris* (ballet), cr Paris. VWB, SWT.
13 May *Hommage aux belles viennoises* (ballet), pdd. Liverpool Ballet Club (guest artist), Crane Hall, Liverpool.
8 June *Pure and Simple* (revue), RH arr dances and ensembles. Cambridge University Footlights Dramatic Club, Arts Th, Cambridge.
8 June BBCTV *Nocturne*. The Young Man. VWB.
9 June *Chopin Waltz* (divt; unidentified, possibly from *Les Sylphides)*, pdd. Gala, Cambridge Th, London.
13 Nov *Les Masques* (ballet), A Personage. Ballet Rambert, Mercury Th, London.
26 Dec–21 Jan 1939 *A Midsummer Night's Dream* (play; revival), Oberon. OV Drama Company, OV.

1939
2 Feb *The Sleeping Princess* (ballet), Prince Charming. VWB (1st company perf), SWT.
12 Feb BBC TV: *Arlecchino* (theatrical capriccio), Arlecchino (acted/danced).
19 Mar *La Danse/LaValse* (ballet), chor RH with Wendy Toye. Royal Academy of Dancing Production Club, Rudolf Steiner Hall, London.
22 Mar *The Sleeping Princess* Acts I and III (ballet) Prince Charming. gala mat ROHCG VWB.
25 Mar BBCTV *The Sleeping Princess* Acts I and III (ballet) Prince Charming. VWB.
27 Mar Prologue from *I Pagliacci* (divt), cr pdd. Royal Matinee, London Coliseum. Also BBC-TV, 19 Apr.
28 Mar *The Taming of the Shrew* (play), Gremio/The Tailor/Nicholas. OV Drama Company, OV.
8 Apr BBCTV *The Rake's Progress* (ballet) The Rake. VWB.
21 Apr *Chopin Prelude in A Flat Major* (divt), cr pdd. Liverpool Ballet Club (guest artist), Crane Th, Liverpool.
22 May BBCTV *The Sleeping Princess* Act III (ballet) Prince Charming VWB.
3 June *Façade* (ballet), Yodelling Song, A Mountaineer/Tango, The Dago. VWB, Arts Th, Cambridge.

6 June *The All-Male Revue* (revue), RH arr dances and ensembles. Cambridge University Footlights Dramatic Club, Arts Th, Cambridge.
3 Sep World War II began. VWB reassembled Cardiff 18 Sep.

1940

9 Jan *The Sleeping Princess* (ballet), Fourth Prince/Prince Charming. VWB, SWT.
23 Jan *Dante Sonata* (ballet), cr Ldg Child of Darkness. VWB, SWT.
3 Apr *Les Patineurs* (ballet). Variation/pd3 VWB, SWT.
15 Apr *Coppélia* (ballet; three-act version), Franz. VWB, SWT.
5 May With VWB to Holland. German invasion. Returned to UK 13 May.
22 May *Swinging the Gate* (revue), impressions. Ambassadors Th, London.
4 July *The Prospect Before Us* (ballet), cr Mr. O'Reilly. SWB, SWT.
23 July *Façade* (ballet), cr Foxtrot. SWB, SWT.
22 Aug *Barabau* (ballet; revised version), Barabau. SWB, SWT.
20 Nov *The Wise Virgins* (ballet chor Ashton), The Father. SWB, OH Manchester.

1941

27 Jan *The Wanderer* (ballet), cr The Wanderer. SWB, New Th, London.
28 May *Orpheus and Eurydice* (ballet), cr Orpheus. SWB, New Th, London.
26 July *The Wise Virgins* (ballet), The Bridegroom. SWB, New Th, London.
4 Aug *Façade* (ballet), Nocturne peruvienne/Tango. SWB, New Th, London.
21 Aug *Fun and Games* (revue), chor RH 'The Old Shoemaker', Saville Th, London.
30 Sep *Coppélia* (ballet), Dr Coppelius. SWB, New Th, London.
6 Oct *The Sleeping Princess* (ballet), Carabosse/Prince Charming. SWB, New Th, London.

1942

14 Jan *Comus* (ballet), chor RH, cr Comus. SWB, New Th, London.
24 Apr *One of Our Aircraft is Missing* (film), De Jong.
30 Apr *Fine and Dandy* (revue), chor RH 'Winterhalter Waltz', Saville Th, London.
18 May BBC radio: Poetry reading. 'And So to Bed'
19 May *Hamlet* (ballet), chor RH, cr Hamlet. SWB, New Th, London.
17 July RH talk, 'Choreographic Criticism', Royal Academy of Dancing AGM, Claridge's; text in *The Dancing Times*, September 1942.
6 Aug *Wild Rose* (musical), chor RH 'Flor Fina Ballet'. Princes Th, London.
24 Nov *The Birds* (ballet), chor. SWB, New Th, London.

1943

4 Mar *The Merry Widow* (operetta), chor RH, HM Th, London.
6 Apr *The Quest* (ballet), cr St George. SWB, New Th, London.
12 Sep *Seascape* (ENSA show), chor RH, pd6 'What Shall We Do with the Drunken Sailor?' Royal Albert Hall, London.
22 Dec BBC radio: Poetry reading, from Bridge's *Testament of Beauty*.

1944

11 Feb–8 Apr *Hamlet* (play), Hamlet. OV Drama Company, New Th, London.
23 Apr BBC radio: *A Midsummer Night's Dream* (play), Oberon.
31 Aug *Peer Gynt* (play), RH arr movement and groupings. OV Drama Company, New Th, London.

26 Oct *Miracle in the Gorbals* (ballet), chor RH, cr The Stranger. SWB, Princes Th, London.

23 Nov *Henry V* (film), The Bishop of Ely.

1945

29 Jan–1 Apr with SWB to Belgium and France.

18 Feb *Promenade* (ballet), The Lepidopterist. SWB, Th Marigny, Paris.

16 Nov–16 Dec with SWB to Germany.

19 Nov BBC Forces Radio, Hamburg: *A Midsummer Night's Dream* (play, excerpts), dir, acted Oberon and Bottom. SWB.

1946

20 Feb *The Sleeping Beauty* (ballet, new production) Carabosse/Prince Florimund, SWB ROHCG.

7 Mar *Song of Norway* (operetta), chor RH 'The Concerto Ballet', Palace Th, London.

10 Apr *Adam Zero* (ballet), chor RH, cr Adam Zero/The Principal Dancer. SWB, ROHCG.

12 Apr *Caravan* (film), Wycroft.

12 Nov *Les Sirènes* (ballet), cr Adeline Canberra. SWB, ROHCG.

12 Dec *The Fairy Queen* (masque), Oberon (acted). CG Opera, ROHCG.

1947

17 Feb *The White Devil* (play), Flamineo. Th Royal, Brighton; Duchess Th, London, 6 Mar–7 June.

Mar/Apr *'A Choreographer Speaks'*, article by RH in *New Theatre*.

15 June Dinner speaker, tribute to Ninette de Valois, Claridge's, London.

17–28 June *He Who Gets Slapped* (play), 'Prince' (i.e., He). Duchess Th, London.

30 Nov Lilian Baylis Commemoration Service, Southwark Cathedral, read 2nd Lesson.

1948

22 Jan Cabaret compère. Vic Wells Costume Ball, Lyceum Th, London.

28 Mar BBC radio: *'The Choreographer at Work'* (talk by RH; 1st given Far Eastern Service, 2 Feb).

31 Mar BBC Radio: *'The Production of Hamlet'*' (talk by RH; 1st given Far Eastern Service, 28 Feb).

15 Apr *King John* (play), King John. Shakespeare Memorial Th, Stratford-upon-Avon.

19 Apr *The Merchant of Venice* (play), Shylock. Shakespeare Memorial Th, Stratford-upon-Avon.

24 Apr *Hamlet* (play), Hamlet. Shakespeare Memorial Th, Stratford-upon-Avon.

5 June *The Winter's Tale* (play), RH arr dance. Shakespeare Memorial Th, Stratford-upon-Avon.

19 June BBC Radio Forces Educational: 'The Ballet Dancer' (talk by RH); text published in *The Listener,* 14 April 1949.

22 July *The Red Shoes* (film), chor RH, 'The Red Shoes Ballet' and extract from 'Hearts of Fire', acted/danced Ivan Boleslawsky.

21 Sep–2 Oct with SWB to Paris.

30 Sep *Steps of the Ballet* (documentary film), Narrator. Prerelease run opened, Marble Arch Pavilion, London. US title: *Birth of a Ballet*.
25 Nov *Don Juan* (ballet), cr Don Juan. SWB, ROHCG.
8 Dec BBC radio: *Gaslight* (play), Jack Manningham.
23 Dec *Cinderella* (ballet), cr A Stepsister. SWB, ROHCG.

1949
27 Feb BBC radio: Poetry reading, selection of poems.
6 Mar *Peter and the Wolf* (music), Narrator. Gaumont State Th, Kilburn, London (frequently repeated with other orchestras).
5 Apr BBC radio: *Caligula* (play), Caligula.
20 May–3 June with SWB to Florence and Copenhagen.
29 Sep *The Olympians* (opera), cr Mercury (mime/dance). CG Opera, ROHCG.
9 Oct *The Sleeping Beauty* (ballet) Prince Florimund. SWB Metropolitan OH, New York.
9 Oct–18 Dec with SWB on tour of USA and Canada.
11 Oct *Love's Labour's Lost* (play), RH arr dances, OV Drama Company, New Th, London.

1950
17 Jan *Madame Butterfly* (opera), dir RH. CG Opera, ROHCG.
30 Jan *Spirits of the Air* from *The Fairy Queen*, pdd. (guest artist) Ny Norske Th, Oslo.
20 Feb *Don Quixote* (ballet; chor de Valois), cr Don Quixote. SWB, ROHCG.
1 Mar *Cabaret*, arr and appeared. Sadler's Wells Ballet Benevolent Fund Ball, Dorchester Hotel, London.
21 Apr–7 May *The Sleeping Beauty* Prince Florimund/Carabosse (guest artist) La Scala, Milan.
15 May – SWB 21st anniversary gala *The Haunted Ballroom* (The Master of Treginnis) and *A Wedding Bouquet* (The Bridegroom).
2 June *The Hussar* (divt), solo; *L'Ile des sirènes* (ballet), The Mariner. Fonteyn–Helpmann Concert Ballet tour, Tunbridge Wells Assembly Hall and other touring dates.
15 June *Golden City* (musical), chor/co-dir RH, Adelphi Th, London.
June 'The Orchestration of Movement', article by RH in book *Diversion* pub Max Parrish.
28 Sep With SWB, Metropolitan OH, New York and USA tour. Resigned from company 12 Nov at San Francisco.
1951
13 Feb *The Prospect Before Us* (ballet) Mr O'Reilly (guest artist) SWTB SWT.
1 Apr *The Tales of Hoffmann* (film), Lindorf/Dr Coppelius/Dapertutto, Dr Miracle. Metropolitan OH, New York.
24 Apr *Caesar and Cleopatra* (play), Apollodorus. OH Manchester, Olivier Drama Company; 10 May St James's Th, London; 19 December Ziegfeld Th, New York.
1 May *Antony and Cleopatra* (play), Octavius Caesar. OH Manchester; Olivier Drama Company; 11 May St James's Th, London; 20 December Ziegfeld Th, New York.
7 Sep Constant Lambert Memorial Service, St Martin-in-the-Fields Church, London, read Lesson.

1952
3 Feb NBC Radio, New York: *The Old Lady Shows Her Medals* (play), Private Dowey. Th Guild production.
5 May *The Millionairess* (play), The Egyptian Doctor. Royal Court Th, Liverpool; 27 June New Th, London; 17 October Shubert Th, New York.
4 Aug *The Wedding Ring* (play), dir RH. OH Manchester.

1953
18 Feb BBC TV: *Box for One* (play), The Caller.
31 Mar *Murder in the Cathedral* (play), dir RH. OV Drama Company, OV.
19 June BBC radio Desert Island Discs, interviewed Roy Plomley.
21 Oct BBC TV: *Music for You*, rehearsing Richard Hearne and Annette Page in 'The Old Shoemaker'.
6 Dec Panel of OV Brains Trust, OV.

1954
7 Jan *Le Coq d'or* (opera), dir/chor RH. CG Opera, ROHCG.
13 Apr *The Tempest* (play), dir/chor RH. OV Drama Company, OV.
10 June *After the Ball* (operetta), dir/chor RH. Globe Th, London.
30 June Received Order of the Star of the North from King Gustavus of Sweden at gala performance of *Le Coq d'or*, ROHCG.
31 Aug *A Midsummer Night's Dream* (play), chor RH, Oberon (acted; danced in Nocturne, chor Ashton). OV Drama Company, Empire Th, Edinburgh; 21 Sep Metropolitan OH, New York and an American tour.
6 Sep *The Soldier's Tale* (theatre piece), chor RH, acted/danced The Devil. Glyndebourne Opera production, King's Th, Edinburgh.
Sep 'Formula for Midsummer Magic', article by RH in *Theatre Arts Monthly*.

1955
1 Mar *As You Like It* (play), dir RH. OV Drama Company, OV.
4 May–26 Nov with OV Drama Company in Australia.
14 May *The Merchant of Venice* (play). Shylock. OV Drama Company, Tivoli Th, Sydney.
24 May *The Taming of the Shrew* (play), Petruchio. OV Drama Company, Tivoli Th, Sydney.
31 May *Measure for Measure* (play), Angelo. OV Drama Company, Tivoli Th, Sydney.
1956
5 May 25th anniversary SWB gala. ROHCG. danced The Rake and The Dago.
12 June *Romeo and Juliet* (play), dir RH. OV Drama Company, OV.
9 Aug *The Iron Petticoat* (film), Ivan Kropotkin.
11 Dec *The Merchant of Venice* (play; new production). Shylock. OV Drama Company, OV.

1957
6 Jan Twelfth Night Party, Vic-Wells Association, appeared in sketch 'Forty Years into the Future, 1997' as Dolly the dresser, who 'remembered the years when they was doing the Folio'.
22 Jan *The Two Gentlemen of Verona* (play). Launce. OV Drama Company, OV.
5 Mar *Antony and Cleopatra* (play), dir RH. OV Drama Company, OV.

23 Apr *Titus Andronicus* (play), Saturninus; *The Comedy of Errors* (play), Dr Pinch. OV Drama Company, OV. Both plays in shortened versions.
29 May *Richard III* (play). Richard III. OV Drama Company, OV.
25 July Awarded Order of Merit of the Cedars of Lebanon, as actor and director with the OV Drama Company, at Baalbek.
19 Aug *Nekrassov* (play). Georges de Valera. Royal Court Company, Lyceum Th, Edinburgh; 17 September Royal Court Th, London.
27 Oct BBC TV: *Coppélia* (ballet), prod Margaret Dale, Dr Coppelius.
25 Nov *Nude with Violin* (play). Sebastien. Globe Th, London.

1958
3 Mar RB season, ROHCG: revivals of *Miracle in the Gorbals* and *Hamlet;* also danced The Rake and Dr Coppelius.
21 Apr *Petrushka* (ballet). Petrushka. RB, ROHCG.
30 May *The Big Money* (film). The Bogus Clergyman.
21 June–25 Oct *Nude with Violin* (play), dir RH. Sebastien. Comedy Th, Melbourne (later in Sydney and New Zealand).
17 Aug ABV2 TV, Melbourne: *Box for One* (play; new production), The Caller.
27 Oct RB Touring Company, Empire Th, Sydney: The Rake, The Dago (Nocturne peruvienne & Tango); 1 November Dr Coppelius; 4 November Hamlet.

1959
22 Sep *The Marriage-go-round* (play). dir RH. Royal Lyceum Th, Edinburgh; 29 Oct Piccadilly Th, London.
17 Dec *Aladdin* (pantomime). dir/chor RH. London Coliseum.

1960
19 Apr *Duel of Angels* (play), dir RH. Helen Hayes Th, New York.
26 July given Queen Elizabeth II Coronation Award, Royal Academy of Dancing.
17 Oct BBC radio Home Service: *The Robert Helpmann Story.*
25 Oct *The Sleeping Beauty* (ballet), staged Act III. De Cuevas Ballet, Th des Champs-Elysées, Paris.
date unknown *Mozart, Prince of Song* (record for children), Narrator. Issued by Conquest Records, Richmond, Surrey; also joint editor of the series.
1961
29 Mar *Finian's Rainbow* (musical), dir/chor RH, Grand Th, Blackpool.
12 July *Duel of Angels* (play; new production), dir RH, OV Drama Company (all plays with Vivien Leigh), HM Th, Melbourne.
25 July *Twelfth Night* (play), dir RH. OV Drama Company, HM Th, Melbourne.
8 Aug *The Lady of the Camellias* (play), dir RH. OV Drama Company, HM Th, Melbourne. Tour continued into 1962: Australia, New Zealand, Japan, Hong Kong, Manila, Bangkok and Bombay. RH was only occasionally involved.
date unknown *The Life of Chopin* and *The Life of Beethoven* (records for children). Narrator. Issued by Conquest Records, Richmond, Surrey.

1962
16 Mar BBC TV: *The Ghost Sonata* (play). The Old Man.
29 Mar–16 May OV Drama Company tour dir RH of Latin America opened in Mexico City. Vivien Leigh in *The Lady of the Camellias, Twelfth Night* and *Great*

Scenes from Shakespeare (recital), in which RH took part. Tour continued to Caracas, Lima, Santiago, Buenos Aires, Montevideo, Sao Paulo and Rio de Janeiro.
6 Dec Fonteyn Gala matinee, dir RH, and danced Tango from *Façade*. Drury Lane Th, London.

1963
26 Mar *Elektra* (ballet), chor RH. RB, ROHCG.
6 May 55 *Days at Peking* (film), Prince Tuan.
26 May BBC TV: *An Evening with Robert Helpmann.*
31 July BBC TV: *Checkmate* (ballet). The White King. RB.
9 Aug–22 Sep Fonteyn–Nureyev 'Sunshine Tour', Athens Festival, dir RH. Tour continued to Nice, Cannes, Israel, Japan and Honolulu.
5 Dec Fonteyn Gala matinee, dir RH. Drury Lane Th, London.
12 Dec *Swan Lake* (ballet), dir RH. RB, ROHCG.

1964
27 Jan 5AD Radio Australia: played pop records by RH of 'Surfer Doll' and 'I Still Could Care'. (Later there was another record, 'Surf Dance' and 'Letta Go My Heart.')
9, 16, 23 Feb 1, 8, 15 Mar BBC radio Children's Hour: *The Story of Ninette de Valois,* produced by Peggy Bacon, told in six parts by RH.
5 Mar ABC TV Australia: *Half an Hour with Robert Helpmann.*
13 Mar *Façade* (concert performance), RH spoke poems. Festival Chamber Group, Union Hall, Adelaide.
14 Mar *The Display* (ballet), chor RH. AB, HM Th, Adelaide.
9 Apr BBC TV: *This Is Your Life* (de Valois), RH appeared.
19 Apr BBC radio: 'Talking of Theatre', RH on *Hamlet* ballet, revived by RB for Shakespeare Quatercentenary Prog ROHCG 2 Apr.
23 Apr Shakespeare Birthday Performance, Yvonne Arnaud Theatre, Guildford, RH acted excerpts from plays with Vivien Leigh.
10 May Shakespeare Commemoration Service, Southwark Cathedral, London, RH read 2nd Lesson.
13 June Awarded C.B.E. (Commander of the Order of the British Empire) in Queen's Birthday Honours, received 17 Nov.
19 Aug *Camelot* (musical), dir/chor RH. Th Royal Drury Lane, London.
29 Sep *The Soldier's Tale* (theatre piece; new version), dir/chor RH. The Devil. Programme for 10th Anniversary of Elizabethan Th Trust, Sydney. Also *Rondino* (solo), chor RH.
30 Sep BBC TV: *Catch as Catch Can* (play). Fouché.
12 Oct *The Soldier's Tale* (film), chor RH. The Devil. Press showing in London.
24 Nov *A Wedding Bouquet* (ballet). Narrator . RB, ROHCG.

1965
18 Feb *Yugen* (ballet), chor RH. AB, HM Th, Adelaide.
4 Mar appointed co-artistic director of AB with Peggy van Praagh.
6 Apr *La Contessa* (play) dir RH, Th Royal Newcastle (UK).
early Nov *The Sleeping Beauty* (ballet), dir RH. Rome Opera Ballet.

1966

15 Jan RH named Australian of the Year 1965.

15 Mar *Elektra* (ballet; revival), chor RH. AB, HM Th, Adelaide.

9 Sep Appointed director of the Adelaide Festival 1970, and consultant for the 1968 Festival.

10 Nov *The Quiller Memorandum* (film), Weng.

1967

6 June Montreal World's Fair 'Expo 67', RH dir. Special Australia Day programme. AB participating as part of overseas tour.

early Dec *The Tempest* (play), dir RH. Japanese National Theatre Company, Nessei Th, Tokyo.

1968

1 Jan Awarded K.B.E. (Knight Commander of the Order of the British Empire) in the New Year Honours, received 29 Oct.

19 Feb–3 May With AB on tour of ten Asian countries.

2 Aug *Sun Music* (ballet), chor RH. AB, HM Th, Sydney.

6 Sep ABC TV Australia: *The Contrabandits*, episode 'In for a Penny'. Don Steele.

16 Dec *Chitty Chitty Bang Bang* (film). The Child Catcher.

1969

25 July *Coppélia* (ballet; revival). Dr Coppelius. AB, HM Th, Sydney.

29 Dec *Cinderella* (ballet; filmed for TV). A Stepsister. RB, ROHCG.

1970

6–28 Mar Sixth Adelaide Festival of Arts, dir RH.

23 Mar *Hamlet* (ballet; revival), chor RH. AB, HM Th, Adelaide.

28 Mar *Don Quixote* (ballet; chor Petipa/Nureyev). Don Quixote. AB, HM Th, Adelaide.

24 July *Tribute to Ashton* (anthology programme). Narrator. RB, ROHCG.

27 July TCN TV Australia: *Don Quixote* (ballet). Don Quixote. AB.

26 Dec AB began tour of United States and Canada at Dorothy Chandler Pavilion, Los Angeles with *Don Quixote,* RH appearing as Don Quixote in some cities.

1971

15 Nov *Don Quixote* staged by Nureyev for Nouveau Ballet at Marseilles OH. He, Aldous and RH guest artists.

14 Dec *Checkmate* (ballet, revival). The Red King. RB, ROHCG.

27 Dec *Peter Pan* (play with music), dir RH. London Coliseum.

1972

17 Mar *Cinderella* (ballet; revival, with Ashton). A Stepsister. AB, Elizabethan Th, Sydney.

early Sep *Cinderella* (ballet). A Stepsister, with Ashton, (guest artist). PACT Ballet, Johannesburg, South Africa.

8 Sep *Façade* (ballet; revival). Nocturne peruvienne/Tango. AB, Princess Th, Melbourne.

5 Dec *Alice's Adventures in Wonderland* (film). The Mad Hatter.

1973
19 July *Don Quixote* (film). Don Quixote. AB, Sydney OH concert hall.
27 July With AB on tour of India and Eastern Europe.
14 Sep ATN7 TV Australia: RH appeared in *The Making of the Don Quixote Film.*
30 Sep BBC TV: *Omnibus, Helpmann.*
9 Dec *The Sleeping Beauty* (ballet; revival), RH co-dir with Peggy van Praagh. AB, Sydney OH.

1974
21 Mar *Perisynthyon* (ballet), chor RH. AB, Adelaide.

1975
1 Jan RH sole artistic dir of AB.
19 May Seminar on the preparation and presentation of a ballet, RH lecture-demonstrator. AB, Sydney OH.
13 Nov *The Merry Widow* (ballet), production/scenario RH. AB, Palais Th, Melbourne.
10 Dec ABC TV, Australia: Summer Festival of Opera and Ballet, RH introduced ballets.

1976
26 Mar *The Sleeping Beauty* new prod dir RH AB.
21 May Australian TV: *The Fool on the Hill* (ballet film). Cr Sergeant Pepper. AB.
12 Dec Australian Tribute to UNICEF Concert, New York, dir RH.
16 Dec *The Sleeping Beauty,* RH dir revival of Mary Skeaping's staging for American Ballet Theatre and danced Carabosse, Kennedy Center OH, Washington, DC.

1977
20 Apr SWRB season, appeared as Dr Coppelius and (23 Apr)The Red King, first at the Pavilion, Bournemouth and then at Sadler's Wells.
16 Dec *The Mango Tree* (film), The Professor.

1978
27 June Stars of World Ballet (presented by Michael Edgley), dir RH. Regent Th, Sydney, then tour of Australia.
11 July Appointed dir designate of the Old Tote Th, Sydney, as of 1 Jan 1979. This came to nothing, as federal finance was withdrawn from the theatre and it had to go into liquidation.
18 Aug *Dracula* (play), dir RH. HM Th, Sydney.
28 Sep *Patrick* (film). Dr Roget.
Sep *Puzzle* (TV film). Buckminster Shepherd.

1979
25 Apr ABN2 Sydney interview with Michael Parkinson. 2nd part 28 July.
23 May Tribute to Margot Fonteyn, RH danced Tango from *Façade.* RB, ROHCG.
24 May RH gave reading at memorial service for Leslie Hurry, St. Paul's Church, Covent Garden
2 July Stars of World Ballet II (presented by Michael Edgley), dir RH (also danced Tango from *Façade*). Tour of Australia.

1980
3 June *Steps, Notes and Squeaks* (coaching programme devised by Maina Gielgud), coached *Swan Lake* and was coached by de Valois in *Checkmate.* OV.
24 Sep Elected to Board of Directors of Sydney Th Company.

1981
2 Mar *Sarah in America* (play), dir RH. Kennedy Center, Washington, DC.
2 Apr *Hamlet* (ballet; revival), staged for RB, ROHCG.
26 June *Alcina* (opera), dir/chor RH. Australian Opera, Sydney OH.

1982
10 Feb *Colette* (musical play). Jacques. 5th Avenue Th, Seattle, Washington.
1 Apr RH appeared in documentary film *50 Years of the Royal Ballet.*
19 May *Valmouth* (musical). Cardinal Pirelli. Chichester Festival Th.

1983
29 Jan *Roméo et Juliette* (opera, Gounod), dir RH. Australian Opera, Sydney OH.
5 Oct *The Cobra* (play), Lord Alfred Douglas. Sydney Th Company, Sydney OH.

1984
13 Apr Reception in Mount Gambier (his birthplace) for the renaming of the Civic Th as The Sir Robert Helpmann Th.
7 Nov *Stardust* (play). The Manservant. Civic Theatre, Newcastle, NSW, then to Queensland and Sydney.

1985
c. 14 Jan ABC TV Australia: *A Country Practice* (soap opera), two-part instalment 'Save the Last Dance for Me'. Sir Adrian Dormin.
3 Feb *The Merry Widow* (operetta), dir RH (with Christopher Brown), San Diego Opera, Civic Theater.
24 June *I Puritani* (opera), dir RH (with Christopher Brown). Australian Opera, Sydney OH.

1986
6 May *Checkmate* (ballet; revival). The Red King. AB, Sydney. Last stage appearance.
24 May.
28 Sep Died of emphysema at Sydney Royal North Shore Hospital.
2 Oct State funeral at St Andrew's Cathedral, Sydney.
15 Oct Memorial Service, State Th, Victorian Arts Centre, Melbourne.
25 Nov Thanksgiving Service, St Paul's Church, Covent Garden.

Index

.